REFRACTED IMAGES:

The Canary Islands Through a New World Lens

TRANSATLANTIC READINGS

MEDIEVAL AND RENAISSANCE
TEXTS AND STUDIES

VOLUME 276

MEDITERRANEAN STUDIES MONOGRAPHS AND TEXTS

VOLUME 3

Guy Mermier, General Editor

REFRACTED IMAGES:

*The Canary Islands Through
a New World Lens*

TRANSATLANTIC READINGS

by

Eyda M. Merediz

Arizona Center for Medieval and Renaissance Studies
Tempe, Arizona
2004

Library of Congress Cataloging-in-Publication Data

Merediz, Eyda M., 1964-
   Refracted images: the Canary Islands through a New World lens:
transatlantic readings / by Eyda M. Merediz
        p. cm. – (Medieval and Renaissance texts & studies; v. 276)
   Includes bibliographical references and index.
   ISBN 0-86698-319-8 (alk. Paper)
   1. Canary Islands—Historiography. 2. Canary Islands—In literature. 3.
Canary Islands—Relations—America. 4. America—Relations—Canary Islands.
5. Cross-cultural studies.   I. Title. II. Medieval & Renaissance Texts &
Studies (Series); v. 276.

DP302.C4M47 2004
964'.9'0072—dc22   2004057487

This book is made to last.
It is set in Garamond
smyth-sewn and printed on acid-free paper
to library specifications.

Printed in the United States of America

To my grandfather, who was born in the Canary Islands and died in Cuba without having learned to read.

A mi madre, que sólo podrá leer esta dedicatoria y las citas en español, por su paciencia y amor infinitos.

A mi padre, in memoriam.

CONTENTS

ACKNOWLEDGMENTS

PERHAPS IT ALL BEGAN WITH THE PICTURE OF MY GRANDFATHER. As I gazed at the walls of the abandoned shack where his long since deceased older sister had lived in the remote Aldea de San Nicolás de Tolentino on the southern shores of Gran Canaria, I came across an enlarged black and white picture of a young man. My newly found relatives assured me that he was the one who had left for Cuba: my grandfather. He stood, hat in hand, in a white suit with the serious glare of the recent emigrant posing for the family he left behind. I, an undergraduate student at the time, treasured the discovery and brought the image back to this side of the Atlantic where it had, in fact, originated.

Perhaps it all really began at Princeton. As I ransacked the stacks of Firestone Library in search of a good dissertation topic, I happened upon a play by Lope de Vega about the Guanches of Tenerife. Rolena Adorno, with her usual keen sense for the relevant source, directed me to a crucial work on the early historiography of the Canary Islands that, as it would turn out, was related to the play. The play was the thing. Torn by the intellectual possibilities that were posed by both Golden Age and Colonial Latin American Studies, I could now allow the play to lead me to a history of intertextuality, of transatlantic crossings in the Early Modern era, which never forced me to take anchor on either side of the Atlantic.

This project may have very well been born of a need to reconcile the photograph and the play — my grandfather and Lope de Vega — a personal journey and an academic pursuit. The result, however, bolsters the profound certainty that there are legitimate connections to be made and intricate byways to be unveiled when the Old World is looked at from the New one and considered through the lens of Colonial Latin American scholarship.

This book could not have been written without the academic and personal support of the many people I would like to acknowledge. My endless gratitude and admiration goes to Rolena Adorno whose scholarship inspired me and whose mentorship and friendship ensured I would neither stray nor despair. The only way I can reciprocate for the amount of time she put into every single page of my dissertation is with this book, which is hers as much as it is mine. To David Adorno, who is no longer with us, my thanks. I also extend my gratitude to Margaret Greer, another passionate scholar and exceptional mentor, whose intellectual contributions were invaluable to my project. For their suggestions, I would like to thank Alban Forcione, Ronald Surtz, and François Rigolot. I thank Clara Estow for pointing me in the direction of MRTS, Robert Bjork for finding my manuscript worth publishing, Richard

Clement for a beautiful typesetting job, and for her extremely meticulous copyediting, Leslie MacCoull.

To those friends who so often helped me clarify my thoughts and expression and who helped me stay sound in mind and spirit, I would like to express my appreciation. I cannot thank enough my dear friends Silvia Bermúdez, Carolina Erdocia, and Nadia Benabid for their never-ending encouragement and for taking the time to read, listen, and offer unconditional intellectual and moral support. Many thanks to other generous friends and conscientious critics: María Cristina Quintero, Sumaiya Hamdani, Patrick Pautz, Nina Gerassi-Navarro, and Raquel Medina.

I thank the numerous friends I met while at Princeton, Margarita Navarro, Jessica Hadlow, Ariadna García-Bryce, Diego Alonso, Roberto Madero, Álvaro Fernández-Bravo, Florencia Garramuño, Cynthia Stone, José Mazzotti, Reem and Morten Iversen, Shirley Cardozo, Astrid Arrarás, Nilüfer Hatemi, Christopher Britt, Arthur Denner, Khaled Fahmy, Hebe Gondicas, Luis Grau, and Joy Montero for the solidarity and the fun. I also thank the friends I met in Schenectady, the companions of my hibernation: Karin Hamm-Ehsani, Bradley Jordan, Peter Meyers, William García, Inés Arribas, Carlos Ortiz, Hyung Ji Park, and Livia Caroll. At Smith College, I received nothing but support; to Ana López and Bryna Keenan my thanks. At the University of Maryland, my gratitude goes to the many colleagues I am fortunate to have as interlocutors, especially Phyllis Peres, Carmen Benito-Vessels, Ana Patricia Rodríguez, Regina Harrison, and Sandra Cypess. I thank the friends who eased my travels in the Canary Islands: Pablo Melcón, Orlando Arencibia, Juan Bethencourt, Paco and Malena, Rosa and Javier; and the wonderful people at El Museo Canario and at the Biblioteca de la Universidad de La Laguna.

The following institutions have provided both financial and structural support: I thank the Graduate School, the then Department of Romance Languages and Literatures, and the Program in Latin American Studies at Princeton University. I also thank the Cultural Division of the Foreign Ministry of Spain, the Committee on Faculty Compensation and Development at Smith College, and the Graduate Research Board of the University of Maryland, College Park.

And most of all, I thank my mother, Acela Monzón, and my father, Pablo Merediz, for their dedication and unwavering support, and my loving family, the Domínguez, Roldán, Tejeda, and recent yet close friends, Humberto González and Manal Fouad, who have provided me with many homes in which I could always take refuge from academic chaos. For all the little important things that I seem to forget, I thank those who remember.

INTRODUCTION

> Island where all becomes clear
> Solid ground beneath your feet
> . . .
> The Tree of Valid Supposition grows here
> with branches disentangled since time immemorial.
> . . .
> For all its charms, the island is uninhabited
> and the faint footprints scattered on its beaches
> turn without exception to the sea.
>
> (Wislawa Szymborska, "Utopia," 127)

WHEN POPE CLEMENT VI decided to announce in Avignon in 1342 that he had created the Principate "of Fortunia" and bestowed a new Prince upon the distant Fortunate Islands, certain distressed English ambassadors in Rome, fearing the imposition of a new king, immediately dispatched a warning messenger to England.[1] This gesture is as much a commentary on the English self-image as it is a reflection on the mobile nature of myths. The Fortunate Islands that concerned the papacy at the moment, however, lay on the edge of the known world, not off the coast of Europe but of Africa. The pope had in mind the recently rediscovered Canary Islands, which at the time were less a real site than a mythical construction.

This phenomenon of identifying various islands as the locus of many myths had prevailed since antiquity, and the Canary Islands were no exception (Martínez Hernández, *Las Islas Canarias*, 19–53). The Greek Elysian Fields, the Islands of the Blessed or Fortunate Islands of the Greeks and Romans, the Christian Earthly Paradise, the remains of Atlantis, the Garden of the Hesperides, and the elusive island of Saint Brendan have all inhabited, in a long history of misplacements, the geographical boundaries of the Canary Islands.[2]

---

[1] This anecdote is quoted by Luis Weckmann (*Las bulas alejandrinas de 1493 y la teoría política del papado medieval* [México: Instituto de Historia, 1949], 238) from P. Heylin's *Cosmographie in Four Books* published in London in 1669 (74 [bk. 4]). The location of the "Happy Isles" was also shifted to northern Europe in Grazioso Benincasa of Ancona's map of 1467 (Jean Delumeau, *History of Paradise*, trans. Matthew O'Connell [New York: Continuum, 1995], 103).

[2] According to Marcos Martínez Hernández (*Las Islas Canarias de la Antigüedad al Renacimiento* [Santa Cruz de Tenerife: Cabildo de Tenerife, 1996], 48–49) and Delumeau (*History of Paradise*, 103–4), the myth of the lost, hidden, or inaccessible island of Saint Brendan (San Borondón, San Brandán, San Blandán) had its origins in the medieval sea-traveling of an Irish bishop (abbot of Clonfert) during the fifth or sixth century. Saint Brendan's voyage to Scotland became legendary; a more fantastic journey was then recorded in a Latin text (a

Myths gradually dissipated or became once again displaced as the Europeans gained empirical knowledge and political and cultural dominion over the Atlantic. Nevertheless, as the Canary Islands played a key experimental role in European colonial history, they also remained emblematic of shifting identities, which linked the islands to the history of the New World.

This study takes as its point of departure the early historical and literary images of the Canary Islands where the coexistence of myths and observations, employed by the Europeans during the fourteenth and fifteenth centuries, would come to serve as the antecedent for further overseas enterprises. I will explore broadly both the literary representations of the islands and the islanders as well as the role of the islands in the legal and political debates that occurred in European religious and royal centers, in order to show how they later proved instrumental in conceptualizing America and the Amerindian.

In Chapter One, I examine the role of the islands in the "Age of Exploration and Discovery" as experimental grounds for the colonization of the New World. My first objective is to emphasize the well-established importance of the Canary Islands in Spanish overseas expansion up to the late fifteenth century. For that purpose, I survey the European exploratory voyages into the Atlantic as well as the different representations of the native islanders in historical narratives, which gradually shaped the role of the islands in papal and royal political designs. As the representative *par excellence* of the "non-European" and "non-Christian" mediating between the Old World and the Caribbean islands, the Canaries allowed for a historiographic, economic, juridical, and political experiment which informed Columbus and the European conquest and colonization of the New World.

In the sixteenth century, Europe witnessed the rise of thinkers like Francisco de Vitoria and Bartolomé de las Casas, who applied a medieval legal framework to the legal, moral, and political issues generated by the colonization of a new continent. However, in this process, unquestionably indebted to the past, they opened the way to the international law of the future. Most importantly, America and Amerindian cultures provided the rich corpus from which numerous ethnographic studies emerged, laying the basis for a more systematic approach to ethnology. Although firmly grounded on previous experience and ancient texts, the European entrance into the New World generated intense debates and a massive body of writings, which later proved to be groundbreaking in the way Europe observed and related to its cultural "others."

The encounter with the New World and its inhabitants eventually overshadowed its homologue in the Old World, and the history of the Canaries, especially of Tenerife, the last of the Canaries to fall under Spanish rule by

medieval novel of adventure) dating from the ninth century and titled *Navegatio Sancti Brendani.* There were about eighty different versions of this story in which Saint Brendan traveled to the "Islands of Happiness."

1497, remained practically unwritten until the end of the sixteenth century. My study, then, concentrates on a number of works produced at the turn of the seventeenth century which constructed the islands as a textual utopia to negotiate Spanish colonial history not only in the Atlantic islands, but also in the New World. Although numerous interdisciplinary studies have documented the role of the Canaries as a conceptual and practical "halfway house" for the Europeans on their voyage from the Old World to the New, what I propose here is precisely to consider the revisiting of the islands on the journey back from the New World to the Old. Thus, I argue in the subsequent chapters that the historical and literary production about the islands at the turn of the seventeenth century is reciprocally informed by the colonization of the New World, the legal and political debates it generated, and the European ethnographic gaze on the Amerindian.

By focusing on the last decade of the sixteenth century and the first decade of the seventeenth, and on three particular texts which predominantly look at the history of Tenerife and the Guanches, I have selected a small yet exemplary corpus to illustrate the arguments of my project. Executed formally with conventions responding to different genres, these three works — a historiographic text, an epic poem, and a drama — are unique in the ways that they reconsider the same historical material from dissimilar positions. I take into consideration how this intertextual dialogue unfolds among the three texts, but I also see them in a more crucial dialogue with the historical and literary production generated about the conquest and colonization of the New World.

In Chapter Two, I examine Alonso de Espinosa's *Del origen y milagros de la Santa Imagen de Nuestra Señora de Candelaria, que apareció en la Isla de Tenerife, con la descripción de esta isla* (Seville, 1594). As many chroniclers of the Indies had previously done, Espinosa, who was a Dominican friar, manipulated the existing historiographic conventions; he made use of ecclesiastical history to construct the first ethnographic history of the Guanches and the history of their European subjugation. Espinosa found in the account of the appearance of the Virgin of Candelaria an effective vehicle for formulating the history of Tenerife and the Guanches — a process which occurred in light of the ethnographic and political ideas expressed by Bartolomé de las Casas primarily about the New World. In fact, Alonso de Espinosa's experience in Guatemala and Mexico and his affiliation with Lascasian thought shaped his perspective, and he modeled his views in part after the *Apologética historia sumaria* which was written by Las Casas and circulated in manuscript form at the time. The Guanches portrayed by Espinosa, despite their apparent primitivism, exhibited individual, social, and political traits that represented true civility as prescribed by Las Casas in his application of Aristotle's theory in the *Politics* to Amerindians.

Espinosa's historical account of the conquest and colonization of Tenerife also illustrated his ideological stance against the legality of the European conquest of Tenerife, just as Las Casas had denounced that of the New World in many of his works. Espinosa restated that the war of conquest waged by Spain in the Canaries as well as in the Indies was unjust and unjustifiable. He also condemned in the same fashion as Las Casas the enslavement resulting from raids and conquests in the Atlantic and practiced by several European powers. By his clear assertions about the injustice of the conquest of the natives, to whom he ascribed the same level of civility and rights of sovereignty as the Europeans, Espinosa's island and its inhabitants became reflections of the victimized image that Las Casas constructed of America and Amerindians. Thus Tenerife and the Canaries, along with the New World, shared the space of the colonized.

In Chapter Three, I discuss the immediate reception that Espinosa's account received in the epic poem *Antigüedades de las Islas Afortunadas de la Gran Canaria, conquista de Tenerife y aparecimiento de la Santa Imagen de Candelaria* written by Antonio de Viana (Seville, 1604). This poet chose yet another genre in which to fuse literary conventions and historical material. The epic poem enabled him to construct a project of cultural unification that rejected Espinosa's critical attempt to identify the colonial experience of Tenerife with that of the New World. In so doing, Viana also rejected Ercilla's problematic epic model of the never-ending violent war of conquest staged on the other side of the Atlantic in Arauco. In contrast, Viana's epic exploits war and the battles between the Spanish and Guanche armies for the aesthetic experience, and turns instead to a project of love and cultural harmony. Viana made Tenerife and the Canaries into a utopian space where the harmonious reconciliation of two cultures occurs in the symbolic marriage of a Guanche princess, Dacil, and a Spanish conquistador, Captain Gonzalo del Castillo. Viana's model features two ethnically homogeneous cultures, which were destined to be united since the immemorial time of the mythical kingdom of Tartessus in Spain, whence the ancient inhabitants of Tenerife were thought to have emigrated. Viana's dream is a replica of the *adelantado* Alonso de Lugo's allegorical dream in the poem: the Spanish conquistador and first governor of Tenerife is taken onto the peak of Mount Teide to marry the only one of seven maidens who remained unmarried, Tenerife. Unlike the troubling image of the New World fostered by Espinosa, Ercilla, and representatives of the Lascasian reformist movement and its legacy, Viana's islands had always been legally and culturally bound to Spain; and so in Viana's work the most basic foundation of colonialism — the colonized devoured by the colonizer — symbolically disappears from Spanish imperial history.

In Chapter Four, I explore Lope de Vega's play *Los guanches de Tenerife y Conquista de Canaria*, written between 1604 and 1609 and published in Madrid and Barcelona in 1618. This drama was directly inspired by Viana's epic poem, although Lope most probably also used other historical sources that dealt with the New World. Following the steps of his main model, Lope de Vega subscribed to Viana's paradigm of cultural integration between Spain and its colonial Atlantic outpost. However, Lope's critical views, expressed as well in others of his plays which feature the history of the New World, reveal the ruptures in Viana's perfect model. By exposing the materialization of such a utopian model only through the direct and forceful intervention of supernatural agents, Lope effectively criticizes the Spanish conquest and colonization of America as violent and greedy. In the drama, any celebration of the conquest of Tenerife embedded in the valid supposition of a symbolic union between Guanches and Spaniards is undermined by Lope's implicit reflection on the clash between Amerindians and Spaniards. Lope's Virgin of Candelaria becomes less of a miraculous icon for the evangelization of the Guanches than an instrument to teach a lesson of Christianity to the Spaniards — a lesson that needed to be learned to apply it not in the consolidated colonial structure of the Canaries, but on the still unsettling reality of the New World. Perhaps most significantly, Lope's inclusion of the Canaries' historical past in his dramatic production reveals that the history of Spain in the New World served as the background stage and that it continued to be an important issue of national concern.

These three works offer the perspective of different authors and distinct visions of history: Alonso de Espinosa's history is formulated from the experiential and intellectual training that the author acquired in the New World; Antonio de Viana's epic poem establishes the author's personal and textual authority on the basis of his birth in the city of La Laguna in Tenerife; and Lope de Vega's play highlights the perspective of the privileged position enjoyed by its author who writes from the center of the empire, Spain. Yet each of these literary works, in one way or another, rethinks Spanish colonial history in the New World by reformulating or reinventing the historical and cultural identity of the Canary Islands.

Once again, these revisited Fortunate Islands are the islands where everything becomes clear, but their historical and imaginary construction always entangles other lands beyond the Atlantic, in the New World, and a multiplicity of cultural identities. Thus, this study will place the Canary Islands in the foreground, above all as a pivotal point in a complex imperial triangulation of transatlantic exchange from the onset of the Modern era through the seventeenth century.

By exploring the dynamics of this transatlantic relationship, the Canaries emerge as the physical "in between," but also symbolic "intermediary" space *par excellence* where Europe and the Americas, and even Africa, repeatedly converge, intertwine and interact. This book studies the Canary Islands as a "contact zone," to use Mary Louise Pratt's (*Imperial Eyes*, 6–7) terminology and definition, which "invoke[s] the spatial and temporal copresence of subjects previously separated by geographic and historical disjunctures ... [and] the interactive, improvisational dimensions of colonial encounters so easily ignored or suppressed by diffusionist accounts of conquest and domination." If Paul Gilroy's work has led the way for a transoceanic perspective in looking at the Anglophone Modern Black Atlantic, the Canary Islands, indeed at the midway of a transatlantic passage, should be read from precisely that perspective. At the crossroads of histories, politics and cultures, these islands are "sites traversed," in James Clifford's words ("Traveling Cultures," 103–4) by the constant movement of peoples and ideas and artifacts, the sites of detours and returns (very much as the Caribbean has been conceived), and ultimately sites of collisions and dialogues.

These notions of "contact," of "culture as travel," of "transatlanticism," which have recently transformed the fields of anthropology, cultural history, and literature are extremely useful in illuminating from a different and interdisciplinary angle spaces, histories and agents that have been neglected by traditional methodologies. In fact, a similar critical apparatus, *avant la lettre*, has been shaping Latin American colonial criticism mostly for the last twenty-five years: that of Silvio Zavala, Edmundo O'Gorman, Rolena Adorno, Mercedes López-Baralt, Sabine MacCormack, Beatriz Pastor, Margarita Zamora, Veronica Salles-Reese, Walter Mignolo, José Rabasa, Serge Gruzinski, Inga Clendinnen, and Peter Hulme, among others. My work springs first and foremost from this set of developments: a critical discourse that emerged, not from the British colonial experience and the post-colonial criticism that it has elicited, but from a less known and less academically featured tradition, that of the Iberian empires and the Hispanic world.[3]

A complete transatlantic paradigm, moreover, must take into further account not only the late imperial cultures, trans-national and post-colonial spaces, but also the beginnings of colonialism, its strategic survival, and its dissenting legacies in the early Atlantic world. This is where the historical and cultural discourse about the Canaries occupies a privileged position in its relation to the "center," Europe, and to the farthest "periphery," the Americas, revealing a fluid model of transatlantic colonial transactions and negotiations. This study seeks to fill an important void by re-mapping a far more inclusive and interdependent Hispanic Atlantic.

---

[3] These ideas have been formulated and expanded in a recent article; see Eyda M. Merediz, "Traveling Icons: The Virgin of Candelaria's Transatlantic Journeys," *Arizona Journal of Hispanic Cultural Studies* 5 (2001): 1–18, here 1–4. For a useful discussion of "transatlantic studies" within the broader context of Hispanic cultural studies, see all the articles that appeared in the above-mentioned volume.

CHAPTER ONE

MEDIEVAL QUESTS:
The West Meets the Savage

> What the seaborne empires all had in common was their
> starting-place on the shores of the Atlantic. For the Atlantic,
> in the age of sail, was a highway that led not only to the im-
> mense, under-exploited, defenseless resource-base of the
> Americas but also to wind-systems that linked with the rest of
> the world. (Felipe Fernández-Armesto, *Millennium*, 257)

IN 1483, AT THE START OF THE CHRISTIAN RECONQUISTA OF GRANADA, the
Catholic monarchs moved their court from Madrid to Cordoba where Boabdil,
the last Muslim king, had been imprisoned. As part of their entourage, Isabella
and Ferdinand had brought with them Tenesor Semidan, better known as Don
Fernando Guanarteme, the king of Gáldar in Gran Canaria.[4] Like Boabdil, he
had also been captured, but had subsequently accepted baptism and submitted
voluntarily to the Spanish crown. Chroniclers narrated that, when Ferdinand of
Aragon rode his horse through the streets of Cordoba, he would do so, proud
to be flanked by the two defeated monarchs, Boabdil and Guanarteme (Rumeu
de Armas, "Don Fernando," 36–37). This symbolic formation stands as the
prophetic vision of the final conquest of the Muslim kingdom of Granada in
1492 and the complete annexation of the Canary Islands by 1497 to the kingdom of Castile. These events would seem to lose their importance in light of
the later discovery, conquest and colonization of the New World, which nevertheless had the imprint of both the Reconquista and the military takeover of
the Fortunate Islands.

The degree to which these two colonizing experiences were influential in
later Spanish imperial expansion has been widely debated, but for obvious
chronological and geographical reasons, they have never been entirely denied.

---

[4] The word *guanarteme* meant "king" or "political authority" in the language of Gran
Canaria (D. Wölfel, *Monumenta Linguae Canariae*, 2 vols. [Graz, 1965; trans. ed. Tenerife,
1996], 2: 536–37). The languages of the islands are thought to be related to North African
Berber dialects (Tuareg, Kabyle). For linguistic references about all the islands' dialects, see
Wölfel's *Monumenta Linguae Canariae* in its original German version or in the recent Spanish
translation. See also Francisco Navarro Artiles, *Teberite, diccionario de la lengua aborigen canaria*
(Las Palmas, 1981).

The conquest of the Canary Islands provided continuity with the Reconquista, yet it posed different questions because of the islands' supposedly primitive inhabitants and the legal issues that arose from their conquest. The conquest of the New World resembled that of the Canary Islands, but it encountered quite different and complex civilizations.

The natural pattern of winds which made Columbus take advantage of the Atlantic outpost of the Canaries speaks for itself, and the strategic geographical location of the islands would play an essential role in westward navigation. If the legal and political issues concerning the discovery and conquest of the islands are more elusive when historians have tried to explain subsequent colonial experiences, the strategic fact that the Canary Islands had finally been annexed to Castile made the conquest of the New World predominately Spanish (Fernández Armesto, *Before Columbus*, 207). Consequently, the Canary Islands were instrumental in the rise of the Spanish empire. After all, Europeans, at first, regarded the discovery of the distant islands in the Ocean Sea as no more significant than the discovery of the Azores or the Canary Islands (Sale, *Conquest of Paradise*, 125). In fact, the Genoese Allegretto Allegretti thought that America was another Canary Island, and it is possible that due to this sort of confusion Castile received the papal donation to conquer those islands "still to be discovered" (Fernández Armesto, *Before Columbus*, 221; Weckmann, *Bulas alejandrinas*, 30). Moreover, the Canary Islands provided an immediate point of reference for the Caribbean islands and the Arawak Indians upon whom Columbus stumbled in 1492.

To clarify the importance of the Canary Islands in the Spanish overseas enterprise up to the late fifteenth century, I will survey the exploratory voyages into the Atlantic which began to shape the Canary Islands in the maps and minds of Europeans. I will also discuss the political problem of the islands' status as seen by popes and monarchs, as well as the different representations of the native islanders in historical accounts, which attempted to redefine a space and a people that throughout the Middle Ages had belonged to the realms of myth.

1. LAND OF INFIDELS: POPES, KINGS, AND LAWS[5]

Several centuries before the Columbian discovery of the New World, Europeans had already been regulating the treatment of non-Europeans.[6] Sinibaldo Fieschi, better known as Pope Innocent IV (1243–1254), can be considered a pioneer in developing the legal guidelines for relations between the Roman Curia and non-Christian societies (Muldoon, *Popes, Lawyers, and Infidels*, 5). Although in the context of the crusades the general theory of just war had justified the war against the infidels and the rightful seizure of the Holy Land, Innocent IV was most interested in applying the same argument to other lands occupied by Muslims (Muldoon, *Popes, Lawyers, and Infidels*, 7). Drawing from the Bible and Roman law, he asserted papal jurisdiction over all infidels, whereby as pope, he alone had the right to authorize an intervention to enforce adherence to natural law if violations such as sexual perversion and idolatry occurred.[7] Infidels were also required to admit into their lands missionaries

---

[5] According to P. E. Russell, the word "infidel" was used vaguely in Medieval Latin to define those who had willfully rejected the Christian faith as well as those who had not been aware of its existence. The word "pagan," however, had recovered, by the early fourteenth century, its correct meaning in Latin and the vernacular languages to refer to those who had never been instructed in the faith ("El descubrimiento de Las Canarias y el debate medieval acerca de los derechos de los príncipes y pueblos paganos," *Revista de historia canaria* 36 [1978]: 2–32, here 11–12). The issue seems to be more complex. The term *infidelis* in Christian Latin had shifted meaning from "untrustworthy" (as in classical Latin) to "unbelieving"; this is what the Muslim Arabic notion of *Kafir* ("infidel") itself got calqued on in late antiquity (cf. *EI²*, 4: 407–9), giving rise to the Western Latin medieval reverse notion of "infidel."

[6] Canon law was concerned at first with schismatic and heretical practices and practitioners, and later with the Jews and Muslims as well as those inhabiting the European eastern borders. See James Muldoon's (*Popes, Lawyers, and Infidels* [Philadelphia: University of Pennsylvania Press, 1979], 29–119) discussion of the Roman Curia's relation to infidels inside and outside of Europe. See also Fernández Armesto's complete study of European Christians' dealings with the "wild men" of Europe in his *Before Columbus* (Philadelphia: University of Pennsylvania Press, 1987). In the specific context of the Canary Islands, both Muldoon and Fernández Armesto are also very useful, as well as D. Wölfel, "La Curia Romana y la Corona de España en defensa de los aborígenes canarios," *Antropos* 25 (1930): 1011–83, and A. Rumeu de Armas, *La política indigenista de Isabel la Católica* (Valladolid: Instituto "Isabel la Católica," 1969), among others.

[7] What triggered Innocent IV's general discussion was the decretal *Quod super his* issued by Pope Innocent III (1198–1216), which had been concerned with crusades to the Holy Land (Muldoon, *Popes, Lawyers, and Infidels*, 6). His particular point regarding papal authority to wage war now applied to infidels the principles that canonists had used unsuccessfully to control war among Christians in Europe (Muldoon, *Popes, Lawyers, and Infidels*, 12). Innocent IV also asserted that his jurisdiction over infidels was *de iure*, not *de facto*, which defines as well papal claims over Christian secular rulers. The Pope could then intervene indirectly in spheres that under normal circumstances were autonomous (Muldoon, *Popes, Lawyers, and Infidels*, 15). This papal figure serves as the starting point of Muldoon's useful book, which

who would facilitate their voluntary conversion. If they failed to do so, Christian armies had the right to invade (Muldoon, *Popes, Lawyers, and Infidels*, 10–12). Innocent IV's views prevailed throughout the Middle Ages in the work of many canonists, but not without opposition from one of his own students, Henry of Segusio, or Hostiensis. In his commentaries on the *Decretales*, Hostiensis strongly supported papal power as his master did, but he denied the rights of infidels to *dominium*, that is, lordship and property. Infidels were defined as usurpers, according to Hostiensis, because with the coming of Christ their previous authority over their domain became unlawful (Muldoon, *Popes, Lawyers, and Infidels*, 15–18).[8] Both opinions circulated widely, and by the fifteenth century canonists seemed cautious about accepting the extreme opinions of Hostiensis, although their explicit support of Innocent was not always evident (Muldoon, *Popes, Lawyers, and Infidels*, 24).[9]

In the late medieval period, the increasing exploratory travels in the Atlantic Ocean raised religious, legal, and political issues with regard to the new lands which were being discovered or rediscovered. The issues that had been discussed in the context of the infidels, mostly Jews and Muslims, had to accommodate another reality: that of the pagans who inhabited the Atlantic islands. The frequency and variety of travels to different islands, as well as attempts to settle them that took place since the 1300s, reveal a European interest in negotiating, within a long-standing tradition of dealings with non-Christians, unsystematic patterns of conquest and inconsistent policies on the part of kings and popes.[10]

---

ties sixteenth-century debates about the rights of Amerindians to a long history of medieval legal thought. The broader theoretical frame of the just war from Augustine to Aquinas, which is complementary to Muldoon's study, is discussed in detail by Frederick Russell, *The Just War in the Middle Ages* (Cambridge: Cambridge University Press, 1975).

[8] Hostiensis's formulation of the argument against infidels' rights to *dominium* was not new. Alanus Anglicus, an English canonist, had already stated it in the early thirteenth century. This, in turn, constituted a variant on the ancient Donatist heresy, a Christian sect which originated in North Africa (A.D. 311) and asserted (among other things) that only priests in a state of grace could exercise sacramental authority in the Church (Muldoon, *Popes, Lawyers, and Infidels*, 16). On the connection between Saint Augustine's debates with Donatists and pagans and Spanish America, especially Peru, see S. MacCormack, "Ubi Ecclesia? Perceptions of Medieval Europe in Spanish America," *Speculum* 69 (1994): 74–100.

[9] Rumeu de Armas has concluded that Hostiensis's views prevailed throughout the Middle Ages (*La política*, 11), but Muldoon's conclusions about their limitations are better supported by the evidence.

[10] If there was a point of clear agreement between popes and monarchs, it was the dream of undermining Muslim power by reuniting those lost Christian kingdoms "believed to exist beyond the Muslim-dominated world" (Muldoon, *Popes, Lawyers, and Infidels*, 103–4), especially the persistent legend of the realm of "Prester John" (identified with Christian Ethiopia).

Four particular periods in the medieval history of the Canary Islands seem to capture the religious, legal, and political conflicts that their conquest generated in Europe at the time. The first centers on Pope Clement VI in the mid-fourteenth century. The second pertains to the French occupation in the early fifteenth century, and the third to the long-standing Castilian-Portuguese dispute, which lasted throughout most of the fifteenth century. The fourth and final period focuses on the reign of the Catholic monarchs, whose overwhelming offensive brought about the islands' total subjugation to the kingdom of Castile by 1497.

In 1342 at Avignon, Pierre Roger de Beaufort, Archbishop of Rouen and professor of theology in Paris, became Pope Clement VI. One of the many projects which occupied the new Pope was the extension of the dominion of the Church by taking a special interest in the Canary Islands.

Two years later, in his bull *Tuae devotionis*, he created what was called the Principate 'of Fortunia' which included the Canary Islands and the island of Jalitā next to Tunisia.[11] Clement VI selected a perfect candidate to become the new prince: Luis de la Cerda, who had previously proposed to the pope the conquest of the islands (Muldoon, *Popes, Lawyers, and Infidels*, 90). Born in Castile and exiled to France, Luis de la Cerda was the grandson of Alfonso X (El Sabio) and of Louis IX, or Saint Louis of France, a fact which probably influenced considerably the pope's decision to support Cerda's candidacy (Serra Ráfols and Martínez Hernández, "Sermón de Clemente VI," 108). Just as in the proclamation of a crusade, requests for aid were sent out to the kingdoms along the western Mediterranean, and bulls and indulgences were issued to Christian princes and missionaries (Fernández Armesto, *Before Columbus*, 172). Clement VI constructed in his *collatio* a comprehensive list of reasons for waging war against the inhabitants of the Canaries who appeared at the time to be the most evident example of primitive pagans. His arguments derived from the medieval papal pretensions to universal dominion and assertions of the rights of the Church to the lands of infidels, which were assumed previously to have been Christian. For Pope Clement, Africa and its islands had been Christian before becoming pagan, and, just as the primitive church had been persecuted by pagans in power, it was now time for the powerful church to do the same to

---

[11] Clement VI's bulls concerning the Canary Islands, in particular *Sicut exhibitae*, can be seen as part of what Luis Weckmann has called the "omni-insular doctrine," which found its zenith in Alexander VI's *Intercaetera* bulls of 1493. According to Weckmann, underlying all papal donations of new islands, including those discovered by Columbus, was an old and strange juridical theory developed by the pontificate in the eleventh century and first enunciated by Urban II (1088–1099) in 1091. This theory, the "omni-insular doctrine," declared that all the islands of the world belonged to the jurisdiction of Saint Peter and his successors who held sovereignty over them (Weckmann, *Las bulas alejandrinas*, 32–33, 229–62). By the fifteenth century, the pope's role as *verus imperator* and the doctrine of his dominion over the lands and seas together determined the legal issues surrounding all new discoveries.

pagans (Serra Ráfols and Martínez Hernández, "Sermón de Clemente VI," 110). As Fernández Armesto (*Before Columbus*, 231) has argued, Clement's views were deeply rooted in the Augustinian tradition which conceived war as the measure taken by a legitimate source of authority for the recovery of usurped possessions or as a mechanism of defense.[12] The twist added by the pope was the fantastic assumption that the island of Capraria, mentioned by Augustine (*Ep.* 48), was one of the Canaries that needed to be recovered. He also affirmed, with little support from canon law, that pagans were required to submit to Christianity by virtue of their paganism (Fernández Armesto, *Before Columbus*, 232). With his sermon, the pope thus authorized Luis de la Cerda to use force if necessary in the conquest of the pagan territories entrusted to him.

The investiture of the Prince of Fortune turned out to be a fiasco. In the words of Petrarch, who was a witness to the ceremony of 15 November 1344, the events occurred as follows:

> while that day he [Luis de la Cerda] was strutting through the city adorned with crown and scepter, suddenly it rained so hard, and he returned home so drenched, that it was taken as an omen that he had been granted dominion over a damp and rainy land. What happened to him thereafter in that land situated outside the world, I do not know; I know however that many things are handed down and have been written according to which the fortune of those lands does not seem to fully correspond with the epithet of fortunate lands.[13]

The humiliating image of the newly proclaimed monarch soaked to the skin, as well as the omen brought about by the storm, determined the fate of Luis de la Cerda and the immediate fate of the lands he was set to rule. The king never exercised his rights to the new kingdom because he never set foot in the Canary Islands nor did he govern them from afar. As for any other attempt to conquer the islands by force, none was made until the Portuguese attempt of 1370; the missionary labor of spiritual conquerors, however, took a more active role (Fernández Armesto, *Before Columbus*, 172).

---

[12] See Russell, *The Just War* and his useful analysis of St. Augustine's ideas on just war (16–39); also idem, "War," in *Augustine Through the Ages*, ed. Allan D. Fitzgerald (Grand Rapids, MI: Eerdmans, 1999), 875–76.

[13] This passage appears in Petrarch's *Vita solitaria*, originally written in Latin, but transcribed, translated, and analyzed thoroughly by Theodore J. Cachey, Jr. ("Petrarch, Boccaccio, and the New World Encounter," *Stanford Italian Review* 10 [1991]: 45–59, here 48–49). This critic has also written a more comprehensive book on the appropriation of the Fortunate Islands in the literature and historiography of the Italian Renaissance (*Le Isole Fortunate* [Rome: Bretschneider, 1995], 11–283).

In the bull *Coelestis Rex regum* (1351), Clement VI desisted in his efforts at holy war and resigned himself to the peaceful work of missionaries. He created the Bishopric of the Fortunate Islands in Telde, Gran Canaria, and sent the Majorcan Carmelite Fray Bernardo there on an evangelical mission in the company of merchants and enslaved natives of the Canaries who had been living in Majorca (Serra Ráfols and Martínez Hernández, "Sermón de Clemente VI," 109; Fernández Armesto, *Before Columbus*, 158–59). Although this phenomenon of peaceful persuasion to the Christian faith is scarcely documented, there is a clear sense of the role of the Franciscan order in the evangelization of the islands. Pope Clement allowed Majorcans to undertake missionary work, which bore the mark of the Franciscan Ramón Llull (1232–1316).[14] The missionary center in Gran Canaria, however, did not survive the 1390s. It was followed by the French military occupation and settlement of other islands under the guidance of Jean de Béthencourt and Gadifer de La Salle, as well as numerous attempts to conquer the most populated islands of Gran Canaria, Palma, and Tenerife (Fernández Armesto, *Before Columbus*, 236).

As exemplified by the dual policy of Clement VI, the medieval history of the Canary Islands seemed to fluctuate between two poles: a proposal for violent conquests on the one hand, and the pursuit of peaceful missions on the other. The political and legal debates became more pressing as the Europeans gained more navigational and geographical knowledge of the lost islands in the Atlantic Ocean.

Unlike Luis de la Cerda, who never completed a journey to the islands, Béthencourt and La Salle set sail from La Rochelle on 1 May 1402, and arrived in Lanzarote by July of the same year, according to a contemporary chronicle.[15] The French expedition was authorized by Charles VI, King of France, without previous consultation with the pope; Béthencourt eventually sought the protection of another Christian prince, Henry III of Castile, and left La Salle's own claims unsupported at the Castilian court (Russell, "El descubrimiento," 10). La

---

[14] Ramón Llull, or Raimundo Lulio, was a famous Catalan theologian and philosopher who was born in Majorca and probably died among the Muslims of Tunis. This Franciscan, who also wrote several scholastic, mystical, and chivalric books, founded the first schools of Arabic language for missionaries. He advocated methods of peaceful evangelization achieved by apostolic example and the learning of the languages of those who were to be converted (Fernández Armesto, *Before Columbus*, 157). Interest in the Canary Islands as a site of missionary work and easy conversion of the natives continued to be acknowledged and registered during the papacy of Urban V (1362–1370) (Muldoon, *Popes, Lawyers, and Infidels*, 140). His bull *Ad hoc semper* of 1369 authorized Catalan missionaries to go to the islands.

[15] The chronicle, ascribed to Pierre Boutier [Bontier] and Jean Le Verrier, is known as *Le Canarien*, ed. and trans. Elías Serra Ráfols and Alejandro Cioranescu, 3 vols. (La Laguna: Instituto de Estudios Canarios and Museo Canario, 1959, 1960, 1964). I will discuss below the particularities of its production in the context of the description of the islands and their inhabitants.

Salle attempted to make his own claims to the king but Henry III favored Béthencourt, compelling La Salle to abandon the enterprise. Béthencourt's status reflected a feudal legal situation in which he was a vassal of the king of Castile (a vassalage which was first established by Henry III and later maintained by John II in 1412), and he was proclaimed in Seville Lord of Canaria — "Seigneur des isles de Canare" (Pérez Voituriez, *Problemas jurídicos*, 29–74). The basis for the investiture of Béthencourt is unknown, but such a process — contrary to Luis de la Cerda's prior investiture — seemed to be regarded as inadequate by the chroniclers of the expedition and by Europeans at the time (Weckmann, *Bulas alejandrinas*, 238–39). The points of debate transcended the conflict between Béthencourt and La Salle and moved the conflict to the sphere of papal and royal rights over the islands on the Atlantic.

This particular historical moment — in which the first colonists disembarked on Lanzarote — initiated substantive contact between the Atlantic pagan world and its European neighbor in the context of a military expedition and political conflict (Russell, "El descubrimiento," 10). With this expedition Europeans recognized the Canary Islands as a place inhabited by true pagans. Thus the legal problems surrounding the respective roles of the papacy and Christian monarchy over pagan nations found a practical application (Russell, "El descubrimiento," 12). Fernández Armesto (*Before Columbus*, 180) states that when the Normans reached the islands in 1402, "the rights of pagans to undisturbed sovereignty was a much debated issue"; however, "the rights of Christians to conquer them, save under serious provocation, was not generally recognized." The islands nevertheless became fertile ground for the debates of papists (*papistas*) and anti-papists who saw the opportunity for demarcating the extent to which the Roman Curia could exercise power over lands that a century before had only been part of an imagined geography.[16]

Papists believed that no pagan or infidel nation could possess *dominium* legitimately: thus the pope had the right to dispose of them, as being the only true emperor of the world (*verus imperator mundi*), to create the only possible legitimate union of the whole Christian people into one body (*societas omnium christianorum* or *congregatio fidelium*). Anti-papists, on the contrary, had simultaneously developed a theory of sovereignty which denied the *congregatio fidelium*, that is, the political, temporal prerogatives that the papists had added to the spiritual ones. The most extreme anti-papists denied the pope the right to intervene in any legitimate human society (*societas humana* or *communitas mortalium*) which comprehended all human beings, regardless of their religious affiliation.

---

[16] The following discussion of papist and anti-papist ideas, as these apply to the Canaries context, is extracted from Russell's summary ("El descubrimiento," 13–14), which in turn derives from a more general study, Michael Wilks, *The Problem of Sovereignty in the Later Middle Ages* (Cambridge: Cambridge University Press, 1969), 105–6.

It was precisely the papist mentality that triggered the authorization to conquer the Canary Islands and convert their inhabitants, as is evident from Anti-Pope Benedict XIII's bull *Apostolatus officium* of 1404 which made the conquest of the Canaries into a crusade by offering indulgences to Béthencourt (Rumeu de Armas, *La política*, 29). By authorizing the establishment of the diocese of Rubicón in the Atlantic Islands in the same bull, the pope proclaimed himself the sovereign of all regions and nations of the world (Russell, "El descubrimiento," 14–15).[17] Upon these ideas the Portuguese built the theoretical and juridical basis for their Atlantic empire in subsequent years, following in the footsteps of Béthencourt and La Salle's first occupation of some of the Canary Islands. The French at first justified waging war against the islanders on the basis of their customs and heathenism, which seemed to them a clear violation of natural law (Fernández Armesto, *Before Columbus*, 180). There were military confrontations with the natives; raids were conducted on most islands, and, due to the treachery of one of La Salle's men (Bertin de Berneval) or as a desperate measure of survival, slaves were taken. Although surrounded by the rhetoric of the crusade in which spiritual conversion was a natural consequence of military conquest, the French settlement seemed to have been rather peaceful: their missionary work in Lanzarote, Fuerteventura, and Hierro christianized most of these islands' populations by 1423 (Russell, "El descubrimiento," 10; Rumeu de Armas, *La política*, 30). The relative success of this settlement[18] and the increas-

---

[17] For a useful and comprehensive chronology of European interventions in the Canaries as well as along the African coast, see Isacio Pérez Fernández's introduction to his own selection of Bartolomé de las Casas's *Historia de las Indias*, entitled *Brevísima relación de la destrucción de África* (Salamanca: Viceconsejería del gobierno de Canarias, 1989), 145–87. Pérez Fernández concentrates on all interventions, political and military as well as religious, offering a useful list of all papal bulls issued to regulate religious activity in the region. Pope Benedict XIII (1394–1417) in his bull *Apostolatus officium* authorized the bishopric of Rubicón in Lanzarote and also named Alfonso de Sanlúcar de Barrameda as its first bishop. The same pope authorized Franciscan missions in the Canaries in his bull *Pia fidelium* of 1416 and renewed the Bishop of Rubicón's license in his bull *Sincerae devotionis* of the same year. Pope Martin V (1417–1431) in his bull *Meritis tuarum* (1423) created the first general vicarship of the Franciscan order in Fuerteventura and named Juan de Baeza as vicar-general. In his bull *Illius caelestis agricolae* (1424), Martin V also established the bishopric of Fuerteventura and named Martín de las Casas as its bishop.

[18] Although Normans, Gascons, and Sevillians managed to settle in Lanzarote, Fuerteventura, and Hierro, they "did not succeed in domesticating the economy of the [two main] islands," which "never benefited directly from the sugar boom that enriched the western islands in the last years of the fifteenth century" (Fernández Armesto, *Before Columbus*, 179, 182–83). Neither could these colonists penetrate Tenerife, Gran Canaria, Palma, or Gomera. Many contenders disputed the conquest of these islands, which suffered continuous attacks until they gradually capitulated to Christian forces (Fernández Armesto, *Before Columbus*, 184). As for Béthencourt, he died in France in 1425, and the government of the islands was left to his nephew, Maciot de Béthencourt, who turned out to be a tyrant and sold the islands first to Enrique de Guzmán, the Count of Niebla (via Captain Pedro Barba Campos from

ingly circulating information about the islands soon precipitated notions of the potential worth of the Atlantic Islands in the calculating minds of two Christian kings.

By the 1430s the Canaries had attracted the political and economic interest of the crowns of Castile and Portugal, both of which had legitimate claims to conquest. Alfonso IV of Portugal and Alfonso XI of Castile had previously accepted Clement VI's concession of the islands to Luis de la Cerda in 1344, but each monarch had also expressed his reservation by writing to the Pope and asserting as early as 1345 his own rights to conquer the Canaries.[19] Facing a prohibition of any further expansion issued by Pope Eugene IV (1431–1437), almost a century later, another Portuguese monarch, King Duarte, wrote to the pope in 1436 to persuade him to lift the ban and issue a bull for a Portuguese crusade to the Canaries.[20] A discussion on infidels' rights was revived on the basis of this letter, and the pope required the help of professional jurists who implicitly favored the arguments made by Duarte (Muldoon, *Popes, Lawyers, and Infidels*, 120–24). Antonio Minucci de Pratovecchio and Antonio de Rosellis, professors of canon law and Roman law, respectively, at the University of Bologna, asserted the rights of Portugal. These jurists did not refer to the Canary Islands or Portugal directly, but dealt with the issue theoretically, responding to the question of whether it was lawful to wage war against pagans in lands never previously occupied by Christians. They agreed that the principles of natural law were violated by the Canary Islanders because they had refused to admit missionaries to their lands; the canonists consented to the right of Christians to

---

Seville), and later to Prince Henry the Navigator of Portugal. The already settled islands passed from hand to hand until their final incorporation into Castile. For a comprehensive summary of the Franco-Norman conquest of some islands, see Elías Serra Ráfols and Alejandro Cioranescu's edition and study of Bountier and Le Verrier's *Le Canarien*, vol. 1.

[19] In February of 1345, Alfonso IV of Portugal wrote to the pope stating the evidence in favor of the Portuguese rights over the Canary Islands. These rights were determined by the facts that the Portuguese occupied them first, that the coast of Portugal was the closest to the islands, and that the Catholic faith needed to be spread to those lands (Alfonso de Cartagena, *Diplomacia y humanismo*, ed. and trans. González Rolán et al., 23). With no less juridical rights, Alfonso XI of Castile also wrote to the pope in March of the same year stating that the lands of Africa and the adjacent islands had belonged to his glorious forefathers and thus to him, as their universal heir (Cartagena, *Diplomacia y humanismo*, 24).

[20] Pope Eugene IV in his bulls *Regimini gregis* and *Creator omnium* of 1434 championed the liberty of the infidel inhabitants of the Canaries. The same pope, however, ordered a crusade of extermination against "Zenaga Berbers (*acenegues*) and Guineans" in his bulls *Rex Regum* of 1436 and 1443 (Rumeu de Armas, *La política*, 30). From the 1430s onward, slavery could not be officially practiced in the islands. The early condemnation of slavery proclaimed by Eugene IV was later ratified by Pius II (1458–1464) in his 1462 bull *Pastor bonus*, which also sought to stimulate and intensify missionary work in the Canaries (Rumeu de Armas, *La política*, 31).

conquer and colonize the islands, favoring the Portuguese crown in the process (Fernández Armesto, *Before Columbus*, 232–33).[21]

Another key figure in the debate, the erudite and accomplished Castilian jurist Alonso de Cartagena or de Santa María (1384/1386–1456), fully agreed with the above reasons except that in his view the rightful agent of conquest could be only Castile.[22] The Castilian diplomat and jurist's ingenious theory refuted each and every one of the legal arguments in favor of the Portuguese, to the point of elaborating a theory of monarchical succession that connected the islands' past to contemporary Castile (Cartagena, *Diplomacia y humanismo*, 57–163; Pérez Voituriez, *Problemas jurídicos*, 87–88). The Portuguese, however, had claimed to be the first legal occupants of the islands of the previously un-occupied sea.[23] Also, the Portuguese had utilized the principle of contiguity to assert that the closest geographical point to the islands was the Cape of San Vicente, which again gave the rights of conquest to Portugal. Cartagena responded to these allegations (that were at least ninety years old) by stating that neither justification, occupation nor vicinity, could be legally used by the Portuguese. The Canary Islands had indeed been occupied before, for they had belonged to the realms of the Visigoths since the time of the domination of the African Tingitania.[24] The Visigothic kings were in turn the direct forebears of Castilian monarchs who inherited the rights to conquer or reconquer the lands that had been part of their own dominion (Pérez Voituriez, *Problemas jurídicos*, 95–97).[25] Alonso de Cartagena did not stop there, but went on to assert (mis-

---

[21] Both Russell ("El descubrimiento," 24–25) and Muldoon (*Popes, Lawyers, and Infidels*, 124–31) present Minucci and Roselli's arguments very extensively. Russell uses them to argue that not only the Castilians but also the Portuguese received their colonial training in the Canaries. Muldoon emphasizes the canonists' arguments regarding the issue of *dominium* for the purpose of exploring the development of theoretical ideas rather than practical political applications (*Popes, Lawyers, and Infidels*, 124–31).

[22] For an excellent and brief overview of Cartagena's diplomatic missions and juridical writings and his greater significance in the Europe of the fifteenth century, see the introductory study of Tomás González Rolán, Fremiot Hernández González, and Pilar Saquero Suárez-Somonte (*Diplomacia y humanismo*, 9–41) to their 1994 bilingual Latin-Spanish edition of Alfonso de Cartagena's *Allegationes super conquesta Canarie* (Madrid: Universidad Nacional de Educación a Distancia, 1994).

[23] The king of Portugal, Alfonso IV, affirmed in 1345 that his kingdom had initiated the subjugation of the Canary Islands by sending an expedition for that purpose. This might have been the journey recorded by Boccaccio, who dated it imprecisely to 1341. Fernández Armesto (*Before Columbus*, 171) states that the evidence suggests that the Portuguese mission was more "an armed reconnaissance, at the private initiative, perhaps of slavers and merchants" than anything else.

[24] Tingitania or Mauretania Tingitana was part of the Roman Empire. Its capital was Tingis, presently Tangiers.

[25] Fernández Armesto (*Before Columbus*, 213) has pointed out that Alfonso XI not only had already used the same argument (mistakenly of course) in the mid-fourteenth century in

takenly) that the Castilian monarchs made Béthencourt recover the island of Lanzarote with the intention of conquering the rest for Castile (Pérez Voituriez, *Problemas jurídicos*, 97); he argued that the occupation of the part yielded to the rights of occupying the totality (Pérez Voituriez, *Problemas jurídicos*, 110–11). His argument became more sophisticated when he combined the principle of occupation with that of contiguity, derived from Roman law. Cartagena argued that the Canary Islands were part of Tingitania, which belonged to Spain; therefore the islands should be rightfully part of the land to which they bore the nearest geographical proximity (Pérez Voituriez, *Problemas jurídicos*, 111–12). When islands are annexed according to the criterion of proximity, it is proportionate to the extension of land that lies in front of them; thus, the Cape of San Vicente in Portugal, according to the jurist, was too narrow to have any validity as the closest and widest point of proximity to the Canary Islands (Pérez Voituriez, *Problemas jurídicos*, 113).

Portugal thought the papacy would be inclined to favor its claims, and indeed Eugene IV issued the bull *Romanus Pontifex* on October of 1436 favoring Portugal (Nicholas V also did so in 1454). However, twenty-two days after issuing that bull, Eugene IV issued another, *Romani Pontificis*, in which he annulled any concession made to King Duarte of Portugal and recognized the rights of John II of Castile over the Atlantic islands (Cartagena, *Diplomacia y humanismo*, 25). Cartagena's elaborate sophism and persuasive forensic discourse provided the legal groundwork for the recognition of Castilian rights of conquest as well as the legal justification for waging war against the heathens who had been occupying the islands for centuries. Despite papal donations, the territories in question continued to be disputed.[26] By 1479, however, the Portuguese and

---

his letter to the pope, but that it continued to be brought up occasionally. It survived during the times of Ferdinand and Isabella when witnesses to the status of the Canarian seigneury in 1476–1477 thought that the islands had belonged to the last Visigothic king. This same argument was also used by Cardinal Carvajal in 1494 while he was on an embassy to Rome (Fernández Armesto, *Before Columbus*, 213). A somewhat similar claim was made much later by the poet Antonio de Viana in 1604, which I will discuss in detail in Chapter Three. With respect to the New World, Gonzalo Fernández de Oviedo (1535) similarly claimed the right of Spain to seize the new lands on the other side of the Atlantic on the basis of an ancient dominion ("así con derecho tan antiquísimo … volvió Dios este señorío a España") (*Historia general y natural de las Indias*, ed. Juan Pérez de Tudela Bueso [Madrid: Atlas, 1959], 20 [bk. 2, chap. 3]; A. Pagden, *The Fall of Natural Man* [Cambridge: Cambridge University Press, 1982], 37).

    [26] The significant moments of the Portuguese-Castilian disputes over the Canaries, according to J. Mercer (*Canary Islanders* [London: Rex Collings, 1980], 181–98), are the following: In 1446, there was a mandate from the Portuguese crown to take over the islands and enforce a *quinto* tax. Fernán Peraza, of Spanish origin, obtained titles to the Canary Islands and began to colonize Gomera. The Peraza-Herrera clan continued to attack or attempted to annex other islands from 1447 to 1476. In 1448, the Portuguese were forced out of the islands by previous settlers, while in 1454 the king of Portugal ordered Prince Henry the Navi-

Castilian dispute was settled by the Treaty of Alcaçovas, and the universal titles provided by occupation, territorial vicinity, papal donation, or treaties were all more or less admitted as legitimate justifications for acquiring sovereignty over new territories (Pérez Voituriez, *Problemas jurídicos*, 100).[27] Castile was finally to have the Canary Islands, while Portugal had jurisdiction over the Azores, the Madeiras, the Cape Verde Islands, and the Guinea Coast (Muldoon, *Popes, Lawyers, and Infidels*, 135). Nevertheless, the ultimate Christian right of waging war against the natives of the islands was never questioned in this dispute. As Muldoon (*Popes, Lawyers, and Infidels*, 136) points out, "the rights of infidels [took] second place to the question of which two conflicting Christian powers would dominate their lands."

In 1479, when Isabella and Ferdinand of Castile and Alfonso V of Portugal signed the treaty of Alcaçovas-Toledo, they agreed upon the territories towards which the two respective kingdoms would expand. The Canary Islands were officially assigned to Castile.[28] Two years earlier, Castile had already claimed the

---

gator to withdraw from the Canaries. In 1468, another Portuguese, Diego de Silva, was sent to the Canaries; he married Herrera's daughter and attacked Gran Canaria without success. In 1477, Castilians and Portuguese battled in Gomera, but the next year the Portuguese managed to assert certain power through an alliance with the Peraza-Herrera family. In 1478, the Catholic monarchs sent Juan Rejón and Alonso de Lugo to the islands, who scored the first victory for the Spaniards by confronting and defeating a Portuguese maritime blockage in Gran Canaria. For a more detailed account of this dispute in the greater context of Spain's involvement in Africa, see A. Rumeu de Armas, *España en el África Atlántica*, 2nd ed., 2 vols. (Las Palmas: Cabildo insular de Gran Canaria, 1996), 1: 81–136, 221–48, 509–41.

[27] Two main principles prevailed. One derived from *ius gentium*, which considered the mere act of occupation without further settlement a right to annexation, *ius ad ocupationem*. The other was the general view that any effective juridical right for settlement needed to be validated by papal donation (A. Pérez Voituriez, *Problemas jurídicos internacionales de la conquista de Canaria* [La Laguna: Universidad de La Laguna, 1958], 91–92). The conquests prior to the fall of Gran Canaria in 1483 seem to have worked more like crusades, following the recommendations of the papacy. Later conquests seem to have followed a more unsystematic approach, since the Spaniards treated Tenerife in the 1490s, for example, as "a sovereign community" (Fernández Armesto, *Before Columbus*, 213–14). Fernández Armesto differentiates between the conquest of the Canary Islands and those in the New World by stating that the latter relied upon papal donation while the former did not (*Before Columbus*, 214). If the 1344 donation, which carried no further action, is disregarded, the complexity of the conquest of the Canaries can be said to encompass all possible kinds of legitimization as these were practiced in the fifteenth century.

[28] This treaty ended the lengthy legal dispute over the Canaries and the coast of West Africa sustained by Castile and Portugal. However, the Portuguese made new claims in 1482 while marriage negotiations (between Prince Alfonso of Portugal and Princess Isabella of Aragon and Castile) were taking place (Fernández Armesto, *Before Columbus*, 192). After Columbus's expedition, Pope Alexander VI's three bulls, *Inter caetera* and *Eximiae* of 3 May and *Inter caetera* of 4 May 1493, continued to demarcate each kingdom's zone of influence. A more definite divisory line between the territories to be conquered by the respective Iberian

right to conquer the larger islands, Gran Canaria, Palma, and Tenerife, and for that purpose the crown had taken action in sending the conquering expedition of Juan Rejón. Since the military campaign needed a legal justification, the Catholic monarchs adjusted papal policy. That is, the bull *Pastoris aeterni*, issued by Sixtus IV in 1472, had urged the conversion of all native Africans; thus, the Catholic monarchs inferred from the bull that if the natives of the Canaries did not want to convert peacefully, forceful military intervention was to be used (Rumeu de Armas, *La política*, 33, 40). This policy accompanied the beginning of one of the more ruthless conquests ever in the history of Castilian expansion: the conquest of Gran Canaria at the hands of Pedro de Vera.[29]

Isabella and Ferdinand commissioned Pedro de Vera in 1480 to take over the government of the Canaries, and under his command Gran Canaria fell to Spain in 1483. The Guanarteme of Telde finally capitulated to Vera and later to the Catholic monarchs, who ratified the peace in 1481. Pedro de Vera nevertheless initiated a policy of enslavement and massive deportation. Don Fernando Guanarteme of Gáldar and forty members of his immediate family were made prisoners in 1483, but in 1485 they obtained a protective royal decree against their enslavement or deportation. While the enslavement of the natives was taking place without the consent of the crown, all deportations during this period had the support and encouragement of the monarchy (Rumeu de Armas, *La política*, 52–53). In 1488, the Gomerans rebelled against Hernán Peraza and killed him, and Pedro de Vera came to the aid of Peraza's wife, Beatriz de Bobadilla. Once the Gomerans were defeated, Vera proceeded to ship men, women, and children to Spain to be sold in the Sevillian markets with the full approval of the crown — at first. The Catholic monarchs saw in Vera's attack the most just of wars because the Gomerans rebelled against their "natural lord"; thus, they considered prisoners taken in such a war to face enslavement rightfully. What the sovereigns did not foresee was the ruthless attitude of Vera, who also sold women and children; Vera's days as governor were

---

powers was not traced until 1494 with the Treaty of Tordesillas. Castile and Portugal agreed to change the zones allocated to each party from one hundred leagues west of the Azores and Cape Verde Islands to three hundred seventy leagues west of those islands. No other papal interventions were sought until there was need to demarcate the discoveries made in the Pacific Ocean between 1514 and the time of the Treaty of Saragossa in 1529 (Muldoon, *Popes, Lawyers, and Infidels*, 139).

[29] In his *Memorias del reinado de los Reyes Católicos* (1500?–1513?), Andrés Bernáldez (77 [chap. 35]) gave an interesting explanation for the Catholic monarchs' choice of Pedro de Vera, Mayor of Arcos, for the conquest of the last Canary Islands. The chronicler stated that Vera was exiled from Castile because he was responsible for the death of Diego de Basurto, the Mayor of Medina Sidonia, and for stealing his property (*hacienda*). As punishment, Vera had to return what he had taken and was sent on a mission to the islands. Incidentally, Pedro de Vera was also the grandfather of Alvar Nuñez Cabeza de Vaca, the famous shipwrecked explorer of the present southwest United States in the 1520s and 1530s.

numbered, however, thanks to his probable denouncement by Bishop Miguel López de la Serna.[30] Isabella and Ferdinand issued several royal decrees for the restoration of the personal freedom of many native islanders, and eventually deposed Vera as governor and brought charges against him for crimes against the legitimate subjects of the Castilian crown (Rumeu de Armas, *La política*, 67–75). Even though the policy of the crown seems to reflect a profound concern for the legal and moral issues surrounding the conquest of the Canary Islands, military expeditions did not cease. On the contrary, Francisco de Maldonado, Vera's successor, organized an unsuccessful attack on Tenerife. Finally the *adelantado* Alonso de Lugo completed the conquest of Palma in 1493 and of Tenerife in 1496–1497 for the crown of Castile (Mercer, *Canary Islanders*, 195–209). The inhabitants of the recently conquered islands continued to live in exile throughout Andalusia and mostly in Seville, and their return home was severely punished unless they participated in the new conquests as part of the Spanish army (Rumeu de Armas, *La política*, 54). The unjust enslavement of many continued, occurring sporadically under Lugo's direction.[31] The crown tried to compensate for some of the injustices committed against the islanders, but in spite of their apparently good intentions, some of the crown's protectionist measures eventually proved to be a kind of *encomienda* or entitlement to conquerors which led to the enslavement of many natives in Andalusia and the islands (Rumeu de Armas, *La política*, 53, 62). As would later occur in the New World, the vigilant eye of the Spanish monarchy would hardly question its legitimate right to rule over infidels and their lands, and it would lose sight and control of the process by which these new territories were acquired and by which their inhabitants were subdued and converted.

2. NAVIGATORS AND CHRONICLERS: REPRESENTATIONS OF THE CANARY ISLANDER

Throughout the centuries historians have rightfully assumed that the Canary Islands had been known in antiquity, although the only description that seems to correspond to the actual islands appeared in Pliny the Elder and later was copied by Solinus and Isidore of Seville (Martínez Hernández, *Las Islas Ca-*

---

[30] Bishop López de la Serna took over the bishopric of the Canary Islands in 1486, after the death of the famous Bishop Juan de Frías who also had defended the rights of the islanders (Rumeu de Armas, *La política*, 61). For a complete chronology of missionary establishments in the Canaries prior to 1499, see Pérez Fernández, introduction, *Brevísima relación*, 145–73.

[31] In Palma, Lugo claimed that the friendly natives were actually enemy forces in order to justify their captivity and sale. He also took hostages who were subsequently sold in violation of a peace treaty. In Tenerife, he might have followed a similar practice with his native allies of the kingdom of Güímar, among others (Rumeu de Armas, *La política*, 84–89).

narias, 201–2; Fernández Armesto, *Before Columbus*, 154). More than ten centuries later, at the apogee of the period of reconnaissance and raiding by European navigators, the islands finally began to take part in the experiential as well as the textual world of late medieval Europe.[32] New realities were still encapsulated by ancient texts, although direct contact with the islands brought about more accurate accounts. Whereas the earliest recorded voyage dates from 1291, when the galleys of the Vivaldi brothers from Genoa took the southward route to India, the navigators never made it back to narrate their trip. Subsequent journeys were more successful; some depicted mythical images in the tradition of the medieval bestiary, and some have left valuable ethnographic descriptions of the islanders: the Canarians of Gran Canaria, the Majos of Lanzarote, the Majoreros of Fuerteventura, the Bimbaches of El Hierro, the Gomeros of La Gomera, the Auaritas of La Palma, and the Guanches of Tenerife. In the following pages, I will concentrate on the same four important moments of medieval Canarian history to describe the information about the islanders, which to a great degree informed the European legal debates and policies discussed above.[33]

---

[32] In this period of reconnaissance and raiding, the islands also received visits from North African navigators, although with less frequency (Fernández Armesto, *Before Columbus*, 154). The Moroccans Ibn Fatima and Mohamed ben Ragano visited the Canaries in the thirteenth and fourteenth centuries; during the latter, raids conducted by Moroccan pirates were frequent (Mercer, *Canary Islanders*, 155). What is clear, however, is that the islands had never been occupied by the Almoravids and Almohads despite their aggressive expansion through the northwest of Africa. The representation of the islands consequently followed a similar mythical path in Arab writings as it did in classical European sources: al-Bakri (eleventh century), Ibn Said (thirteenth century), Sams-ed-Din Dimašqi [Shams al-Dīn al-Dimishķī] (fourteenth century), and Ibn Khaldun (fourteenth century) (M. Martínez Hernández, *Canarias en la mitología* [Santa Cruz de Tenerife: Centro de la Cultura Popular Canaria, 1992]; 82–85. In Arabic the islands were called "al-Kalidat" or "Kalidat" [*al-Djazā'ir al-Khālida*], a name which had its origin in a translation of the Latin denomination "Fortunatae" (B. Bonnet, "Las Canarias y el primer libro de geografía medieval," *Revista de historia canaria* 10 [1944]: 205–27, here 217; Martínez Hernández, *Canarias en la mitología*, 84–85; cf. *EI²*, 2: 522).

[33] In the mid-fourteenth century, imaginary and realistic accounts coexisted. I will concentrate on the voyages that collected some important empirical data. David Abulafia ("Neolithic Meets Medieval: First Encounters in the Canary Islands," in *The Medieval Frontier: Concepts and Practices*, ed. David Abulafia and Nora Berend [Aldershot: Ashgate, 2002], 255–78) has argued for a serious reconsideration of the ethnographic material of these early texts. It is worth noting here, however, that between 1348 and 1350 an anonymous Franciscan wrote a work entitled *Libro del conosçimiento de todos los reinos et tierras et señorios que son por el mundo, et de las señales et armas que han cada tierra et señorio por sy et de los reyes y señores que los proveen*. In this book, the friar takes an imaginary trip that leads him eventually to Africa and the Caridat Islands (Canaries), which he probably knew from Majorcan and Catalan explorers' letters and maps. The names of the islands are confused and some were duplicated, but most importantly a depiction of their inhabitants in manuscript R showed that they were one-legged (cf. Bonnet, "Las Canarias," 216–20; Marco Jiménez de la Espada, ed. *Libro del conoscimiento*

Two prominent writers of the Italian Renaissance, Boccaccio and Petrarch, handed down accounts which most vividly exemplified a break with the mythical image of the islands. The source of Boccaccio's *De Canaria et insulis reliquis ultra Hispaniam noviter repertis* is uncertain. It is possible that the journey of exploration undertaken by Lanzarotto (Lancelotto or Lanzarote Maloncelo) sometime prior to 1339, in the course of which he found and named the island of Lanzarote, was recorded by Boccaccio and misdated to 1341. This was partly a Portuguese enterprise, the account of which could have reached Florence via the community of Italian merchants in Seville; their medium of communication, the mercantile familiar letter, may have been the source of Boccaccio's text (Cachey, "Petrarch," 54). Boccaccio's account could also have been based on the Portuguese-sponsored reconnaissance mission of 1345, also misdated. Boccaccio described the newly discovered island of Canaria and its inhabitants by emphasizing that they were "much more civilized than many Spaniards: "et satis domestici, ultra quam sint multi ex Ispanis" (Cachey, "Petrarch," 54).

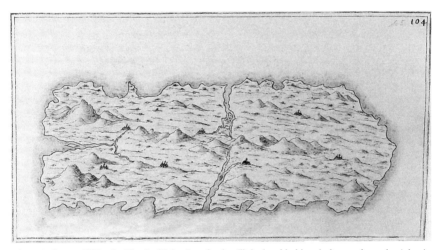

Fig. 1. As late as 1590s, the island of Saint Brendan is still depicted in historical texts about the Atlantic. This is Leonardo Torriani's rendition of the island in his *Descrittione et historia del regno del Isole Canarie gia dette le Fortunate con il parere delle loro fortificationi*. The original is housed at the General Library of the University of Coimbra (Codex 314).

[Madrid: Imprenta de T. Fortanet, 1877]). See the English translation of the text, *The Book of Knowledge of All Kingdoms*, ed. and trans. Nancy F. Marino, MRTS 198 (Tempe, AZ: Medieval and Renaissance Texts and Studies, 1999). Some of the cartographic texts which delineated the Canaries were by Dulcert in 1339, Mediceo in 1351, Pizzigano in 1367, Abraham Cresques in 1375, and others (Martínez Hernández, *Las Islas Canarias*, 167–68).

Boccaccio also insisted that the island to which the Europeans were taken was the most populous (probably Gran Canaria). The natives were addressed in many languages, but they did not understand; they responded to signs and gestures in the same manner. They were of the same height as the Europeans, robust, brave, and intelligent. They seemed to have a king who dressed differently (with an apron of palm leaves) and was shown deference by his subordinates. The others dressed in red and yellow reeds. They tasted bread for the first time and seem to like it, but they absolutely refused to drink wine and drank only water. The islanders ate wheat and barley, cheese and meat, and had plenty of goats, sheep, and wild dogs. Although they were shown gold and silver money, they ignored the use of it as well as of any kind of spice. They observed marriage, and married women wore aprons as well, but the single ones were naked and were not ashamed of it. They were also very loyal and honest and shared the food they were given with the rest.[34]

Regardless of the source, Boccaccio's *De Canaria* is not alone. His contemporary Francesco Petrarch, in his *Vita solitaria* (c. 1346), offered another significant description. For Petrarch, the Fortunate Islands were quite inferior to their name, and their inhabitants were "so savage in their customs and so similar to beasts that they were totally ruled by natural instinct, and roamed in the company of animals" ("Ceterum gentem illam pre cunctis ferme mortalibus solitudine gaudere, moribus tamen incultam adeoque non absimilem beluis ut, nature magis instinctu quam electione sic agentem, non tam solitarie vivere quam in

---

[34] The above summary comes from Cachey's quotation ("Petrarch," 55–57 n. 22) of Richard Henry Major's translation. Boccaccio's original text reads as follows:

Insula autem ex qua sublati sunt Canaria dicitur, magis ceteris habitata. Hii nichil penitus ex ydiomate aliquo intelligunt, cum ex variis et pluribus eis locutum sit. Magnitudinem vero nostram non excedunt, membruti satis, audaces et fortes et magni intellectus ut comprehendi potest. Nutibus loquitur eis et nutibus ipsi respondent mutorum more. Honorabant se invicem: verum alterum eorum magis quam reliquos, et hic femoralia palme habet, reliqui vero iuncorum, picta croceo et rufo. Cantant dulciter et fere more gallico tripudiant. Ridentes sunt et alacres et satis domestici, ultra quam sint multi ex Ispanis.

Hii postquam in navi positi sunt panem et ficus comederunt, et eis sapit panis cum ante numquam commedissent [sic]. Vinum omnino renuunt, aquam potantes. Comedunt similiter frumentum et ordea plenis manibus et caseum et carnes quarum his, et binarum, permaxima copia est. Boves autem aut camelos vel asinos non habent, sed capras plurimum et pecudes et silvestres apros. Ostensa sunt eis aurea et argentea numismata, omnino eis incognita. Similiter et aromata nullius materiei cognoscunt. Monilia aurea, vasa celata, enses, gladii ostensi eis non apparet ut viderint umquam vel se penes habeant.

Fidei et legalitis videntur permaxime: nil enim esibile datur uni quin antequam gustet equis portionibus diverserit ceterisque portionem suam dederit.

Mulieres eorum nubunt, et que homines noverunt more virorum femoralia gerunt; virgines autem omnino nude incedunt, nullam verecundiam ducentes sic incedere.

solitudinibus errare seu cum feris seu cum gregibus suis dicas").[35] These two writers, who witnessed the rediscovery of the islands, ended the "classical conception of the Fortunate Islands in literary as well as geo-historical terms," according to Cachey ("Petrarch," 47), and offered instead paradigmatic but divergent examples of the European anthropological gaze.

Cachey's ("Petrarch," 46–47) argument challenges Fernández Armesto's labeling of both canonical figures as similar in their exemplary humanist outlook. Cachey argues convincingly that although both writers shared the same European frame of reference, the two Renaissance views were representative of two opposite currents. That is, Petrarch's negative view fully supported his patron Clement VI's sermon "in its moral and cultural indictment of primitivism," while Boccaccio's more positive perspective represented the merging of both "humanistic and mercantile" cultures which constituted a prefiguration of Montaigne's and Voltaire's rhetorical use of cannibals and Hurons respectively to speak about Europe as well as its cultural others (Cachey, "Petrarch," 54, 58–59). As Cachey suggests, it is this bifurcated model which continued to characterize succeeding European encounters with other cultures.[36]

Similar representations of the Canary Islands proliferated throughout the fifteenth century, sometimes too interwoven to tell them apart as clearly as in the Italian writers, but emanating from a commonplace picture of primitivist societies.[37] Increasingly, the islands and their inhabitants were made out to fit

---

[35] Petrarch affirmed that native islanders enjoyed solitude more than any other people, but "they do not so much live alone as err/roam in desert places, with the wild beasts or with their flocks ... " (quoted and translated by Cachey ["Petrarch," 52 n. 15] from *Vita solitaria* [bk. 2, chap. 3]). In the sixteenth century, Bartolomé de las Casas would later disagree with Petrarch, stating that the famous writer transcribed hearsay which was not the truth (*Historia de las Indias*, ed. A. Millares Carlo, 3 vols. [Mexico: FCE, 1986], 1: 117–18 [bk. 1, chap. 21]).

[36] Such is the case of pirates' accounts that coincided with Petrarch in their assessment of the natives. *De nobilitate et rusticitate*, written by Felix Malloli, or Hemmerlin (1389–1457/1464), canon of Zurich, contradicted those accounts, agreeing in a fundamental way with Boccaccio's view, although Hemmerlin used Franciscan missionaries' accounts as his main source (Fernández Armesto, *Before Columbus*, 234–35; Martínez Hernández, *Las Islas Canarias*, 166).

[37] In his reference to the New World, Pagden offers a useful survey of the "primitivist topoi" that prevailed throughout the Middle Ages and well into the sixteenth century. He describes the "age of the natural man" in which an image of vegetarianism predominated, and in which there was no search for gain, no technology (*Fall of Natural Man*, 52), no iron (91), and in which human beings depended on nature for survival. Along with these characteristics, however, men of exotic lands were also constructed as being anthropophagi and filth-eaters (Pagden, *Fall of Natural Man*, 80–84). The representations of the inhabitants of the Canaries — which Pagden (58) does not explore as antecedent for those of the Amerindians — categorized the islanders in terms of some of the stereotypical attributes that I will describe below.

particular agendas, and descriptions began to become more specific to each of the islands which numbered "seven and were inhabited by infidels of different religions and different languages" ("sont sept, habitées de gens mescreans de diverses loys et de divers lengages"), according to the testimony of the French explorers and settlers in 1402 (Boutier and Le Verrier, *Le Canarien*, 3: 32–33). *Le Canarien*, written by Pierre Boutier and Jean Le Verrier, the two clerics who accompanied La Salle and Béthencourt, respectively, to the Canary Islands, described the islanders as "infidels who did not acknowledge their creator and lived in part like beasts and whose souls were on their way to damnation" (*Le Canarien*, 3: 84–85).[38] Thus, the French intervention was justified on the basis of the pagan status of the natives and the necessity to spread the Christian faith. Above all, however, this encounter proved once and for all that the inhabitants of the Canary Islands had nothing to do with the Muslim world. In fact, the chronicle stated that there was no region of non-Christians (*sarrazins*) or pagans (*paiens*) that could be so easily conquered; thus, a clear distinction was

---

[38] Elías Serra Ráfols and Alejandro Cioranescu have edited and extensively commented on the two extant manuscripts of *Le Canarien* in a bilingual French-Spanish edition in three volumes (above, n. 15). There are two versions of the French chronicle.

The first manuscript, written by Boutier and Le Verrier, is considered older and more accurate. It voiced Gadifer La Salle's complaint against Béthencourt's injustices and insisted on the former's more important role in the exploration and settlement of the islands. Serra Ráfols and Cioranescu call it manuscript G (*Le Canarien*, 1: 230–54; 2: 7–10); it was discovered in 1889 and is currently housed in the British Museum, MS. Egerton 2709.

The second version is apparently also written by Boutier and Le Verrier, but it is amended and continues beyond the events narrated by the previous manuscript (beyond 1404). This one is called manuscript B by Serra Ráfols and Cioranescu (*Le Canarien*, 1: 255–70; 2: 7–8), and it constitutes a later and somewhat careless rewriting (dating probably between 1488 and 1491) of a common source which was manipulated to defend the role and interest of Béthencourt. It is currently in the Municipal Library of Rouen, MS. Montruffet (*Le Canarien*, 1: 262). In the mid-seventeenth century, this version, included in Bergeron's *Traité des navigations* (Paris 1630), was translated into Spanish and circulated in the Canary Islands in manuscript form; see Serra Ráfols and Cioranescu's study (Boutier and Le Verrier, *Le Canarien*, 1: 256–57, 259).

Critics suspect, with no conclusive evidence, that manuscript G was written by Boutier, while manuscript B was written by Le Verrier, since these two clerics were the loyal companions of La Salle and Béthencourt respectively. However, an heir of the French conquistador, Jean V de Béthencourt, is thought to have revisited the original manuscript and finished what is known as manuscript B around 1491 (Boutier and Le Verrier, *Le Canarien*, 1: 256). I quote primarily from manuscript G since it is the older and most reliable source, but I also include some of the emendations made by manuscript B. As for the name "Boutier," it is worth mentioning here that the French editions of *Le Canarien* adopted the form "Bontier," but Serra Ráfols and Cioranescu opted for Boutier after researching family names in the Thouars region (*Le Canarien*, 1: 162).

The English translations are mine, except where I indicate my partial reliance on previous translations (Mercer, *Canary Islanders*, 162–197).

made between the Muslims and the Canary Islanders (Boutier and Le Verrier, *Le Canarien*, 3: 96–97; Russell, "El descubrimiento," 12).[39] The islanders, in addition to being ignorant of the arts of war and lacking effective weapons, could not be aided by the Berbers/Barbarians (*barbarins*), who were separated from the islands by distance and great mountains (Boutier and Le Verrier, *Le Canarien*, 3: 96–97). The French descriptions emphasized the economic potential of the land, much as Columbus's accounts of the Caribbean Islands would do nearly a century later, and they attempted to describe the native islanders as destined for the evangelical mission.[40] Their descriptions varied depending on the amount of knowledge that they had of the different islands; Lanzarote and Fuerteventura were, of course, portrayed in greater detail.

The French chroniclers said of Lanzarote's natives that the men were naked except for a sort of cape which fell to about the back of their knees and that they did not seem ashamed of exposing their bodies. The women were beautiful and dressed decently, with long tunics made of skins that reached down to the ground. Most women had three husbands who would rotate in month-long turns. The next husband in line would spend the month as a servant for the woman and her current husband.[41] The women bore many children who were described as handsome, delightful, and as white as European children at birth though they became quite tan as their naked skins were exposed to the wind. The women could not produce milk so they used their mouth to feed their children. This practice accounted for the women's enlarged lower lips which the French found quite repulsive. This divergence seemed characteristic only of Lanzarote, and the French chroniclers noted that the children of other islands were breast-fed as was the practice in Christian territories (Boutier and Le Verrier, *Le Canarien*, 3: 140–41).

Of Fuerteventura, which the French also called Erbania, they said the following: the inhabitants were few in number and ate meat and milk. Both men

---

[39] It is interesting that the word *sarazin* to define a king from Lanzarote was used in manuscript B (Boutier and Le Verrier, *Le Canarien*, 2: 30–31). From the context, however, Serra and Cioranescu have concluded that the word meant "non-Christian" rather than "Muslim" (Boutier and Le Verrier, *Le Canarien*, 2: 29 n. 10). The use of term "saracens" for non-Muslim pagans (like Lithuanians) was widespread; nevertheless, Fernández Armesto (*Before Columbus*, 214) seems to believe that toward the end of the fifteenth century the image of the native islanders was not totally exempted from association with the "Moors," as in the case of a Venetian Ambassador for whom Don Fernando Guanarteme was a "Saracen king."

[40] Jennifer R. Goodman in *Chivalry and Exploration (1298–1630)* (Woodbridge, UK: Boydell Press, 1998) here 106, points out how Béthencourt and Columbus had a similar "contractual approach" to exploration and conquest. However, Goodman's main concern is Gadifer and his inscription in a long tradition of chivalric literary heroes that becomes evident even in his real adventure in the Canaries. Goodman's excellent readings of transatlantic texts, among them *Le Canarien*, is quite successful in undermining the artificial border between "factual literature of travel" and voyages "of imaginative fiction" (*Chivalry*, 219).

[41] I follow Mercer's English version in this section (*Canary Islanders*, 163).

and women were described as tall. The accounts depicted them as being so fervent in their religious beliefs that it was quite difficult to take them alive. If one of them were to return after allowing himself to be captured by Christians, he would be killed without mercy (Boutier and Le Verrier, *Le Canarien*, 3: 136–37). They all walked about naked, especially the men, who wore only a hairy animal skin tied around their shoulders. The women wore a similar cape as well as two others tied around the waist, one in front and one behind, reaching to their knees. The women also wore shoes without heels, and had long curly hair which they cut across the forehead, as the men did. *Le Canarien* noted again that, in contrast to Lanzarote, children on this island were breast-fed (Boutier and Le Verrier, *Le Canarien*, 3: 136–37). Later, the second account (manuscript B) would add that besides being firm in their faith, the natives were doltish ("de dur entendement") and had a temple in which to offer sacrifices. The natives did not have salt, but nonetheless had the ability to dry meat. This meat was hung up to dry in their homes, thereby making the houses smell rather bad, yet the resulting product was much better than the corresponding jerky produced in France. The natives also ate suet (*suyf*) with the same gusto with which Europeans ate bread (Boutier and Le Verrier, *Le Canarien*, 2: 248–51 [chap. 68]).

Of Gran Canaria, the French chroniclers observe that it was the most celebrated of all the islands. The native social structure was made up of six thousand noble men ("gentilz homes") as well as people of other classes. Men were naked apart from a loin-covering made of palm leaves, and a great many of them were tattooed with diverse emblems. They wore their hair back in a type of braid. As a people, they were attractive and well-proportioned, and their women were beautiful and dressed in skins to cover their shameful parts (Boutier and Le Verrier, *Le Canarien*, 3: 130–31). The French also attempted to describe what they called the "Island of Inferno" ("L'isle d'Enfer"), also known as Tenerife, and thought to be one of the best islands. They said of this island, which they had only circumnavigated, that it was inhabited by the bravest of all people who lived on these islands although they were of small stature.[42] They also were never raided nor taken into slavery (Boutier and Le Verrier, *Le Canarien*, 3: 128–29).

---

[42] It is interesting to note here that manuscript B eliminated the reference to the short stature of the Guanches (Boutier and Le Verrier, *Le Canarien*, 2: 240–41 [chap. 66]). Perhaps by the later date in which this version was rewritten other information about the Guanches had reached the author. In the sixteenth century the Guanches were thought to have had great giants among their ancient people, and this mythical image passed from one account to another. The writings of the Florentine Cristóbal Landino in the late 1400s, for example, speak of islanders who were very tall and robust, with hair only on their heads, and who lived for four hundred years (Martínez Hernández, *Las Islas Canarias*, 171, 219–20). This imaginative description was made after most of the islands had already been conquered by Europeans.

The chroniclers stated that Gomera was heavily populated by people who spoke the strangest language of all these parts. They spoke with their lips ("des baulievrez") as if they had no tongue, and it was said that a great prince had exiled them to the islands and cut off their tongues because of an unknown crime. The French confessed that they were inclined to believe this explanation because of the Gomerans' unusual speech (Boutier and Le Verrier, *Le Canarien*, 3: 126–27). In Hierro, the French explorers encountered few inhabitants due to yearly raids and massive enslavement (Boutier and Le Verrier, *Le Canarien*, 3: 76–77). The chronicle described the people of the island as simple, good-natured, and predisposed to European influence (Boutier and Le Verrier, *Le Canarien*, 3: 76–77). The second version of the chronicle (manuscript B) would later add that both the men and the women were handsome, and that the men carried long wooden lances without a metal point (because they did not possess or know about any metals).[43]

The French writers also described Palma, which they called "L'isle de Palmes." They found the island to be heavily populated, since it had not been raided to the same extent as the others. Its inhabitants were characterized as handsome people who ate nothing but meat, and manuscript B added that the natives hardly fell sick and that they lived a long time (Boutier and Le Verrier, *Le Canarien*, 2: 236–37 [chap. 64]). The French thought Palma was the most attractive (*delitable*) island, although their knowledge of it was rather superficial (Boutier and Le Verrier, *Le Canarien*, 3: 126–27).

Years later, the Portuguese historian Gomes Eanes de Zurara or Azurara wrote the *Crónica dos feitos notáveis que se passaram na conquista de Guiné por mandado do Infante D. Henrique* (1452–1453), in which, upon narrating the great deeds of Prince Henry the Navigator of Portugal, he dedicated a few chapters to the Canary Islands and their inhabitants. Zurara concentrated on the four islands that were not subjugated by the French and that offered real economic possibilities for Portugal. He related that the Gomerans walked about completely naked and ate milk and herbs like beasts ("como bestas"), and also that they ate dirty animals and insects ("Comem coisas torpes e sujas, como sejam ratos, pulgas e piolhos e garrapatos ...") (Zurara, *Crónicas*, 2: 461 [bk. 3, chap. 80]). As would be expected from such a degree of bestiality, Zurara continued describing the Gomerans' sexual practices as rather open and relaxed: women were commonly shared and men lent married women to strangers as a gesture of hospitality. Men, therefore, left their wealth to their sister's son and not to their

---

[43] Manuscript G lacks a page between the narration of the return of La Salle to Fuerteventura and the description of the islanders, and then it goes on to describe the islands beyond Hierro (Boutier and Le Verrier, *Le Canarien*, 3: 122–25 n. 48). Manuscript B took this passage to refer to the natives of Hierro (Boutier and Le Verrier, *Le Canarien*, 2: 232–35 [chap. 63]), which is probably correct, since there are no other specific physical descriptions of them in the text.

own. The natives lived in caves and huts and their fighting was done with jave-lins. Above all, the Gomerans spent a great deal of time singing and dancing. They believed in one God, but followed no laws (Zurara, *Crónicas*, 2: 462 [bk. 3, chap. 80]). This was not the case for the natives of Palma, whom Zurara con-sidered very primitive ("muito bestiais") to the point of being without God or faith, unlike the rest of the islanders who knew of the existence of God. He also pointed out that their fighting was done using staves with horn tips (Zurara, *Crónicas*, 2: 465–66 [bk. 3, chap. 82]).

Gran Canaria and Tenerife were considered the most populous and civi-lized islands and thus the Portuguese chronicler described them in greater de-tail. Zurara talked about Gran Canaria in terms of a more sophisticated society which had a king, a duke (*duque*), and about 190 to 200 knights whose lineage had never been mixed with other classes ("sem mistura de vilãos").[44] Since the natives had reason ("são entendidos") and possessed knowledge of the Creator, they had an understanding that those who did good would be rewarded and that those who did evil would be punished (Zurara, *Crónicas*, 2: 456 [bk. 3, chap. 79]). The general population, according to Zurara, believed in what the knowl-edgeable knights did and there was no disagreement of opinion among them. Furthermore, all maidens in Gran Canaria had to be deflowered by the knights, and the natives practiced a curious bride-fattening ritual, which was believed to help improve their childbearing capacity. Before a maiden was to be married she was fattened, and Zurara stated that the women's skins became so bloated that they resembled soaked figs.[45] The nobles had the right to the first night with the fattened brides, who would first parade naked in front of the noble men in order to be chosen; those who were too fat were sent to the ocean to "swim it off." After having been with the nobles, the women went home to their fathers who could only then marry them off (Zurara, *Crónicas*, 2: 457 [bk. 3, chap. 79]). Children were fed not by their mothers, but by nanny goats (Zurara, *Crónicas*, 2: 460 [bk. 3, chap. 79]).

Zurara also wrote about the natives' prejudices against those who killed animals, an act that was considered a great sin; thus the butcher caste was the lowest and none of the others would mix with them. The task could also fall to captured Christians, when available (Zurara, *Crónicas*, 2: 459–60 [bk. 3, chap.

---

[44] Besides having two kings or *guanartemes* in the position of political authority, the is-land of Gran Canaria had two *faycanes* or religious authorities (A. Tejera Gaspar, "Sociedad y cultura indígena," in *Historia de Canaria*, ed. A Béthencourt Massieu [Las Palmas: Cabildo Insular de Gran Canaria, 1995], 116).

[45] Zurara's phrase "o coiro delas se arregoa como fazem os figos" has been translated by Mercer (*Canary Islanders*, 185) as "their skins are wrinkled like ripe figs." The Portuguese verb *arregoar*, however, may denote here the more appropriate notion of irrigating or flood-ing.

79]).[46] They had wheat and barley from which they made only flour but not bread. When the chronicler remarked on the absence of metals in the island, he also emphasized that the natives saw no value in gold, silver, or other metal ("têm em desprezo").[47] Zurara used his ethnographic description to also make clear his political stance in favor of the Portuguese rights to the islands. He insisted that among the natives of Gran Canaria many called themselves Christian after Prince Henry the Navigator had sent an expedition under Fernando de Castro in 1424. Zurara concluded that the evangelizing mission initiated by the Portuguese would have been more successful if the Castilian king had not interfered by reclaiming the island for Castile (*Crónicas*, 2: 459 [bk. 3, chap. 79]).

Zurara saw the inhabitants of the "Ilha do Inferno ou de Tanarife"[48] as well off and more civilized than other islanders ("e vivem mais como homens que alguns destes outros"). The Guanches dressed in animal skins and kept their genitals well covered except when they procreated or urinated. Men were strong and wives were not shared among them. Tenerife was divided into eight or nine territories, and the inhabitants of that island fought among themselves regularly with fire-hardened pinewood spears. The chief of each territory kept his predecessor's remains near him, unburied; his own successor threw the penultimate relics in a pit replacing them with the latest remains. The disposal of a set of relics was marked by the bearer saying, "May he go to salvation." Zurara's Guanches, of course, believed in God (*Crónicas*, 2: 463–64 [bk. 3, chap. 81]; Mercer, *Canary Islanders*, 197).[49]

---

[46] According to Mercer (*Canary Islanders*, 185), Zurara added some details that have traditionally been attributed to Tenerife but that the critic claims referred to Gran Canaria as well. The natives painted themselves with green, red, and yellow designs. Polygamy was normal, and the installation of a new leader was celebrated with a ritual in a deep valley followed by a voluntary human sacrifice. The leader then became indebted to the person's family. This information, however, appears in Alvise Ca' da Mosto's account (*Viagens* [Lisboa: Academia Portuguesa da Historia, 1947], 13–14) and not in Zurara's history as Mercer suggests. A similar description of the ritual appears in Diogo Gómez de Sintra's *De insulis*, in which the volunteer for the sacrifice, carrying the entrails of the dead king, jumped off a cliff (B. Bonnet, "Un manuscrito del siglo XV," *Revista de historia canaria* 7 [1940]: 92–100, here 98–99).

[47] According to Zurara (*Crónica*, 2: 458 [bk. 3, chap. 79]), the natives valued only one metal, iron, which was used to make fishing hooks. However, iron is generally thought not to have been known by the islanders. Based on this information, Las Casas, following João de Barros's *Asia*, rewrote this passage in the sixteenth century. He indicated that the natives valued any piece of iron (like nails) that happened to come into their possession, and that they turned them into fishing hooks (*Historia de las Indias*, 1: 117 [bk. 1, chap. 21]).

[48] Although in modern times the natives of all the Canary Islands have generally been called Guanches, this term can be appropriately used only for those who inhabited Tenerife. Zurara did not call the natives Guanches. The term came into use at the turn of the sixteenth century.

[49] The Venetian Alvise da Mosto or Ca' da Mosto (c. 1455), who traveled on behalf of the Portuguese as well, left another valuable description, although a less detailed one than

Despite their different emphases, an important point of agreement in Portuguese and French narratives concerned the "pagan" nature of the Canary Islanders. For the economic empire being built under Prince Henry the Navigator, the Portuguese chroniclers pretended that sub-Saharan Africa was indistinguishable from Muslim Africa (Russell, "El descubrimiento," 12). However, it was hard to make such a claim about the Canary Islands after some of the islands had been conquered and settled, especially given the fact that most islanders had been observed and described by many travelers, while many others were living and serving in several European urban centers. For Prince Henry and the Portuguese, their enemies were either "saracens" or "homines silvestri" (Fernández Armesto, *Before Columbus*, 187). Luckily, the natives of the Canaries fell in the second category, which nevertheless did not prevent Europeans from seeking their conquest and enslavement.

Castilian chroniclers were also interested in narrating the conquest of the Canaries. They offered, however, an image of the natives which added very little to the information gathered by the Portuguese.[50] The islands whose de-

---

Zurara's. About the inhabitants of the four conquered islands (including Gomera, which had been occupied by Fernán Peraza), Ca' da Mosto (*Viagens*, 12) said that: "They have not been subdued in the mountains"; he also heard other stories about Tenerife, which sometimes agreed and some times disagreed with Zurara. Ca' da Mosto (*Viagens*, 12) stated that the Guanches greased their bodies with a mixture of goat fat and herb juices, and that their animal skin garments alone were not adequate against the winter cold. They did not have huts. The position of leader was not inherited but went to the strongest; therefore, the nine leaders (*duci*) were not natural lords ("non sono segnori per natura"). They had no Christian faith, nor God. Some worshipped the sun, others the moon, and others the stars, with strange idolatrous fancies (Ca' da Mosto, *Viagens*, 13). Ca' da Mosto's account is based on inaccurate narratives in which the natives appeared more primitive than the ones described by Zurara, due mostly to the fact that Ca' da Mosto (*Viagens*, 14) affirmed that he had visited only Gomera and Hierro and circumnavigated Palma. For this reason the three islands, which were not under Christian subjection, are also treated as if they were an encompassing and confusing whole in Ca' da Mosto's account. According to Bonnet ("Un manuscrito del siglo XV," 92–100), shortly after Zurara's chronicle was finished, another Portuguese navigator, Diogo Gómez de Sintra, reported information mostly about Gran Canaria, Tenerife, and Palma. Diogo Gómez in his *De insulis primo inventa in mari oceano occidentis, et primo de Insulis Fortunatis, quae nunc de Canaria vocuntur* (1460–1463) narrated that in Gran Canaria natives adored the sun as God, were repulsed by meat, shared their wives with guests, and used goats as matrimonial dowry. In Tenerife, natives were short but fierce and had a ritual of human sacrifice after a royal succession. In Palma, as population control, natives practiced infanticide by crushing children's skulls with stones. Diogo Gómez insisted that Christians were put to death in the same way when their numbers exceeded that which was stipulated on the island.

[50] Information about the islands can be found, according to Martínez Hernández (*Las Islas Canarias*, 172–73), in López de Ayala's *Crónica de Enrique III* or in Álvar García de Santa María's *Crónica de Juan II* (the latter is also attributed to Fernán Pérez de Guzmán or to Juan de Mena), and in Alonso de Palencia's *Décadas*, specifically in *Cuarta Década* (see José López

scriptions presented more interest were the ones still to be conquered, a feat that would contribute to the military glory and religious righteousness of Castile and the Catholic monarchs. Most descriptions of the islanders thus appeared in the writings of chroniclers narrating the deeds of Ferdinand and Isabella. Mosén Diego de Valera, for example, did not even engage in any description of the islands or islanders, while he explained in detail the conquest of Gran Canaria (*Crónica de los Reyes Católicos*, ed. de Mata Carriazo, 108–14 [chap. 37]). Hernando del Pulgar offered a rather brief and generic description of the inhabitants of Gran Canaria. He mentioned in passing that they were all naked from the waist up while from the waist down they covered their loins with leaves and skins; he emphasized instead the information directly related to Pedro de Vera's conquering mission. The natives fought very well because war was frequent among them and the island was won, according to Pulgar, because one of the two kings (the *Guanarteme* of Gáldar) joined forces with Pedro de Vera against the other native king ("Crónica de los Señores Reyes Católicos," ed. Rosell, 382 [bk. 4, chap. 18]). He also enumerated succinctly the general customs of Gran Canaria's natives ("Crónica de los Señores Reyes Católicos," ed. Rosell, 330–31 [bk. 2, chap. 76]), which I will discuss later, as these appear in a richer form in Andrés Bernáldez's history. The focus of the above-mentioned texts lies beyond the Canaries, and consequently the islands are practically ignored.

Such is not the case in Andrés Bernáldez's *Memorias del reinado de los Reyes Católicos* (1500?–1513?), which offered a comprehensive description of at least one island, Gran Canaria. The conquests of Palma and Tenerife were perhaps too recent for him to have had access to any substantial information or written sources. According to Bernáldez (*Memorias*, ed. Gómez-Moreno and Mata Carriazo, 137–39 [chap. 64]), before Christians came to the islands, all islanders, both men and women, went about as naked as the day they were born, except in Gran Canaria, where they wore undergarments made of leaves — which could not cover their shameful parts properly because they were open under-

---

del Toro, ed., *Cuarta Década*, 2 vols. [Madrid: Real Academia de la Historia, 1970–1974]; see also the most recent edition of Palencia's *Décadas* under the original Latin title, *Gesta hispaniensia ex annalibus suorum dierum collecta*, ed. and trans. Brian Tate and Jeremy Lawrance [Madrid: Real Academia de la Historia, 1998]). More information can also be found in Esteban Pérez del Cabitos's *Información*, among others (Martínez Hernández, *Las Islas Canarias*, 172–73). Apparently Palencia wrote *Mores et ritus idolatrici incolarum insularum Fortunatarum quas Canarias appellant* or *Costumbres y falsas religiones de los canarios*, which is now lost, but was known in manuscript form by Bartolomé de las Casas (Martínez Hernández, *Las Islas Canarias*, 172–73; Palencia, *Cuarta Década*, ed. López del Toro, 1:92 n. 92). Also, references to the Canaries (Martínez Hernández, *Las Islas Canarias*, 174–76) appeared in another type of texts, the *Isolarii* (the books about all the islands in the world): that is the case of C. Buondelmonti's *Liber insularum* (c. 1420) and Domenico Silvestri's *De insulis et earum proprietatibus* (late 1300s). The islands also appeared in many other encyclopedic medieval works of the *Imago Mundi* or *Cosmographia* types.

neath. He also remarked that the skin of the many goats living on the islands served the islanders for the fabrication of covers and *tamarcos*, which hung from their shoulders and backs. Interestingly, in his early account, Bernáldez used the word *tamarco*, which was later attributed to the Guanche lexicon to mean "tunic" or "dress." Each man had one or more women, but marriage could be dissolved for the slightest of reasons, and both sexes were free to interact with whomever they pleased.

For Bernáldez, islanders were "idolaters without law" ("idólatras sin ley"). To support this claim, Bernáldez narrated that in Gran Canaria the natives had a house of prayer called "Toriña" in which they adored a wooden image of a naked woman half a lance tall. In front of this image, Bernáldez (*Memorias*, 138 [chap. 64]) continued, there was another image of a wooden female goat positioned before the wooden figure of a male goat, both suggesting the act of conception. There the islanders spilled milk and lard as if in an offering, and the whole place reeked of milk and lard. However, when the old men were asked about their ancestors, said Bernáldez, they responded that God put them there and forgot about them. And then, pointing towards Spain, they added that God had prophesied that an eye or a light would appear from that direction to illuminate them. The apparently primitive religion practiced in Gran Canaria was, for Bernáldez, a forgotten part of Christianity awaiting the light. The islanders were indeed characterized as "reasonable, intelligent and sharp witted ... loyal, charitable, honest and good Christians" ("razonables de buenos entendimientos, y de agudo injenio ... gente fiel, y caritativa, y de verdad, y buenos cristianos") (*Memorias*, 139 [chap. 64]).

With respect to Gran Canaria, Bernáldez affirmed the existence of nobles and knights who were respected and obeyed. He elaborated on Zurara's description of the bride-fattening practice, although, unlike the Portuguese chronicler, he claimed that the women slept with the noblemen of their choice. He showed his disapproval by summarizing that the natives had other such heathen customs ("como de alimañas") and that like beasts they felt no shame for their nakedness (*Memorias*, 144 [chap. 66]) — which could very well have been understood to be spiritual as well as physical.

Regarding the island of Palma, Bernáldez stated only that Alonso de Lugo conquered people who were naked barbarians, idolaters, and enemies of the Catholic faith (*Memorias*, 337–38 [chap. 132]). This might have referred to Lugo's claims of having to confront fierce enemies to justify the natives' captivity. Of Tenerife, Bernáldez (*Memorias*, 339–41 [chap. 134]) briefly related that the islands had nine kingdoms and that the inhabitants were called "Guanchos" instead of Guanches. Sevillians, Andalusians, and other natives of the Canaries themselves participated in the conquest of Tenerife, which, despite the natives' predisposition to surrender, was done by force. According to "the priest of Los Palacios" ("el cura de Los Palacios"), as Bernáldez was known, the war took place because "the greedy Christians desired eagerly to have slaves and booty rather than to serve God" ("los christianos, con mucha cobdicia antes de haber esclavos y esclavas y despojos, que no por servir a Dios") (Bernáldez, *Memorias*, 339 [chap. 134]).

Bernáldez's image of the islanders was, like those of his predecessors, the result of distortions and displacements for areas where precise geographical sites as well as empirical information were rather elusive. His description of Gran Canaria, however, offered the details and value judgments of one who was to some degree fascinated by another culture, its customs and rituals. His comments on the conquest of Tenerife, moreover, openly criticized European war practices. Above all, Bernáldez voiced a more than a century-old dilemma surrounding the Canaries, but also one that he had already seen reenacted in the context of the New World, especifically in the Caribbean. On the one hand, there was the clear recognition of the Atlantic islanders as "wild men" outside of true civilization and religion, although for Bernáldez they had already fostered a myth that prefigured Christianity. On the other hand, there was the evidence that the war waged against them and the enslavement suffered by many of them were very difficult to justify either legally or morally.

With slight variations, the image of the Canary Islands and their inhabitants continued to be constructed in the European imagination more homogeneously than the cultural differences among the islands called for. The sixteenth century, however, saw the discovery of many other more distant, diverse, and far more sensational "fortunate islands." Not until the end of the sixteenth century would there be a serious attempt by historians and poets to reconstruct the history of the Canary Islands. These would have the history not only of the Canaries and their inhabitants in mind, but also of the islands and islanders of the New World.

3. THE CANARY ISLANDS AND THE NEW WORLD: MUTUAL INFLUENCES

Most of the legal and moral arguments surrounding the Canaries up to the fifteenth century found an echo in the debates surrounding the Amerindians. To the same degree, European textual representations of the islands and their inhabitants prior to 1492 find similar reproductions in sixteenth-century texts dealing with the recently discovered continent. The New World, according to Fernández Armesto (*Before Columbus*, 244), posed no new challenge that had not already been proposed or discussed previously in the context of the Canary Islands and the African rim, "except perhaps for the evolving of a scientific ethnology."[51] Fernández Armesto has arrived at this conclusion by analyzing the documentation and debates of humanists, missionaries, and jurists which

---

[51] Anthony Pagden (*Fall of Natural Man*, 119–75) has called it "comparative ethnology" in his discussion of Las Casas's and Acosta's ethnographic works about the Amerindians.

Fig. 2. Mapa Mundi by Abraham Ortelio in his *Theatrum Orbis Terrarum* (Antuerpiae: Balthasaris Moreti, 1626). Courtesy of the General Library at Salamanca University.

somewhat resembled the more famous debates of Charles V's court in the six-teenth century. Fernández Armesto's position is very much like that which mo-tivated Muldoon's study of medieval canon law, which regulated the relation-ship between the spiritual and secular powers of the Christian world with that of the infidels. If the sixteenth century's polemics about the Amerindians were indebted to medieval juridical debates, it is also true that such canonistic mod-els proved defective because popes and lawyers failed to assimilate into their arguments the rapidly increasing European incursions into the non-European and non-Christian worlds (Muldoon, *Popes, Lawyers, and Infidels*, 155). Muldoon (*Popes, Lawyers, and Infidels*, 157) further asserts that the same failure was later experienced in the sixteenth century by Vitoria and Las Casas who were work-ing within a canonistic framework rendered obsolete by the actual reality of the conquest.

For those interested in writing the history of the Canary Islands, however, the New World and the debates generated around it did pose new challenges. Theorists and thinkers like Vitoria or Las Casas not only appropriated a series of medieval legal arguments, but also elaborated a coherent and systematic ap-proach to the legal, moral, and political dilemmas facing Spain in the sixteenth century. These famous debates played an extraordinary role in the later development of a more sophisticated international law. If the legal and moral status of the conquest of the Canaries informed those that later took place in the New World, the debates generated by the latter informed the manner in which the history of the Canary Islands was revisited at the turn of the seventeenth century.

The legal framework that served as the basis for Las Casas's anthropological outlook and his defense of the rights of the Amerindians underlies the textual practices which set out to reconsider the history of Spain overseas at the turn of the seventeenth century. It is true that Las Casas's influential presence was felt in Charles V's court and Rome and that it helped shape secular policies as well as papal bulls, only to see them fail when implemented. His writings, however, inspired another Dominican, Alonso de Espinosa, to write a historical account that reformulated the history of the Guanches and the European conquest of Tenerife and that ultimately did justice to the spiritual and political legacy of Bartolomé de las Casas.

CHAPTER TWO

BETWEEN NARRATION AND DIGRESSION: ALONSO DE ESPINOSA AND THE HISTORIOGRAPHY OF THE CANARY ISLANDS

> Andaban todos desnudos como su madre los parió ... muy bien hechos, de muy hermosos y lindos cuerpos y muy buenas caras ... y ellos son de la color de los canarios, ni negros ni blancos ....

> [They were all naked as their mothers brought them into the world ... well built, of handsome and beautiful bodies and good faces ... and they are of the same color as the Canarians, neither black nor white ....]

THESE WERE THE WORDS OF CHRISTOPHER COLUMBUS, according to Las Casas in his *Historia de las Indias*, when the Admiral first encountered the Arawak Indians in 1492. By making such a comparison, Columbus made use of a very important and well-known point of reference in his times: the Canary Islands (*Historia de las Indias*, 1: 204 [bk. 1, chap. 40]).[52] The use of the islands as intermediary between the Old and the New World was not exclusively a Columbian practice; on the contrary, the chroniclers of the Indies mentioned the history of the islands as antecedent to the history of the New World. Gonzalo Fernández de Oviedo y Valdés, for example, in his *Historia general y natural de las Indias* (1535), wrote a few paragraphs about the islands "which the ancients

---

[52] All translations are mine unless otherwise indicated. This is the first reference to the color of the skin of the Canarians in comparison to that of the Arawaks. When Las Casas gives more detailed descriptions of the Caribbean islanders, he repeats the comparison (*Historia de las Indias*, 1: 205 [bk. 1, chap. 40]; 1: 231 [bk. 1, chap. 46]). He makes additional comparisons, mainly geographical ones, between the Canary Islands and some of the Caribbean islands such as Tortuga or Jamaica (*Historia de las Indias*, 1: 265 [bk. 1, chap. 55]; 1: 394 [bk. 1, chap. 97]). For a complete summary of the references to the Canary Islands in the chronicles of Indies, see Francisco Morales Padrón, *Sevilla, Canarias y América* (Las Palmas: Cabildo Insular de Gran Canaria, 1970), 189–253.

called the Fortunate Islands" ("que los antiguos llaman Fortunadas") (ed. Pérez de Tudela, 1: 24 [bk. 2, chap. 5]), while Francisco López de Gómara included in his *Historia general de las Indias* (1552) three brief chapters on the subject: "because the Canary Islands are on the route to America and have been reconquered, I write here of their conquest" ("Por ser las islas de Canaria camino para las Indias, y nuevamente conquistadas, escribo aquí su conquista") (ed. Gurría Lacroix, 315 [chaps. 221–23]). Sharing the brevity of other historians, Bartolomé de las Casas nevertheless took up the role of the islands as a geographic and experimental space for the later conquests in the New World. By recounting the details of the conflict between Portugal and Castile and condemning the slave trade and the treatment of the natives, he initiated a serious and comprehensive inquiry into the historical place of the Canary Islands among Columbus's contemporaries in exploration as well as among his own sixteenth-century contemporaries in history writing, the chroniclers of the Indies.[53]

The relevance of the Islands within the greater project of Spanish imperial expansion has been further studied by numerous contemporary historians. John Elliott, for example, has stated that:

> Castile's occupation of the Canaries was an event of major importance in the history of its overseas expansion. Their geographical position was to make them of exceptional value as an indispensable staging-post on the route to America: all Columbus's four expeditions put in at the Canary archipelago. But they were also to provide the perfect laboratory for Castile's colonial experiments, serving as the natural link between the Reconquista in Spain and the conquest of America (*Imperial Spain*, 58).

---

[53] For the medieval accounts about the re-discovery, exploration, conquest, and pacification of the Canary Islands up to 1500, see the previous chapter. During the fifteenth and sixteenth centuries, the history of the islands appeared in various works by Spanish and Italian geographers, Portuguese travelers and chroniclers, and Spanish royal chroniclers. Fernández Armesto, *Before Columbus* offers a detailed study of these explorations from 1229 to 1492, and Martínez Hernández, *Las Islas Canarias* also offers a descriptive overview of references to the islands made from antiquity to the Renaissance. See also Morales Padrón, *Sevilla*, 189–253. Some local chronicles — known as the manuscripts *Ovetense, Lacunense, Matritense, López de Ulloa, Cedeño* and *Escudero* — explored the history of the conquest, mainly of Gran Canaria, of which only eighteenth-century copies are extant (see F. Morales Padrón, *Canarias: Crónicas de su conquista* [Las Palmas: Museo Canario, 1978], 9–468). Espinosa's chronicle, however, is the first devoted exclusively to the islands, Tenerife in particular, and was the first one to be published in the Spanish-speaking world by 1594. Thomas Nichols's *A Pleasant Description of the Fortunate Ilandes* was published approximately ten years before Espinosa's, but in England. See Alejandro Cioranescu, ed., *Thomas Nichols: Mercader de azúcar, hispanista y hereje* (La Laguna de Tenerife: Instituto de Estudios Canarios, 1963).

Fig. 3. Title page; woodcut of the image of the Virgin of Candelaria in Alonso de Espinosa's *Del origen y milagros de la Santa Imagen de Nuestra Señora de Candelaria, que apareció en la Isla de Tenerife, con la descripción de esta isla* (Seville, 1594). Courtesy of The Hispanic Society of America, New York.

Others have echoed this argument, showing that the process of Spanish colonial experimentation took place at the judicial, administrative, and economic levels as well as in the implementation of organizational and behavioral structures, which were repeated or modified in subsequent explorations and conquests.[54] These studies illustrate that the cultural relevance of the Canaries

---

[54] Antonio Pérez Voituricz (*Problemas jurídicos*) and Peter Russell ("El descubrimiento") deal with the judicial and administrative models, as do Antonio Rumeu de Armas (*La política*) and Silvio Zavala (*Las conquistas de Canaria y América* [Las Palmas: Cabildo Insular de Gran Canaria, 1991]). Morales Padrón (*Sevilla*), José Peraza de Ayala (*El regimen comercial de Canarias con las Indias en los siglos XVI, XVII y XVIII* [Sevilla: Universidad de Sevilla, 1977]), and Eduardo Aznar Vallejo (*La integración de las Islas Canarias en la Corona de Castilla (1478–1526)* [Madrid: Universidad de La Laguna, 1982]), among others, study the economic aspects. Fernández Armesto (*Before Columbus*) also offers a panoramic study of the role of the Canaries in European expansion for which John Kicza ("Patterns in Early Spanish Overseas Expansion," *William and Mary Quarterly* 49 [1992]: 229–53) is also useful. Anthony Stevens-Arroyo ("The Inter-Atlantic Paradigm," *Comparative Studies in Society and History* 35 [1993]:

to the Americas can be documented not only in the chronicles of the Indies, but also by recent interdisciplinary works which have explored its particularities. I am persuaded, however, that the cultural network from America to the Canaries needs further exploration, in particular the historical and literary production about the islands at the turn of the seventeenth century.[55]

Although the final conquest of the Canary Islands occurred as early as 1497 with the fall of Tenerife, as an event in its own right it was so eclipsed by the discovery and colonization of the Americas that the history of the Canaries was practically ignored. Almost one hundred years after the conquest of Tenerife, the Canaries became the subject of literary and historical reflections destined to rescue the islands from the histories of the New World which had marginalized the legacy of the islanders and the account of their conquest. In 1594, Alonso de Espinosa published in Seville his *Del origen y milagros de la Santa Imagen de Nuestra Señora de Candelaria, que apareció en la isla de Tenerife, con la descripción de esta isla* [*Of the Origin and Miracles of the Holy Image of Our Lady of Candelaria which Appeared in Tenerife, With the Description of This Island*]. Espinosa's attempt to place in the foreground the historical past of Tenerife, which was effectively buried in the chronicles of the Indies, could, however, not escape the historical paradigm of the New World. Despite the limited scope of Espinosa's Marian book, I shall argue here that his history emerged from the historiographic and literary treatment of the conquest of America and that it was mediated or filtered by the chronicles of the Indies and by the European vision of the Amerindians. Espinosa's effort to revise Canarian history as it had been told before his times was the conscious work of someone whose living experience had flourished within the colonial and missionary world of Central America and whose intellectual training had been marked by the evangelical and political struggles of Bartolomé de las Casas. Such experiential and intellectual backgrounds resulted in the writing of a work that challenged both historiographic practices and historical truths.

515–43) has more recently offered an extensive view of what he has called the Inter-Atlantic paradigm. Although his article constitutes a somewhat specific comparison between the Canary and the Caribbean Islands, it is nevertheless illuminating insofar as it shows the slow transition undergone by medieval models of expansion, conquest, and colonization between the Reconquista and the final conquest of the great American civilizations (516–43). See also Peter Hulme, "Tales of Distinction: European Ethnography and the Caribbean," in *Implicit Understandings*, ed. S. B. Schwartz (Cambridge: Cambridge University Press, 1994), 157–97, about ethnographic constructions of the Caribbean and its precedents.

[55] Many of the studies on the Canary Islands that deal with the arts concentrate on painting, architecture, and religious iconography rather than literature. See, for example, *Coloquio de Historia Canario-Americana III (1978)* (Las Palmas: Cabildo Insular de Gran Canaria, 1980). The limited criticism to date which has dealt with early historical and literary works will be examined in the present study.

Alonso de Espinosa, a Dominican friar ordained in Guatemala, wrote by 1591 a history whose "main purpose" ("principal intento"), as he expressed it in the prologue, was to record an account of the origin of the Virgin of Candelaria and the miracles ascribed to her in Tenerife. With his book, the friar (*Historia*, ed. Cioranescu, 15–16) claimed he intended to invigorate devotion to the image, which had been diminished and forgotten due to the increasingly common occurrence of miracles. Although he stated as his main objective the writing of the history of the Virgin of Candelaria, he also announced that he would describe the island, its inhabitants, and the war of conquest waged by the Spaniards, with as much accuracy as his sources permitted (Espinosa, *Historia*, 17–18).

With his pious objective in mind, Espinosa described briefly in the first book of his history (Espinosa, *Historia*, 24–46 [bk. 1, chaps. 1–10]) all the conjectures surrounding the etymological beginnings and geography of the Canary Islands, specifically of Tenerife, as well as the ethnic and cultural background of all their inhabitants. He then depicted in detail all the customs, practices, and social and political structures of the Guanches, who were the ancient inhabitants of Tenerife. In the second book (Espinosa, *Historia*, 48–83 [bk. 2, chaps. 1–15]), Espinosa narrated the appearance of the Virgin of Candelaria to the natives around 1400. The statue of the Virgin had apparently appeared to Guanche shepherds upon a rock near the beach of Chimisay in Güímar. Espinosa described the commotion caused by the early miracles of the Virgin, who immobilized the arm of one shepherd and made the other cut himself. Then he mentioned how processions of angels illuminated a nearby beach and left traces of green wax.[56] This happened repeatedly from the time of the Vir-

---

[56] For a comprehensive look at the history of the myth and cult of the Virgin Mary in Europe, Marina Warner, *Alone of All Her Sex* (New York: Knopf, 1976), 3–398, continues to be an important point of departure. The specific case of the apparition of the Virgin of Candelaria and the documentation of her miracles follow the general characteristics traced by the excellent study that William Christian (*Apparitions in Late Medieval and Renaissance Spain* [Princeton: Princeton University Press, 1981], esp. 203–6) has done on apparitions in Late Medieval Castile and Catalunya. This *advocación* (names and representations by which the Virgin Mary is venerated), like many others, pertains to a "local devotional system," which gradually acquired "political meaning" as the Spanish empire gained enemies from the sixteenth to the eighteenth centuries; this, in turn, is a clear parallel with the structure of political domination disguised under the religious banner of the Marian cult that flourished during the thirteenth century. According to Christian's classification (*Apparitions*, 8), apparitions fall into three categories: 1) a divine figure who appears to seers; 2) a sign (*signum*) that can be verified by the senses; 3) the finding of statues or paintings. The legend of the Virgin of Candelaria was far from an isolated phenomenon: apparitions and legends often became the same thing (*Apparitions*, 208); visionaries were often shepherds (208); the cure of paralyzed arms was indeed a common sign (76), and so was the miraculous wax that frequently appeared on the beach.

gin's first appearance until as late as 1497, when it was officially documented by sworn witnesses. He explored how, by the 1420s, the natives became aware of the true identity of the image thanks to Antón Guanche who had been indoctrinated into the Christian faith. Espinosa also narrated how neighboring Christians, who were settled on other islands, learned about the new manifestation of the Virgin and unsuccessfully tried to take the image away from the islanders.

He finished this section by describing the physical form and image of the Virgin. Her complexion was dark, although her cheeks flushed miraculously and her eyes constantly followed the movements of her visitors. Her hair was long and cascaded down her back in six golden locks. She was dressed in a golden tunic, which displayed an indecipherable cryptic message (a series of letters that perhaps hid a message in Latin). She held a child (holding a golden bird) on her right arm and a green candle in her left hand, whence the name Candelaria.[57]

In the third book (Espinosa, *Historia*, 86–142 [bk. 3, chaps. 1–17]), Espinosa narrated the history of the conquest and colonization of Tenerife at the behest of Ferdinand and Isabella and under the military direction of Alonso de Lugo. Espinosa also briefly explored the social, political, and religious structuring of Tenerife's colonial society up to the year of 1558. In doing so, he touched upon the history of the cult of the Virgin of Candelaria, which under Spanish rule had passed to the hands of the Dominican Order. In the fourth book (Espinosa, *Historia*, 144–212 [bk. 4]), Espinosa simply enumerated all the miracles attributed to the apparition in the 1500s; only some of the miracles were documented, and the list Espinosa constructed followed a rather loose chronology.

Espinosa's work, despite his religious subject, was one of the first manifestations of an interest in the re-articulation of the history of the Canary Islands, which, as noted above, had been widely mistold or simply ignored. His interest was not an isolated phenomenon but rather formed part of a greater interest in

---

As for the literary corpus from which the Marian tradition emerged in Spain, the *Cantigas de Santa María* of Alfonso X El Sabio and Berceo's *Milagros de Nuestra Señora* (who followed a European trend) are the most relevant poetic examples in medieval literature. During the Renaissance and Baroque, many epic poems honored the Mother of God and her miraculous actions, while many ecclesiastical histories were written about particular *advocaciones* of the Virgin: Espinosa's is one of them. See also Merediz ("Traveling Icons," 1–18) for a summary of many of the ideas presented in this chapter.

[57] According to María Jesús Riquelme Pérez, the child Jesus was often depicted in the fifteenth century with a book, a globe, or a bird symbolizing the human soul (*La Virgen de Candelaria y las Islas Canarias* [Santa Cruz de Tenerife: Cabildo de Tenerife, 1990], 59). This conventional element of the bird, however, acquires more significance in the case of the Canary Islands in which the golden bird symbology encompasses "nationalistic" overtones.

the arts and literature among a group of learned men on the islands.[58] Espinosa wrote his work in the same period as Leonardo Torriani wrote his *Descrittione et historia del regno del Isole Canarie gia dette le Fortunate con il parere delle loro fortificationi* [*The Description and History of the Canary Islands, called before Fortunate Islands with a Description of their Fortifications*] (1592) and Juan de Abreu y Galindo produced his *Historia de la conquista de las siete Islas de Canaria* [*History of the Conquest of the Seven Islands of Canaria*] (1602). Torriani's work was not published until 1940. While Abreu y Galindo's work had been published for the first time in 1632, Alejandro Cioranescu successfully demonstrated that it had been completed by 1602 (Abreu y Galindo, *Historia de la conquista*, ed. Cioranescu, ix–xvii).[59] There was a community of writers who recognized the lack of historical and literary narratives about the islands, but Espinosa's chronicle became the most important primary source for the ethnographic description of the Guanches; due to its early publication, it became a common source of reference for later historians.[60] Espinosa's chronicle also became the immediate target for attack by another writer, Antonio de Viana, who was a native of the islands. For Viana and the descendants of the conquistador Lope Fernández de la Guerra, Espinosa's revision of the history of Tenerife proved to be too critical of the Guanches and some of the conquistadors. With his project financed by the prominent Guerra family, Viana hastened to write the first epic poem (in Spanish) about the heroism of the natives and their conquerors. It was published in Seville in 1604.

---

[58] Many writers attended Bartolomé Cairasco de Figueroa's literary meetings in Las Palmas between 1580 and 1600. Cairasco himself translated Tasso's *Jerusalem Delivered* into Spanish, and wrote an epic poem called *Templo Militante* and several dramatic pieces. Alonso de Espinosa, Leonardo Torriani, and Antonio de Viana were presumably part of Cairasco's literary circle. See A. Millares Carlo and M. Hernández Suárez, *Biobibliografía de escritores canarios (siglos XVI, XVII y XVIII)* (Las Palmas: Museo Canario, 1977), 2: 124. Silvestre de Balboa, the author of *Espejo de Paciencia* (c. 1604) which is considered to be the first epic poem of Cuba, is also thought to have been part of this group.

[59] Espinosa (*Historia*, 87 [bk. 3, chap. 1]) mentioned two of his contemporaries who were involved in projects similar to his own, one of whom was Torriani and the other Fiesco, of whom nothing has been known thereafter (see A. Cioranescu, "El doctor Fiesco, historiador de Gran Canaria," *Revista de historia canaria* 25 [1959]: 203–9). As for Abreu y Galindo, since there is no documented evidence of his existence on the islands, scholars suspect this name to be a pseudonym. Rumeu de Armas (*La conquista de Tenerife* [Tenerife: Aula de Cultura, 1975], 10–11) has argued that Espinosa and his contemporaries must have had a common written source, which has been lost in modern times.

[60] Espinosa called his work a "history," but I use the term interchangeably with "chronicle." In the sixteenth century, according to Walter Mignolo's comprehensive study of what he calls the "historical meta-text," both terms came to mean the same thing as expressed in treatises and historical prologues of the time. Mignolo ("El metatexto historiográfico y la historiografía indiana," *Modern Language Notes* 96 [1981]: 358–402, here 372, 374–76, 384–85) argues that, even though history and chronicle belonged in their origins to different discursive types, the new narrative demands imposed on historiography by the conquest and colonization of the New World made both terms synonymous.

Without dismissing the common European background shared by the majority of historians at the time, I wish to take into account the rich and complex path that Espinosa's life and work took with respect to the New World. It is precisely in light of Espinosa's connection with the New World that this first Spanish-language chronicle about the Canary Islands must be studied. The American context of Espinosa's work evolved, at first, from the biographical experience of the author, who was born in Alcalá de Henares in 1543 and in 1550 at the age of seven moved with his family to Guatemala. His schooling made his bond with the New World even more relevant since he received his complete education within the monastic and intellectual tradition of the Order of Preachers. As a Dominican, he also took part in the censorship and expurgation of books undertaken by the Mexican Inquisition, and he was exposed to the prolific historical and literary production generated by interest in the New World and its cultures which redefined the boundaries of historiography.[61] Above all, Espinosa was exposed to the writings of Bartolomé de las Casas (1484–1566).

I will argue that Espinosa's American experience would later influence how he chose to tell the history of the Virgin of Candelaria, how he depicted the origins of the Guanches of Tenerife, and how he narrated the European conquest and colonization of the island. A textual analysis of Espinosa's chronicle must therefore take into consideration how the author's intellectual training in the New World and his encounter with Lascasian thought conditioned his writings.

1. The Monastery and the Mission: Dominican Intellectual Training

Since the late 1520s when Domingo de Betanzos made the first attempt to found the Dominican convent of Santiago de los Caballeros in Guatemala, the region was closely associated with the name of Fray Bartolomé de las Casas, who arrived in the area after 1535 (after a frustrated attempt to travel to Peru)

---

[61] Unless otherwise indicated, most of the following biographical information about Espinosa comes from his own declaration made in 1591 for a formal complaint brought against him by the Holy Office of the Inquisition in Las Palmas in 1590. A. Millares Carlo ("Proceso inquisitorial contra fray Alonso de Espinosa, dominico (1590–1592)," *El Museo Canario* 1 [1933]: 150–216) has transcribed all the original documents. See also Buenaventura Bonnet, "La obra del p[adre] Alonso de Espinosa," *Revista de historia canaria* 6 (1932): 33–42, and idem, "El p[adre] Alonso de Espinosa y su historia," *El Museo Canario* 12 (1952) 31–49; and the more complete introduction by A. Cioranescu Espinosa, *Historia*, ed. idem (Santa Cruz de Tenerife: Goya, 1968), ix–xxxvii.

and would serve from 1543 to 1550 as the second Bishop of Chiapas.[62] Betanzos left the mother-convent in the province of Mexico to found a new house in neighboring Guatemala; the new foundation was almost immediately abandoned due to an insufficient number of religious members available. At the request of Francisco Marroquín, the newly appointed bishop of Guatemala, Las Casas, Luis de Cáncer, and Pedro de Angulo returned from Nicaragua to occupy the abandoned house (Remesal, *Historia general*, 1: 200 [bk. 3, chap. 5]). Although the convent served as a base for important missionary incursions into less hospitable areas, it was not fully functioning as a center of religious and educational training. Not until 1538, when interest in evangelizing the region revived, was the convent authorized to train novices and ordain new friars. To this end four more members of the order arrived, and in 1539 Angulo was named vicar of the convent to replace Las Casas, who traveled to Spain in the company of Cáncer and Rodrigo de Ladrada in 1540 (Remesal, *Historia general*, 1: 244–45 [bk. 3, chap. 20]; Wagner and Parish, *Life and Writings*, 96–98). The founding of the convent in Santiago de los Caballeros in Guatemala led to the foundation of several others, including Ciudad Real de Chiapas, El Salvador, Cobán in Verapaz, and six additional Dominican houses (Remesal, *Historia general*, 2: 388 [bk. 11, chap. 4]) which were initially under the auspices of the province of Mexico, to which the new region belonged for a period of twelve years. In 1551, two distinct provinces were delineated, that of Mexico and the new one of San Vicente de Chiapas, which had as its main city Guatemala (Remesal, *Historia general*, 2: 235 [bk. 9, chap. 13]; Dávila Padilla, *Provincia de Santiago de México*, 111 [bk. 1, chap. 36]). It was to this newly founded province of Guatemala that Alonso de Espinosa came as a child and there encountered the long-felt presence of Bartolomé de las Casas's teachings.

From the 1530s onward, Las Casas had made this region one of his battlegrounds to challenge the oppressive slave system of the *encomienda* and also to test the method of peaceful evangelization in the "War Zone" (Zona de

---

[62] Antonio de Remesal (*Historia general de las Indias Occidentales y particular de la gobernación de Chiapa y Guatemala*, ed. C. Sáenz de Santa María [Madrid: Atlas, 1964], 1: 193 [bk. 3, chap. 4]) dated Las Casas's arrival earlier. However, the extensive research done by Henry R. Wagner and Helen R. Parish corrects the date to 1536 (*The Life and Writings of Bartolomé de las Casas* [Albuquerque: University of New Mexico Press, 1967], 85). Using a variety of sources, these critics have revealed the inaccuracies of Remesal and other texts to arrive at a more reliable biography of the famous Dominican. Las Casas had first arrived in Hispaniola in 1502 at the age of eighteen, while his first visit to Mexico took place during 1535. He returned to Mexico in 1536 and then was sent south to Guatemala. For Las Casas's activities in Mexico see H. R. Parish and H. E. Weidman, *Las Casas en México* (México: Fondo de Cultura Económica, 1992), and for his role as Bishop of Chiapas see Parish, *Las Casas as a Bishop* (Washington, D. C.: Library of Congress, 1980). For a brief yet most up-to-date biography of Las Casas, see eadem, introduction to Las Casas, *The Only Way*, ed. eadem (New York: Paulist Press, 1992), 9–58.

Guerra), which later became known as "True Peace" (Verapaz) (Wagner and Parish, *Life and Writings*, 86–93). These two pillars of political and missionary activity would prove quite influential in Espinosa's project; Espinosa would later apply to the Canary Islands Las Casas's anti-slavery ideas as well as his theory about peaceful evangelization.

Las Casas's struggle against the *encomenderos'* abuses of the Amerindians had led him to design a guide for confessors consisting of ten rules which clerics were to consider before confessing and absolving any parishioner: this guide was intended to reinforce the New Laws promulgated in 1542 abolishing *encomienda*. The implications of this document reached far beyond its premises, as noted by Parish (Parish and Weidman, *Las Casas en México*, 64), since it implied that the conquest of America and the subjugation of the natives were illegal and immoral, and anyone who participated in reaping benefit therefrom would be excommunicated if they failed to make proper restitution to the Indians whose possessions, land, and labor they took. Of this *Confesionario*, Remesal (*Historia general*, 2: 111 [bk. 8, chap. 5]) explained that Las Casas had not intended it to be shown to any layman, but copies of the document became common and caused such a scandal that a royal mandate of 1548 ordered their confiscation. In fact, the Franciscan friar Toribio de Benavente (Motolinía), one of Las Casas's most vicious detractors, observed with satisfaction in 1555 that copies of the treatise had been publicly burned by Don Antonio de Mendoza, then viceroy of Mexico, in a zealous attempt to control the potential outrage of the Spanish citizenry (*Carta al Emperador*, ed. Bravo, 57; Parish and Weidman, *Las Casas en México*, 71). In a clear act of defiance, Las Casas nevertheless also published an extended version of the confessional guide in Seville in 1552. While Bishop of Chiapas, Las Casas tried tenaciously to implement his ten rules for confessors; he upheld the New Laws and demanded help from the *Audiencia* in enforcing them. After threats were made against his life, and being unable to effect reform locally, the bishop-elect abandoned his see to return to Spain for the last time in 1550. There he continued his struggle at the Castilian court where he had been successful previously in helping create the controversial legislation whose aim was to abolish Indian slavery and the Spanish *encomienda* system (Wagner and Parish, *Life and Writings*, 121–69).

Espinosa was not the only adherent of Las Casas's ideas to take up an anti-slavery stance sometime later: the Dominicans of Ciudad Real de Chiapas adopted Las Casas's recommendations in his *Confesionario* just two years before Espinosa decided to leave Guatemala to establish himself in the Canary Islands. The legacy of Las Casas was ardently felt during a remarkable incident that occurred in Ciudad Real de Chiapas that was either not known or purposely dismissed by the Dominican chroniclers Remesal and Dávila Padilla and that reflected divisions within the Dominican Order.

A Dominican named Pedro de Feria had been appointed by the king to the bishopric of Chiapas in 1575, and by 1579 he had encountered difficulties with his own brothers and subordinates, according to a *memorial* he wrote to Philip II (*Cartas de Indias*, 2: 451–59). In 1577, the Dominican friars who resided in the bishopric — perhaps the sixteen inhabiting the convent of Ciudad Real or the thirty-four or thirty-five residing in the five convents of the province — publicly rejected before the bishop the official assessment of tributes that had been set three or four years earlier by Cristóbal de Axcueta, judge (*oidor*) of the Royal Audiencia of Guatemala. Since the friars considered the tributes to be unjustly high and in need of immediate reassessment, they registered their opposition by using the radical Lascasian method of refusing to confess any *encomendero* during Lent. Pedro de Feria disagreed with his brothers and instructed the clerics in the Cathedral to continue exercising their pastoral duties. The Dominican friars reacted with equal harshness. Pedro de Feria (*Cartas de Indias*, 2: 457) declared:

> los religiosos reçibieron tanta pesadumbre de que yo no siguiese su pareçer, y admitiese á la confesión á los que ellos excluian, que me declararon y publicaron por inabsoluble; y desde entonçes asta ahora no an querido ni quieren confesarme, ni á quién me confiesa, ni á quién confiesa a los dichos encomenderos; del qual pecado yo nunca me e confesado ni pienso confesar.

> [the friars were so perturbed that I did not share their opinion and that I admitted to confession all those they had excluded that they declared publicly that I was to be denied absolution. Since then and until now they have refused to confess me and anyone who confesses me or the aforementioned *encomenderos*; but to such a sin I have never confessed nor do I ever intend to do so.]

The consequences did not stop there. With the hope of moderating the opinions of the Dominicans, the furious citizens of Ciudad Real called for the introduction and settlement of Franciscans in the area. The Dominicans found the dealings of Bishop Feria with the Franciscans intolerable and once more denied him absolution. The case apparently continued and was brought to trial. Pedro de Feria tried to resign his position two years later, but the king did not accept his resignation; thus Feria died, still holding the office of Bishop of Chiapas, in 1588 (García Icazbalceta, *Bibliografía mexicana del siglo XVI*, 205–6). At this point, Las Casas had been physically absent from the New World for thirty years and deceased for the last eleven; nevertheless, his ideas still held currency among the present generation of missionaries. Espinosa must have been among those who witnessed and supported such drastic measures as the denial of confession and absolution, which caused so much public unrest among the citizens of Ciudad Real.

Espinosa's affiliation with Lascasian thought would not be limited to the controversial anti-slavery ideas which made Las Casas the target of the most fierce hatred among the *encomenderos* of the New World. Espinosa would also embrace Las Casas's theoretical postulates regarding the nature of Christian apostolic work among the Amerindians. Las Casas's missionary efforts, put into practice at Verapaz, were described in his *De unico vocationis modo omnium gentium ad veram religionem* [*Del único modo de atraer a todas las gentes a la verdadera fe*]. Here he proclaimed the principles of peaceful evangelization and engaged in a debate against the mass baptism of adults (widely practiced by the Franciscans) which triggered the vigorous enmity of Motolinía (Wagner and Parish, *Life and Writings*, 98–99; Parish and Weidman, *Las Casas en México*, 319–21). This document was as notorious as the *Confesionario* if not more so. Parish (Parish and Weidman, *Las Casas en México*, 36) has successfully demonstrated that the now lost original of *De unico vocationis modo* served as the basis for the encyclical *Sublimis Deus* issued by Pope Paul III in 1537.[63]

Other evidence suggests that the *De unico vocationis modo* was widely read in the sixteenth century. Remesal mentioned, for instance, that by 1615 he had seen four identical handwritten copies of the treatise, one of which was in New Spain and another in the hands of a priest in Mazaltenango, Guatemala (*Historia general*, 2: 370 [bk. 10, chap. 24]). Remesal owned his own copy and summarized parts of the treatise in his *Historia general* (1: 209–12 [bk. 3, chap. 9]). This does not constitute the only instance in which he referred to Las Casas's writings; on the contrary, his references and quotations are found throughout his work, since Remesal had access to all of Las Casas's published and unpublished writings which were kept in the convent of San Gregorio of Valladolid. To a lesser degree, the Dominican friar and contemporary of Espinosa, Agustín Dávila Padilla, who published his *Historia de la fundación y discurso de la provincia de Santiago de México de la Orden de Predicadores* in 1596, also spoke of and quoted some of the published treatises; he complained however, that it was almost a miracle to find one in his times (*Provincia de Santiago de México*, 309 [bk. 1, chap. 98]).[64]

---

[63] The encyclicals *Sublimis Deus* and *Pastorale Officium* (1537) proclaimed the Indians' capacity for receiving religious instruction and their sovereign rights to their territories and possessions. Therefore, any servitude or exploitation of the natives was condemned as an obstacle to their conversion to the faith of Christ. Las Casas's recommendation that the *encomenderos* were to be sanctioned with excommunication for their crimes against the natives had much less success in Rome, since it faced revocation. However, the famous Dominican was instrumental in gaining the approval and implementation of the bull *Altitudo divini consilii* in 1539, which mandated that adults were to be instructed in the faith before baptism (Parish and Weidman, *Las Casas en México*, 38–45).

[64] The date and place offered by Remesal for the writing of *De unico vocationis modo*, 1536 in Guatemala, were corrected by Wagner and Parish, who have argued that the treatise was mostly written or at least finished in Mexico between 1538 and 1540 (*Life and Writings*, 98–102). Cioranescu has followed the erroneous affirmation in his introduction to Espinosa's

Although some of Las Casas's contemporaries observed that his works were fiercely persecuted, the uncontrollable and prolific writings of Las Casas were not confined within the walls of the convent of San Gregorio. On the contrary, Las Casas's works were disseminated among other Dominicans and, as the example of the *licenciado* Antonio Prieto de Villegas in Mazaltenango reveals, among secular priests as well. Las Casas's ideas continued to be a source of inspiration and a target of attack by successive generations, but his works and ideas could never be dismissed entirely. His serious scholarship — as evidenced by the virtual transcription of his *Historia de las Indias* in the *Historia general de los hechos de los castellanos en las islas y Tierra Firme del mar Océano* (1601–1615) of the royal chronicler Antonio de Herrera y Tordesillas — as well as his persuasive rhetoric and his political influence endured well beyond the end of his life. The impact of his apostolic work among the Indians and his political work at the Castilian court, which never ceased to be critical and militant, was highly influential for many years after his death in 1566. When Alonso de Espinosa arrived in Guatemala in the mid-sixteenth century, he was to live and be educated in a region and a monastery deeply marked by the passage of Las Casas, his teachings, and his writings. Alonso de Espinosa's history, written in 1594, bears witness to the survival of Lascasian thought, which in turn provides an important key to understanding the character of Espinosa's writing on the Canary Islands.

The scarce surviving biographical data about Espinosa can be traced to his life in Guatemala and other nearby areas. It indicates that he took his vows in the Dominican Order in 1564, as stated by Remesal (*Historia general*, 2: 246 [bk. 9, chap. 16]), who was familiar with Espinosa's *Del origen y milagros de la santa imagen de Nuestra Señora de Candelaria*. Remesal also pointed out that Espinosa's death occurred outside Guatemala.[65] At the age of twenty-one, Espinosa had

---

text (*Historia*, xi n. 1). Parish (Parish and Weidman, *Las Casas en México*, 29–45) has subsequently argued that Las Casas had begun to write the *De unico vocationis modo* in Santo Domingo after the peaceful surrender of the Indian rebel leader Enriquillo in 1534.

[65] Remesal made the mistake of considering Espinosa Guatemala-born (*Historia general*, 2: 246 [bk. 9, chap. 16]). But, according to Pedro Henríquez Ureña ("El primer libro de escritor americano," *Romanic Review* 7 [1916]: 284–87), Remesal's contemporary, Juan de Marieta, in his *Historia eclesiástica de España* (Cuenca, 1594–1596), understood that Espinosa was born in Alcalá de Henares. Remesal's error, along with Nicolás Antonio's erroneous dating of the publication of Espinosa's history to 1541, and the existence of another Alonso de Espinosa in Santo Domingo, led Carlos M. Trelles to label the book as the first written by a writer born in the New World in his *Ensayo de bibliografía cubana de los siglos XVII y XVIII* (1907). Henríquez Ureña corrected this false claim in 1916. Following J. García Icazbalceta and J. Toribio Medina, Henríquez Ureña reaffirmed that the first American-born writer was Fray Juan de Guevara, author of a now lost *Doctrina cristiana en lengua huasteca* (Mexico, 1548), while Fray Pedro de Agurto published his *Tractado de que se deben administrar los Sacramentos de la Sancta Eucharistia y Extrema Unction a los indios de esta Nueva España* in Mexico in 1573. For a critical survey of the information (and misinformation) regarding Espinosa's birth and the

already studied grammar, that is, Latin and rhetoric, under the direction of a teacher named Pedrosa. He had requested admission to the Dominican order, which implied a formal investigation of his family origins (for the *limpieza de sangre* statutes) and educational background and the approval of his application by three examiners. He had received the white habit in sign of purity and sincerity and the black cape to remind him of mortification and penitence. He had professed and made his three vows of poverty, chastity, and obedience, and was ready to continue his studies in the liberal arts and theology.[66]

As Espinosa himself stated in the transcript of his appearance before the Inquisition in Las Palmas de Gran Canaria from 1590 to 1592, his studies had been carried out over a period of seven years, from 1564 to approximately 1570; Alonso de Ximénez taught him the liberal arts, while Tomás de Vitoria and Juan de Castro directed his instruction in theology.[67] The last two were quite renowned for their exemplary role in the mendicant order. Tomás de Vitoria, educated in Salamanca and Valladolid, arrived in Guatemala in 1554 and learned two indigenous languages; he was a famous preacher in Santiago de los Caballeros. Until his death in 1570, he occupied several prominent positions, which included his appointment as the first friar from Guatemala to become prior of the convent of Ciudad Real de Chiapas in 1567. Like this mentor, Espinosa later would exercise care in documenting the few words and expressions of the ancient Guanche language which managed to survive almost a century in the oral tradition. He must have been influenced as well by the debates

---

publication of his history, see also Cioranescu's introduction (*Historia*, xxii) to Espinosa's text, and Bonnet, "El p[adre] Alonso de Espinosa," 44 n. 1.

[66] The steps to become a Dominican friar are well described by Dávila Padilla in his narration of the life of Tomás del Rosario, whose small and fragile body provoked doubts among his superiors as to whether he would meet the requirements for entering the order. First, the candidate studied grammar; then he petitioned to be admitted to the order, for which his family origins were investigated; and finally, he had to pass an exam before a committee of three examiners. He then received the habit and became a novice for a period of one year. Then he professed and made the three vows. There was a period during which further studies were conducted in theology and the liberal arts. The novice was then ordained as a priest and later examined again in order to prove his merit to be authorized to preach. This final examination was to be made by five examiners after the new ordinances of 1590 (Dávila Padilla, *Provincia de Santiago de México*, 343–46 [bk. 2, chap. 1]). As proven by the mentioned ordinance and the many meetings of the chapters, the order showed increasing interest in improving and standardizing the education of new friars, especially those being ordained in the New World.

[67] The following biographical information is contained in Remesal, *Historia general.* For Tomás de Vitoria, see 2: 256 [bk. 9, chap. 18]; 2: 279–80 [bk. 10, chap. 3]; and 2: 351 [bk. 10, chap. 20]. For Juan de Castro, see 2: 384 [bk. 11, chap. 4]; 2: 393–405 [bk. 11, chaps. 5–8]; 2: 421 [bk. 11, chap. 11] and 2: 434–35 [bk. 11, chap. 14]. Of Alonso de Ximénez, Remesal (*Historia general,* 2: 421 [bk. 11, chap. 11]) mentioned only that he was born in Madrilejos, educated in Salamanca, and went to the Philippines, as Castro had done.

generated around the learning of indigenous languages for the purposes of proselytizing the Indians in America, which resulted in a great number of publications of catechisms and vocabularies by the printing establishment in New Spain.[68] In fact, Espinosa occasionally received the assignment of correcting such books in Mexico.[69]

The other theologian who instructed Espinosa, Juan de Castro, was elected vicar-provincial of the Dominican Order in Guatemala in 1572 and again in 1584. He then took his apostolic work to the Philippines in 1587 where he became vicar-general and first vicar-provincial. In 1590, the king offered Castro the bishopric of Verapaz, but contrary to what Cioranescu affirmed (Espinosa, *Historia*, ed. Cioranescu, x), Castro refused and prepared for another mission, this time to China. Castro inspired Espinosa with the importance of carrying out apostolic work not in the New World but in the Old. In doing so, Espinosa carried with him a rich cultural experience, a proper intellectual training, and one self-confessed interest, the Virgin of Candelaria. Thus, after seven or eight years of preaching, Espinosa left Guatemala in 1579 for Sanlúcar de Barrameda, where he spent six months before finally arriving in the Canary Islands the following year.

Espinosa began his journey back to the Old World as a son of Saint Dominic and as a disciple of some prominent Dominicans in the New World. Above all, however, he was an admirer of Las Casas, whose example shaped the vision of history that Espinosa was to depict in his writings. When Espinosa left America for the Canary Islands, the world into which he was entering had very little to do with the ardent polemics that reformers like Las Casas generated in the New World, but he was involved in polemics related to the administration of the sanctuary of the Virgin of Candelaria.[70] Cioranescu has searched the ar-

---

[68] For an inventory of works, which were published in Mexico in the sixteenth century, see J. García Icazbalceta, *Bibliografía mexicana del siglo XVI*, ed. A. Millares Carlo (México: Fodo de Cultura Económica, 1954). See also the more comprehensive study by J. T. Medina, *La imprenta en México: 1539–1821*, 8 vols. (Amsterdam: N. Israel, 1965); and the more recent article and statistical survey by A. Rodríguez-Buckingham, "The Arm of Spain," in *Latin American Library Materials* (Austin: University of Texas Press, 1979), 249–80, which examines the printing presses of both Mexico and Peru.

[69] The nature of Espinosa's work for the Archbishop of New Spain in the correction of books is unclear. The friar only mentioned it without specifying whether he worked as censor or expurgator ("el arçobispo de México, siendo inquisidor en México, le encomendó la corrección de algunos libros") (Millares Carlo, "Proceso inquisitorial," 184).

[70] The convent of Our Lady of Candelaria had been founded by 1530, according to a "Testimonio de los conventos y estudios con sus estatutos, observancias y méritos de la Provincia de Santo Domingo de Canarias," written in April 1743, and certified by Joseph Isidro Uque Osorio (the document is housed at the library of the University of La Laguna, call number C / IV-8). This document also indicates the order in which the Dominican convents were founded on all the islands: the dates given reveal that the first foundation occurred later than those in America: San Pedro Mártir (Canaria) in 1522, Santo Domingo de la

chives to document the presence of Espinosa on the islands, and has found Espinosa's first documented presence to be 1582; he was in Santo Domingo de La Laguna until 1584, in 1585 in Palma, and in 1585–1587 in Arucas whence he returned to Las Palmas de Gran Canaria. Espinosa returned briefly to La Laguna by 1588 and visited the nearby Iglesia de la Concepción in Orotava; the following year he was a few miles away in the Dominican convent of Candelaria where he began his research on the miracles of the Virgin and the origins of the Guanches (Cioranescu in Espinosa, *Historia*, ed. Cioranescu, xviii–xxi). There were no *encomenderos* to reprimand or Indians to protect, but there was a surviving native community whose history had yet to be written and a tradition of a miraculous appearance of a Virgin whose miracles had yet to be recorded.

While Las Casas was rarely called by his proper name by his many enemies who in their letters referred to him as the "Antichrist" or the "Devil" (Remesal, *Historia general*, 2: 64–65 [bk. 7, chap. 16]), his name was often silenced even by his followers. Such was the case of Alonso de Espinosa, who nevertheless managed to indicate his having been deeply influenced by Las Casas without ever mentioning the name that had elicited so much controversy and hatred in the New World.

2. The Writing of History: Dilemmas, Debates, and Miracles

The historiographical practices of the chroniclers of the Indies in the sixteenth and seventeenth centuries responded to the need to design new strategies to justify the inclusion of indigenous rituals and customs in their historical writings.[71] In other words, these authors did not try to solve a problem that pertained to the writing of history, but rather one that pertained first and foremost to the description and representation of non-European, non-Christian cultures. These historians faced the dilemma of exploiting "the fabulous and sensational aspects of their representations" on the one hand, while disassociating them-

---

Concepción de La Laguna (Tenerife) in 1527, San Miguel de la Palma in 1530, at the same time as that of Candelaria; the rest of the convents were founded after San Benito de la Orotava (Tenerife) in 1593. Thus Espinosa was preaching in an area of active Dominican growth. For a more detailed explanation see the eighteenth-century historian J. de Viera y Clavijo, *Noticias de la historia general de las Islas Canarias*, ed. A. Cioranescu and M. G. Martínez Hernández, 2 vols. (Santa Cruz de Tenerife: Goya, 1982), 2: 737–65 (bk. 18, chaps. 24–36), who, in an obvious retrospective attempt to claim the authority of antiquity and tradition, declared that the first convent must have been founded by 1516 (near the time of King Ferdinand's death). See also Jesús Pérez Morera, "Fray Domingo de Mendoza y las primeras fundaciones de la orden dominica en Canarias y América," *El Museo Canario* 53 (1998): 327–66, on the foundation of Dominican convents in America and the Canaries.

71 See Rolena Adorno, "Literary Production and Suppression: Reading and Writing About Amerindians in Colonial Spanish America," *Dispositio* 11 (1986): 1–25, here 2–4.

selves from "the kinds of writing which were condemned by moralists and censors" on the other (Adorno, "Literary Production," 2). In writing about the Canary Islands, Espinosa faced a similar rhetorical dilemma, which he had to confront by designing his own historiographic strategies.

Espinosa's project ran into the obstacle, faced so many times by the chroniclers, of how to negotiate between religious and human history, between synchronic description and diachronic narration, and ultimately between narration and digression.[72] I argue that Espinosa's work reveals a complex clash between two different types of narratives and that he seems to invert their hierarchical order, even though his explicit comments tend to support that order. That is, Espinosa announces to his reader that his history pertains to the ecclesiastical realm, when in reality his text gives precedence to another history belonging to the human realm of Guanches and Spaniards. Espinosa's work thus struggles with the rigidity of categorization of historical writing (which lacks validity for his particular project), and his work reveals how precepts are undermined by practice in the historical-literary production of the sixteenth century.

As the author repeatedly mentioned in his anecdotal prologue, his historical account was inspired by his search for the origin of the miracles of the Virgin of Candelaria. The already established and widespread cult of the image had apparently fascinated him in Guatemala to such a degree that he decided to plan a project for the investigation of its origins.[73] Espinosa (*Historia*, 16–17)

---

[72] History was understood as either divine or human within the historiographical tradition of Golden Age Spain. Luis Cabrera de Córdoba, who wrote the treatise *De historia, para entenderla y escribirla*, published in 1611, described divine history as that which dealt with the sacred or ecclesiastical, while human history concerned natural, moral, particular, or public phenomena (*De historia*, ed. S. Montero Díaz [Madrid: Instituto de Estudios Políticos, 1948], 34).

[73] The cult of the Virgin of Candelaria, which is celebrated mainly on 2 February (the feast of Candlemas), had been taking root in the New World for some time and would later acquire great importance, as evidenced primarily by the Virgin's most famous *advocación*, that of Copacabana in Lake Titicaca, Bolivia. Around 1582, according to the Augustinian friar Alonso Ramos Gavilán in his *Historia del célebre santuario de Nuestra Señora de Copacabana* (Lima, 1621), an Indian artist, Francisco Tito Yupanqui, searched for an image of the Virgin to use as a model and found one of Candelaria in a Dominican church (*Historia*, ed. I. Prado Pastor [Lima: I. Prado, 1988], 235). The statue sculpted by Yupanqui and installed in the Virgin's new sanctuary would then become the protagonist of many miracles, out of which one hundred and thirty-two were narrated and interpreted by Ramos Gavilán. The Catholic symbol, in this case, substituted yet provided continuity for pre-Inka and Inka cults in the Island of the Sun and the greater lake region, as has been argued mainly in iconographic representations by Teresa Gisbert, *Iconografía y mitos indígenas en el arte*, 2nd ed. (La Paz: Gisbert, 1994), 17–22, 51–60, and in sacred, cultural, and political terms by Veronica Salles-Reese, *From Viracocha to the Virgin of Copacabana* (Austin: University of Texas Press, 1997), 18–44, 159–71. As argued by Salles-Reese, in the case of Ramos Gavilán, the Marian narrative offered "an

confessed, however, that once in Tenerife he could not elicit the support of his superiors in his first attempt to write and publish a history of the appearance of the Virgin. After giving an account of his long interest in the subject, he emphasized (17) the rigorous character of his investigations and once again stated his purpose of writing an account of "the origin of this holy image of the Virgin as well as the miracles which she has performed" ("el origen de esta santa imagen como de los milagros que ha hecho"). In fact, he dedicated his book to the Virgin of Candelaria herself. Other evidence in the text suggests that, besides this devotional motif, the friar was concerned with other ecclesiastical issues: the necessity to demonstrate and consolidate the Dominican monopoly over this *advocación* of the Virgin and the miracles attributed to her, and to administer the revenues generated by the cult celebrating those miracles. It becomes clear that the control of the cult of the Virgin of Candelaria had always been surrounded by controversy, and that in his work Espinosa tried to lay this controversy to rest.

Espinosa's history addressed the controversy that involved not only the Dominicans and other ecclesiastical agencies but also the Guanches and the Spanish state. According to Espinosa, the devotion to the Virgin had declined so much by 1530 that the bishop of the Canary Islands, Luis Cabeza de Vaca (1523–1537), decided to turn to the Order of Preachers to ask them to take over the hermitage and guard the cave of Achbinicó or San Blás where the religious image had resided since its initial appearance (Espinosa, *Historia*, 129 [bk. 3, chap. 15]). The Dominicans did not proceed without difficulties; on the contrary, the prosperity of the sanctuary provoked the envy of certain church officials who protested the bishop's orders favoring Dominican control. In 1539 several priests disguised as pilgrims and carrying concealed arms seized the house and drove the Dominican friars from their convent (Espinosa, *Historia*, 138–42 [bk. 3, chap. 17]). Although these internal disputes ended by 1542, the threat of external attacks by Muslim pirates from North Africa kept prelates and clerics debating whether to move the image to the safer location of Santa Cruz; this in turn provoked debate among the worshippers about whether the move was the right measure or Santa Cruz was the right place (Viera y Clavijo, *Noticias*, 2: 748 [bk. 18, chap. 27]). There were, in addition, legal disputes between natives and prominent laymen and clergy regarding the rights to carry

exemplary history of the Christianization of the Titicaca region and present[ed] an alternative model for missionary work which differed significantly from the official policy of extirpation [of idolatries]" (*Virgin of Copacabana*, 170). Espinosa, like Ramos Gavilán, was engaged in a similar historiographic and religious project on the other side of the Atlantic but these two Marian narratives had very different political implications. See also Merediz, "Traveling Icons," 1–18.

the image in procession during the 15 August feast of the Assumption of the Virgin.[74]

The existence of two separate dates honoring the Virgin of Candelaria, the Assumption of the Virgin on 15 August and the Purification of the Virgin on 2 February (the feast of Candlemas), reveals how an old controversy had a novel solution. The summer festivity was (and still is) associated with the Guanche population because it coincides with the native ritual of the *beñesmet* or collection of the harvest; the winter one, "solemn and aristocratic," remains that of the conquistadors, in memory of the visit paid by Alonso de Lugo to the Virgin after the conquest of Tenerife on 2 February 1497.[75] Espinosa explicitly spoke of the main feast of the Virgin of Candelaria being celebrated on the day of Purification (*Historia*, 69 [bk. 2, chap. 7]; 75 [bk. 2, chap. 13]). Despite his statement, however, his insistence on the "pre-evangelization" (that is, the knowledge of the Gospel received before the arrival of Europeans to Tenerife) of the Guanches through the intercession of the Virgin may indicate that he implicitly favored the summer feast, which coincided with the direct evangelization of the natives of Tenerife by the Virgin's appearance.[76]

While these polemics over the appropriation of the Virgin's cult may have conditioned the emergence of Espinosa's history to a certain degree, I would argue that the weaving of textual accounts in Espinosa's work takes a different path and leads away from ecclesiastical issues. Espinosa's eagerness to tell the

---

[74] In the introduction to *Historia de la Virgen de Candelaria*, ed. E Serra Ráfols, B. Bonnet, and N. Álamo (Santa Cruz de Tenerife: Goya, 1952), the historian Buenaventura Bonnet (xxiii–xxv) examines the legal documents in which the natives reclaimed the right to carry the image of the Virgin of Candelaria during her procession and festivities. This right had been under attack by members of the clergy and the lay elite since 1587, but eventually the rights of the Guanche population were ratified by civil authorities in the early 1600s.

[75] The celebration of the two feasts has been addressed by Bonnet in the introduction to the 1952 edition of the text (above n. 74) from which I quote here (xxiii). See also A. Díaz Núñez, *Memoria cronológica del establecimiento, propagación y permanencia de la religión católica, apostólica y romana en Islas Canarias* (Madrid: Pérez Dubrull, 1865), 236–37, for more details. Alonso de Lugo led the final offensive against the Guanches in 1494 and won the island mostly by 1496. Rumeu de Armas (*La conquista*, 175–78, 281–83) has shown 1494 to be the correct date for the first entrance of Lugo into Tenerife despite discrepancies in the different historical texts — Espinosa mistakenly gave 1493 as the pertinent date.

[76] The feasts of the other well-known Candelaria, the Virgin of Copacabana in Bolivia, had a similar history, since not only 2 February is celebrated, but also 6 August (Salles-Reese, *Virgin of Copacabana*, 18). Unlike 15 August that marks the Assumption of the Virgin, 6 August would later mark Bolivia's Independence Day. More importantly, however, the second feast corresponds in the Inka religious calendar (as in the Guanches') to the harvesting season, a ritual of not only agricultural relevance but political and social significance; see S. MacCormack ("Time, Space and Ritual Action: The Inka and Christian Calendars in Early Colonial Perú," in *Native Traditions in the Postconquest World*, ed. E. H. Boone and T. Cummins [Washington, D. C.: Dumbarton Oaks, 1998], 295–343, here 338).

history of the Guanches and their conquest by the Europeans indicates instead his own undermining of his repeatedly stated devotional purpose. The pious objective of narrating the origin and miracles of the Virgin serves as the pretext for his more important goal of constructing the (ethno)history of the natives and their customs while denouncing the unjust war of conquest that finally subjected the Guanches to the crown of Castile. It is precisely in these digressions that the author exhibits an ideological consistency aimed at the exemplary demonstration of human and political concerns over those of religious powers. By taking this broad approach, he articulated concerns that were indeed similar to those expressed by Las Casas about the New World several decades earlier.

Espinosa began by attempting in the prologue to justify why he had taken up the pen to write the history of the Virgin. He was nevertheless quite conscious of the pioneering character of his work with regard to the history of the native islanders and their conquest. He made the reader aware of this (*History*, 16, 17–18) in the description of his sources, which seem to originate mostly in the oral tradition and some documents:

> Y aunque algunos han querido tomar este trabajo y han escrito algunas hojas, se han quedado en blanco, por no haber guardado el orden que el derecho dispone, ni haber proseguido en su intento adelante ..., así por no haber escrituras de que aprovecharse, como por falta de curiosos que tuvieran en la memoria los casos sucedidos. ... También advierto que lo que escribo de esta isla y de los naturales de ella y de sus costumbres, lo he averiguado con la más certidumbre que he podido, escogiendo de lo mucho lo más cierto y llegado a razón y más recibido. Mas lo que trate de conquista, guerras y conquistadores, parte, y la más, es de oídas, y parte es sacado de los archivos y escritorios que en pleitos ... sobre tierras y posesiones he hallado; y si no fuere tan por extenso todo contado como ello pasó, no es culpa mía, pues no me pude hallar presente ... ni hay hombre en las islas todas que lo viese; y vale más saber algo, aunque breve y confuso que no quedar de todo ayuno.[77]

---

[77] All quotations in Spanish of Espinosa's *Del origen y milagros de la santa imagen de Nuestra Señora de la Candelaria* are from Espinosa, *Historia de la Virgen de Candelaria*, ed. A. Cioranescu. My English translations are based on *The Guanches of Tenerife, the Holy Image of Our Lady of Candelaria, and the Spanish Conquest and Settlement*, trans. Sir Clements Markham (London: Hakluyt Society, 1907) which I have modified when necessary. In addition to the first edition of Seville (1594) and the two mentioned above (Cioranescu's and Markham's), Espinosa's history was also published in Santa Cruz de Tenerife by the Imprenta Isleña in 1848, an edition that excluded the fourth book and parts of the prologue. There is also a 1940 edition which is merely a reprint of the latter (cf. Bonnet, "El p[adre] Alonso de Espinosa," 46). A more

[And even though some have desired to take up this task and
have written a few pages, they have remained blank, because
their authors neither have kept the rightful order nor continued in their endeavors to the end ...; on account of there being no writings of which to make use, and because of the lack
of such diligent persons who might have kept in their memo-
ries the events that occurred.... I also note that what I write
about this island, the inhabitants of it, and their customs, I
have determined with as much certainty as possible, selecting
from much material that which is the most certain in accor-
dance to reason and most universally accepted. But that
which treats of the conquest, of wars and conquistadors, derives from (and it is the greater part) the accounts of others;
another portion is taken from the archives and writings in legal disputes ... about land and possessions; if these events
are not told as extensively as they occurred, it is not my fault
for I was not present ... nor is there a man now in all these
islands who has witnessed them; at any rate, it is better to
know a part, however brief and confusing it might be, than to
be completely ignorant of any aspect of it whatsoever.]

Espinosa sought to assure his reader that his main topic, the Virgin of Candelaria, needed to be complemented by a history of the inhabitants of Tenerife as
well as the history of their conquest. He began his first book by announcing
that it was only reasonable to digress first in order to have knowledge about the
place in which the Virgin had appeared and about the people among whom the
cult had flourished (*Historia*, 25 [bk. 1, chap. 1]). He began his third book by
justifying his chosen topic of the history of the conquest of the island of Tenerife and subsequent events up to the year 1558. Thus he attempted (*Historia*, 87
[bk. 3, chap. 1]) to deflect potential readers' criticisms that he had departed
from his divine topic:

> Aunque no fue mi intento ni el principal motivo de mi es-
> critura ser historiador desta isla, no puedo dejar de tocar al-
> gunas cosas de ella, para más claridad de lo que entre manos
> tengo, porque en el orden de proceder no haya falta, y tam-
> bién porque no voy fuera de propósito, pues todo va a un fin
> dirigido.

---

critically sound edition appeared in Santa Cruz de Tenerife in 1952 under the direction of
Serra Ráfols, Bonnet, and Álamo, which was superseded by the 1968 edition by Cioranescu
(see above, notes 61 and 74).

[Although it was not my intention nor the main purpose of
my writings to be the historian of this island, I cannot refrain
from touching upon certain aspects of its history in order to
clarify the task at hand and maintain the proper order. I am
not going beyond my subject because everything is directed
toward the same end.]

These justifications obliged Espinosa to spell out the connection between the
Virgin's miracles to the Guanches and the conquest of Tenerife. In doing so,
however, Espinosa was able to engage in the exploration of the significance of
the miracles within his greater project, rather than vice versa, as he seemed to
claim to his readers.

His history deliberately followed a structure which revealed that in order to
arrive at the fourth book, which contained a description of all the attested and
documented miracles, it was necessary to travel geographically, culturally, and
chronologically through the Canary Islands to explore the context of the appearance of the Virgin and the very first miracles. By the same token, the justification for the appearance of the religious image "to infidels and in the land of
infidels" ("a infieles y en tierra de infieles") provided the perfect pretext for
Espinosa's ethnographic description of the Guanches and their evangelical fate
(*Historia*, 50 [bk. 2, chap. 1]). Espinosa considered such play of narratives to be
an obligatory step which did not divert attention from the purpose of the text,
but rather allowed for the perfect crafting of his own historical account.

Thus, in my view, the miraculous appearance of the Virgin serves as the
point of departure for the emergence of other arguments regarding the nature
of the pagan islanders, how best to evangelize them, and whether peaceful conversion was the only effective means to do so. Like Las Casas before him,
Espinosa was involved in debating positions such as that of José de Acosta,
who, in his *De Procuranda Indorum Salute*, addressed the troubling issue of the
lack of miracles in the conquest and apostolic missions of the New World (see
Adorno, *Guaman Poma*, 31–32). Acosta traced evangelization back to the apostles themselves and elaborated an explanation for the proliferation of miraculous occurrences at that time: in short, the Greeks and Romans were highly
rational and the preachers of the faith required extraordinary measures to reach
them. In America, affirmed Acosta, miracles were scarce not only because
modern preachers were more sophisticated (although less pious), but also because dealing with Amerindians was like "making friends with wild boars or
crocodiles" ("pretender entablar amistad con jabalíes o cocodrilos"). The possibility of evangelizing Amerindians with supernatural help and the absence of
military protection was unattainable because "knowing the lack of judgment
and prudence of hogs and dogs we should think that Christ has ordered us not
to throw pearls in vain at their feet only so they can trample on them and rebel

against us and then mangle us" ("conociendo la falta de juicio y la imprudencia de los puercos y los perros hemos de pensar que también nos es mandado por Cristo no arrojar en vano las preciosas margaritas delante de ellos para que las pisen, y revólviendose contra nosotros nos destrocen").[78]

In contrast, Espinosa demonstrated throughout the pages of his history that in the Canary Islands miracles were previously and presently abundant. He effectively offered a detailed account of the early (therefore undocumented) miracles, to anticipate the fourth book in which he proceeded to present a series of documented and witnessed miracles that had presumably occurred since 1530.[79] Indirectly, this evidence of an abundance of divine interventions implied that the Guanches of Tenerife, like Las Casas's Amerindians, were very different from the image of pagan peoples portrayed by Acosta. The Virgin of Candelaria became indeed the sign of the Guanches' favor with God. In any case, Espinosa set the stage for offering an ethnographic description of the natives. The miracles of the Virgin are not only the professed goal of this history but also the means by which the oral narratives of the Guanche population would be transcribed and the history of their origins and their European subjugation told.

Through the conventional mechanism of digression, Espinosa offers a powerful narrative which reveals other tensions: on the one hand, the author tries to inscribe his text within the boundaries of well-known historiographic

---

[78] Acosta summarized these ideas essentially in three chapters of *De Procuranda Indorum Salute*, ed. F. Mateos (Madrid: Atlas, 1954), 387–608, here 442–48 (bk. 2, chaps. 8–10).

[79] Critics have accused Espinosa of arbitrarily changing the details of the first appearance of the Virgin: see Serra Ráfols and Bonnet's introduction to their 1952 edition of Espinosa's *Del origen y milagros* (xv–xviii). Espinosa's version differed from the more popular tradition found in accounts such as Juan González de Mendoza's 1585 *Historia de las cosas más notables, ritos y costumbres del reino de la China*, Diego Pérez de Mesa's 1590 *Grandezas y cosas notables de España*, and Fray João dos Santos's 1622 *Ethiopia Oriental*. All these texts narrated with little variation the story of the Virgin who appeared in a cave to a native shepherd, who in turn tried to throw a stone at her only to find his arm immobilized until the day he died. Espinosa's account had the Virgin appear standing upon a rock. This Virgin not only performed the miracle of the inert arm but also made a second shepherd wound himself with a *tabona* (native knife) that he had aimed at her moments before (*Historia*, 51–53 [bk. 2, chap. 2]). With respect to the change of location, one can only speculate that it was an intentional attempt to devalue the place of appearance in order to emphasize the cult which, in present times, had a nearby sanctuary visited by many pilgrims. Or perhaps he was influenced by apparitions that took place in the New World on pre-Hispanic religious sites, as I have suggested (Merediz, "Traveling Icons," 10–11). The occurrence of a second miracle serves Espinosa's purpose of proving that a number of miraculous events occurred. The date provided by Espinosa for the appearance of the Virgin in the form of a statue was approximately 1400. Rumeu de Armas, however, has argued convincingly that the statue seems to have been sculpted between 1430 and 1450 (*La conquista*, 45–60). For an overview of the polemics surrounding the dating and iconographic characteristics of the primitive image of the Virgin of Candelaria, see Riquelme Pérez, *La Virgen de Candelaria*, 45–63.

models, and on the other, he shows a clear ideological affiliation with Lascasian thought in his view of the natives and the European conquest. Espinosa thus chose to modify or reshape his historiographical model to fit his ideological aim; he was involved in the task of elliptically offering an ethnographic history and the account of an unjust war of conquest under the seemingly non-controversial guise of ecclesiastical history.

The centrality of Las Casas's most famous arguments in Espinosa's work becomes quite evident. In 1952, Buenaventura Bonnet ("El p[adre] Alonso de Espinosa," 42–43) and María Rosa Alonso (*El poema de Viana*, 61) noted that Espinosa's denouncement of the injustice of the war had repeated Bartolomé de las Casas's well-known condemnatory remarks.[80] But in fact Las Casas and Espinosa's shared perspective on non-European pagan peoples and on the na-ture of just war operates as the basis for the emergence of Espinosa's text as a whole. Any further discussion of Espinosa's textual strategies (which offer an implicit Lascasian narrative) needs first to address the written sources from which Espinosa benefited either directly or indirectly.

3. ESPINOSA READS LAS CASAS: THE SOURCE AND THE GAZE

Several critics have attempted to explore the points of connection between Espinosa and Las Casas by focusing on the question of what Lascasian sources Espinosa might have used. Bonnet, for example, has rightfully suggested as a possible source for this connection the *Brevísima relación de la destrucción de las Indias*, while Alejandro Cioranescu has suggested the unpublished *Historia de las Indias*. Given the problem of circulation confronted by the latter, Cioranescu (*Colón*, 73–88) has speculated that perhaps the *Historia de las Indias* was meant to be used as refectory reading within the Dominican convents, where it easily could have been received by Espinosa. The search for Espinosa's Lascasian sources should be located more appropriately among those works published in Seville in 1552–1553.[81] The *Brevísima* is the most well-known of the treatises,

---

[80] In 1930, Wölfel ("La Curia Romana," 1013) had already pointed out that it was very probable that Espinosa had met Las Casas or read his works.

[81] Las Casas published the following treatises: *Brevísima relación de la destrucción de las In-dias*, *Lo que sigue es un pedazo de una carta*, *Aquí se contiene una disputa*, *Aquí se contienen treinta pro-posiciones*, *Sobre la materia de los indios que se han hecho esclavos*, *Entre los remedios*, *Aquí se contienen los avisos y reglas para los confesores*, *Tratado comprobatorio del imperio soberano*, and *Algunos principios que deben servir de punto de partida* (*Tratados* [México: Fondo de Cultura Económica, 1965], 1.2: 3–1273). The *Brevísima* was first circulated and translated in Europe a dozen years after Las Casas's death. At present, the library at the University of La Laguna holds a *suelta* edition of the *Brevísima* and two other treatises dating from 1552 (*Entre los remedios*, *Aquí se contiene*), and one more from 1553 (*Tratado comprobatorio*). Although it is hard to trace the travels of these early editions, they could have belonged since the sixteenth century to one of the island's

although it is not the most typical example among Las Casas's extensive written works; its specific rhetorical structure was designed to persuade the Court of Castile and the Council of the Indies to promulgate the New Laws in 1542.[82] Although there is a possibility that the *Historia de las Indias* as well as the published treatises might have fallen into Espinosa's hands, I would argue that another of Las Casas's writings provided Espinosa with the necessary optics to guide his ethnological gaze.

Las Casas's *Apologética historia sumaria* is likely the most plausible source for Espinosa's ethnographic description of the Guanches. Although this monumental work was not published in the sixteenth century, solid evidence exists of its transmission in Jerónimo Román y Zamora's *Las repúblicas del mundo*, which was first published in 1575 and re-edited in 1595 — a case of successful plagiarism that managed to evade censorship.[83] Espinosa likely had access to Las Casas's text through Román y Zamora's printed book or in manuscript form during the many years he lived in Guatemala and Mexico. The original manuscript of the *Apologética*, in fact, could have been the whole ream of paper entitled *Del bien y favor de los Indios* in the possession of the Dominican convent in Chiapas, which Dávila Padilla (*Provincia de Santiago de México*, 31 [bk. 1, chap. 98]) mentioned in his history of the Order. Dávila Padilla further commented that Domingo de la Anunciación, in his capacity as prior of the convent of Santiago de México, had the manuscript of *Del bien y favor* copied for the library in Mexico between approximately 1560 and 1585 (*Provincia de Santiago de México*, 31 [bk. 1, chap. 98]).[84] The dates are not exact, since Dávila Padilla provided a

---

convents, which constitute the main source for the rare book collection of the library. The library of the Dominican convent was considered the best on the island in the eighteenth century (A. Cabrera Perera, *Las bibliotecas en Las Palmas* [Las Palmas: Cabildo Insular, 1982], 9). In the sale of church property or *desamortización*, ordered by the Minister of Finance, Juan Álvarez Mendizábal, in 1837, all books ceased to be in ecclesiastical ownership and became part of provincial libraries; in the case of Tenerife, they became the property of the Instituto Provincial de Canarias, which in turn became the university. The provenance of the three treatises mentioned is not given, although they all carry the seal of the Institute, indicating that they probably arrived as a result of the *desamortización*. In any case, the sanctuary of Candelaria was burned on 15 February 1789. While the original image of the Virgin survived until 1826, such was not the case with the library and archive of the convent, which were destroyed by the fire in 1789 (Díaz Núñez, *Memoria cronológica*, 238).

[82] See Wagner and Parish, *Life and Writings*, 108–20. See also Las Casas, *Brevísima*, ed. A. Saint-Lu (Madrid: Cátedra, 1984), introduction (11–53).

[83] Remesal noted in 1620 Román y Zamora's massive borrowings from the *Apologética*: see Remesal, *Historia general*, ed. Sáenz de Santa María, 33. See also Wagner and Parish, *Life and Writings*, 288–89, and, for a more complete analysis, R. Adorno, "Censorship and its Evasion: The Case of fray Jerónimo Román y Zamora's *Repúblicas del Mundo* [1575, 1595]," *Hispania* 75 (1992): 812–27.

[84] The text uses the word *trasladar*, which means that the document was copied or (figuratively) moved from one convent to the other.

biography of Domingo de la Anunciación that reveals that the latter occupied the position of prior in Mexico on two occasions, subsequent to his failed missionary journey to Florida in 1558 and prior to his definitive seclusion in the convent due to his blindness in 1585 (*Provincia de Santiago de México*, 609–11 [bk. 2, chap. 78]; 623–25 [bk. 2, chap. 88]).[85] The historical period of 1558 to approximately 1585 coincides fully with the presence in Guatemala of Alonso de Espinosa, who had become a Dominican by 1564 and was already preaching by 1573; he was also present in Mexico where he worked for the Archbishop and Inquisitor on the correction and expurgation of manuscripts destined for the press up until the time of his departure for Spain in 1579. The volume of a *resma* of paper or 500 *pliegos*, to which Dávila Padilla referred, could correspond to either of the two extensive histories written by Las Casas. Judging by the reference to the work's title, however, the few words given, "of the goodness and favor of the Indians," indicate that the *Apológetica historia sumaria*, which was devoted to defending the worthiness of Amerindian civilizations, was most likely the work Dávila Padilla had in mind.

In the *Apológetica*, Las Casas engaged in an extensive study of indigenous civilizations of the New World and compared them to classical cultures in order to demonstrate that they exhibited every characteristic of civil order as established in Aristotle's *Politics*. As individuals, Las Casas's Amerindians exhibited characteristics regarded as signs of the most refined humanity: intelligence, courage, notable beauty, chastity, peacefulness, excellent intellect, good judgment, and good control over themselves and their domestic economies. In other words, they possessed monastic and economic temperance. As nations, Las Casas's Amerindian societies lived in communities where civil ceremonies were performed and social groups were divided into farmers, artisans, soldiers, grandees (*ricoshombres*), priests, and judges or public officials; they exhibited political prudence. Not surprisingly, Las Casas found parallels between Amerindian practices and the most traditional structures of ancient Old World and European societies. In the words of Sabine MacCormack (*Religion in the Andes*, 206), who has masterfully summarized Las Casas's strategies in the *Apológetica*, such a project had been undertaken previously, but only Las Casas utilized "the ancient evidence in an incomparably more systematic and deliberate fashion." MacCormack (*Religion in the Andes*, 207) further explains that Las Casas arrives at the conclusion that the New World religions "were indeed erroneous, but

---

[85] The reference to such a manuscript seems to be trustworthy. Domingo de la Anunciación and Vicente de las Casas started to compose a history of the ecclesiastical province that served as the basis for Dávila Padilla's book, and both elderly friars revised and added to Dávila Padilla's history before its publication in 1595 (Dávila Padilla, *Provincia de Santiago de México*, 625 [bk. 2, chap. 83]; 653 [bk. 2, last chap.]). The *Apológetica*, in manuscript form, was also used in Mexico by the Franciscan friar Jerónimo de Mendieta (1528?–1604) in his *Historia eclesiástica* (1596), and it is likely that there were other circulating copies of the manuscript in Mexico and Central America (Wagner and Parish, *Life and Writings*, 288).

comparison demonstrated that the error was not specific to the Americas." In fact, the difference that these religions exhibited from those of the Greco-Roman world was that the former "had been performed with exemplary and sober dignity and that they had, in effect, enshrined a certain theological truth" (MacCormack, *Religion in the Andes*, 207). This conclusion serves as the premise for Las Casas's argument (*Apologética*, ed. O'Gorman, 1: 370 [bk. 3, chap. 71]) that "all human beings have the capacity to understand that there is a supreme God, and to seek him by acts of worship and sacrifice" (MacCormack, *Religion in the Andes*, 209).

As a reader of Las Casas, Espinosa embarked on a similar pursuit. Even though the Guanche culture did not resemble that of the Aztecs or Mexicas, Mayas, or Inkas, the friar set out to prove that the Guanches worshipped one God and lived in a civil society, just as had been claimed by Las Casas for the Amerindians. Following the structure of the *Apologética*, Espinosa began his first chapter by offering a geographical description of Tenerife and its place in antiquity. He continued in the following chapter by describing the natural beauty of the island, the fertility of the land, and the utility of the rest of its natural resources. He described very briefly the curious natural phenomenon by which the island was known many years earlier, mainly its volcanic activity ("Isla del Infierno"), which was evident in the barrenness of a certain middle region of the island. He asserted that Tenerife must have experienced a volcanic eruption such as the one he once witnessed in Palma in 1585, which brought up so much "fire from the entrails of the earth" that it reached the sea, heated the water, and cooked the fish (Espinosa, *Historia*, 25–31 [bk. 1, chaps. 1–3]).

Just as Las Casas (*Apologética*, ed. O'Gorman, 1: 109–12 [bk. 1, chap. 22]) provided evidence to assert that the Indies of the West and their inhabitants were related in the ancient past to the Indies of the East, Espinosa (*Historia*, 33 [bk. 1, chap. 4]) described the various theories regarding the origins of the inhabitants of the Canaries, to suggest finally that they were of African origin because of their territorial proximity, the common language, and similar customs and diet. He expressed his opinion bluntly, mentioning that the old Guanches from whom he had received his information spoke of a myth of origin that was not attached to any particular geographical location. According to the natives, a group of sixty people arrived from an unknown place and made their home in Icod and called it "the place for the settlement of the son of the great one" ("Lugar del ayuntamiento del hijo del grande"). The emphasis here is not on the place of geographical origin of the first inhabitants, but rather on the obvious divine interventions that presumably occurred at the birth of their culture (*Historia*, 33 [bk. 1, chap. 4]). In Espinosa's opinion, the Guanches were African by descent, that is, from that continent well-known for its antagonism to Christianity; he reported that regardless of this origin, the Guanches were pagans without law or gods or rituals like other nations. In the following pages of his book, he developed this initial generalization to redeem the apparent primitivism of the Guanches in imitation of Las Casas's ethnographic theory about the Amerindians.

Espinosa's account of the people native to the island began in chapter five of Book One with the description of their system of beliefs and the assertion of their confused knowledge of the Judeo-Christian God, whom they described as "the great, the sublime; he who sustains all things" ("el grande, el sublime, el que todo lo sustenta"). Although they had no rituals of prayer or sacrifices as Aristotle (and later Las Casas) had prescribed for a civil society, Espinosa (*Historia*, 34 [bk. 1, chap. 4]) mentioned that the natives prayed in times of drought with a ceremony called "bleating of the sheep" ("baladero de las obejas"). Torriani, who wrote at the same time as Espinosa, and Abreu y Galindo, who knew of Espinosa's book, presented similar descriptions of the Guanches, thus corroborating their view of the importance of the Dominican friar's (ethno)historical inquiry. The ceremony of the bleating of the sheep appears in Abreu y Galindo's *Historia de la conquista* (ed. Cioranescu, 294 [bk. 3, chap. 11]), which is remarkably faithful to Espinosa's account. Although the ceremony does not appear in Torriani's work, the latter work (*Descrittione et historia del regno del Isole Canarie*) otherwise coincides with Espinosa's on general religious and social aspects of Guanche life, such as their knowledge of God and the devil and the structure of their government. By attributing to the Guanches at least one religious ritual, Espinosa made them conform in a generalized manner to the model of civility adopted by Las Casas. Significantly, he left out any indication of idolatry.

Espinosa's natives also knew of the existence of hell, which they held to be the peak of Mount Teide, and they called the devil "Guayota." If the knowledge of God was confusing to the natives, Espinosa (*Historia*, 35 [bk. 1, chap. 5]) made clear that they distinguished rather sharply between good and evil; in fact, they even performed a ceremony of a kind of baptism. They practiced it rigorously on newborns, not as a sacrament but perhaps as a reminiscence of the ancient evangelical visit that Blandano, Maclovio, and three thousand missionaries had paid to the islands in times of the Emperor Justinian, according to Espinosa.[86] Both Espinosa and Abreu y Galindo portrayed the ceremony as a

---

[86] Blandano and Maclovio's legendary travels are the origins of the myth of the elusive island of Saint Brendan (see note 2 in the Introduction). Espinosa extracted the information about Blandano and Maclovio from the *Martirologium* or *Kalenda Romana*, as did Torriani who quoted a *Calendario* by Maurolicio. Cioranescu (in Torriani, *Descripción*, 180 n. 2) has established that the text referred to here is Francesco Maurolico's *Martyrologium*, published in Venice in 1568. The legend of the visit, transcribed and translated by Espinosa (*Historia*, 33–34 [bk. 1, chap. 4]), says the following: "In them [the Canary Islands] there was a fair man of great abstinence, a native of Scotland, father and shepherd of three thousand monks, for the space of seven years. He was there with the blessed Maclovio who resuscitated a dead giant and baptized him. The giant recounted and explained the pains that Jews and pagans suffer in hell, and shortly afterwards he died again, in the time of the Emperor Justinian" ("Hic

cleansing experience which for the latter pertained to the hygiene of the infant's whole body (Abreu y Galindo, *Historia de la conquista*, ed. Cioranescu, 294 [bk. 3, chap. 11]) and for Espinosa involved only the head, which invested the infant's cleansing with the religious overtones of Christian baptism. Torriani (*Die Kanarischen Inseln*, ed. Wölfel, 166 [chap. 51]; *Descripción*, ed. Cioranescu, 179 [chap. 51]) offered his own version with a few differences. Contrary to Espinosa and Abreu, Torriani made an explicit connection: "they had baptism with water" ("haueuano battesimo d'acqua"), which of course could be established only after the evangelization by the legendary Blandano and Maclovio.[87]

Torriani also made a further distinction between inhabitants of Tenerife before and after evangelization, which opposes Espinosa's description. Of the pre-evangelized Guanches or pre-Maclovio and Blandano period, Torriani wrote: "It was of common belief that among these islanders there was no religion and that they had relations with any woman except their mothers, and that they had no justice nor government. They were all thieves and totally pagan" ("si crede che fra questi Isolani non ui [ci] fosse religione alcuna, et che comunemente usassero con le donne, eccetto era la madre, et non haueuano giustitia, ne gouerno, ma che tutti fossero ladroni, et totalmente gentili") (*Die Kanarischen Inseln*, ed. Wölfel, 166 [chap. 51]; *Descripción*, ed. Cioranescu, 180–81 [chap. 51]). Intelligently and conventionally, Torriani chose to place the most negative primitivism in the distant past while elevating the present-day Guanches to a

---

Blandanus, magnae abstinentiae vir ex Scotia pater trium millium monachorum, cum beato Maclovio has insulas septennio perlustrat. Hic dictus Maclovius gigantem mortuum suscitat, qui baptisatus iudaeorum ac paganorum penas refert, et paulo post iterum moritur, tempore Iustiniani imperatoris… Que quiere decir … En ellas estuvo Blandano, varón de grande abstinencia, natural de Escocia, padre y pastor de tres mil monjes, por espacio de siete años, con el bienaventurado Maclovio, el cual resucitó un gigante muerto y, bautizado, contaba y refería las penas que los judíos y paganos padecen en el infierno, y de ahí a poco murió otra vez, en tiempo de Justiniano emperador").

[87] I quote from D. J. Wölfel, *Die Kanarischen Inseln und ihre Ureinwohner* (Leipzig: Koehler, 1940), and I also subsequently give the page numbers in *Descripción e historia de las Islas Canarias*, ed. and trans. A. Cioranescu (Santa Cruz de Tenerife: Goya, 1978). Cioranescu's translation of the Italian manuscript into Spanish is most useful and his introduction provides a very complete account of Torriani's life and work (i–xliii). When in 1940 Wölfel published the manuscript in a bilingual Italian-German edition with a general introduction (*Die Kanarischen Inseln*), the unpublished manuscript had already been known in the islands since the end of the nineteenth century. Unfortunately, Wölfel's edition appeared during the Second World War and its circulation was consequently limited (C. Díaz Alayón, "Los estudios canarios de Dominik Josef Wölfel," *Anuario de estudios atlánticos* 35 [1989]: 363–93, here 363–74). Most recently, however, Torriani's text has also been translated into Portuguese by José Manuel Azevedo e Silva and published in Lisbon with very comprehensive annotations: Torriani, *Descrição e História do Reino das Ilhas Canárias*, ed. and trans. José Manuel Azevedo e Silva (Lisboa: Cosmos, 1999). The original manuscript is housed in the library of the University of Coimbra, Portugal.

certain civility, which they enjoyed only after the time of Blandano and Maclovio's supposed evangelical mission; this reference to Blandano and Maclovio had at least the appeal of accountability, for their visit was reported in the *Kalenda Romana* from which Espinosa also quoted.

Espinosa erased such a distinction. Rather than claiming that the islanders had been transformed by the visit of Blandano and Maclovio, as Torriani suggested, Espinosa claimed that the Guanches had always been exposed to evangelization. According to Espinosa (*Historia*, 33 [bk. 1, chap. 4]), the apostles themselves sent a bishop to the islands; unfortunately, his name was unknown to the friar ("cuyo nombre me han prometido decir"). Espinosa attributed to all Guanches the pre-evangelization characteristics or dubious civil practices, which Torriani highlighted in the pre-evangelized population of the islands, in a plausible attempt to be truthful to the information handed down to him. Espinosa's Guanches, however, were worthy of the consideration of Christ's own apostles. This argument is the first in a series of textual strategies designed by Espinosa to negotiate his commitment as a historian to "truthfulness" while managing to portray the Guanche population in a positive light.

Espinosa's efforts were directed implicitly and explicitly towards the justification of the natives' predisposition to the true Christian religion and civility despite a series of practices that Espinosa's readers might have considered to be idolatrous. He wrote (*Historia*, 35 [bk. 1, chap. 5]):

> Y aunque gente sin ley, no vivían fuera della, porque en algunas cosas se sujetaban y llegaban a razón: como es en tener superior y conocer vasallaje, en contraer matrimonio y diferenciar los hijos legítimos de los bastardos, en hacer leyes y sujetarse a ellas … que en el transcurso de la historia se verán.

> [Although they were people without law, they did not live altogether outside the law, for in some things they constrained themselves and exercised reason. Such were their subjugation to superiors and their knowledge of vassalage, also their contracts of marriage and their distinction between legitimate children and bastards, their making and obeying ordinances … and other things which will be seen in the course of this history.]

As he did when he overlooked the absence of a writing system by which to preserve the memory of the past, Espinosa disguised the Guanches' primitivism by emphasizing the elements that were considered by neo-Aristotelians truly to represent civil society. He took advantage of the medieval arguments about natural law by investing the Guanches with the exercise of reason, the creation of a social structure, and the institution of a system of government.

After such a general statement, Espinosa wrote briefly about the education of the Guanches, which included learning the physical skills (jumping, running, and throwing) that constituted the basis of their warrior culture. Tenerife was the last island conquered by the Europeans, and the Guanches had the reputation since the fifteenth century of being skilful and bellicose soldiers. Espinosa addressed this known element to show that not only were the majority of the Guanches educated in the arts of war as in any civil society, but that such soldiers were so disciplined and respectful that when they encountered a woman walking alone, they were not allowed to look at her or talk to her unless she addressed them first. Furthermore, any dishonest word on the part of the soldier was punished by death. Despite overtly considering Guanche society primitive, Espinosa argued that such characteristics bespoke a highly refined military and civil order. Abreu y Galindo (*Historia de la conquista*, ed. Cioranescu, 300 [bk. 3, chap. 13]), who borrowed copiously from Espinosa and showed himself to be a follower of Las Casas as well, took the exercise of justice one step further by arguing that the Guanches did not practice the death penalty because "only he who was in the heavens" could punish criminality with death.

As expected in a work like Espinosa's, the natives are physically described as paradigms of beauty: possessing perfect faces, being tall and of well-proportioned bodies. Espinosa, however, added certain particularities. He mentioned reluctantly the myths of the giants fourteen feet tall who had supposedly inhabited the islands, and he described a racial configuration that did not conform totally to that of the New World. He explained that while in the south of the island the Guanches were darker, perhaps due to exposure to the sun or biological inheritance ("de generación"), the northern islanders were white, and their women blonde and beautiful (*Historia*, 36–37 [bk. 1, chap. 6]).[88] This information coincides perfectly with Espinosa's aims of disassociating anything that might be unfamiliar, such as physical oddities or deformities, from the image of the Guanches. In fact, his description of the Guanches' ethnic composition suggests that they resembled Europeans, and it offers nuances to Columbus's famous reference to the Arawaks' uniform color as being like that of the Canary Islanders.

Espinosa's description of the nutritional diet of the Guanches (which consisted of ground barley [*gofio*], milk, lard, goat and pork meats, and a kind of honey from a fruit called *mocán*) is followed by his description of the many tournaments the natives held on the islands to show their physical skills in ath-

---

[88] Recent archeological studies have confirmed the existence of different ethnic and cultural characteristics within each island and between islands. This has been explained by the diversity in the ethnic composition of the Berber communities from whom the Guanches are thought to descend. For an accessible and comprehensive description of the Guanches of Tenerife based on early historical texts and archeological evidence, see Antonio Tejera Gaspar, *Tenerife y los Guanches* (Santa Cruz de Tenerife: Biblioteca Canaria, 1992), 9–106.

letics and dances. Espinosa (*Historia*, 38 [bk. 1, chap. 6]) affirmed that it was reason for admiration that such a rudimentary diet produced men of great courage, strength, and agility, and of such a delicate intellect. The description of the diet also served as an introduction to the natives' agricultural practices. Once again, the practice of agriculture and the existence of a class of farmers was an indication of the civil order of a society. Thus Espinosa described how the natives had a sort of feudal system in which they cultivated the lands of the king, which had been divided among the subjects according to the quality of their service. In a passing parenthetical remark, Espinosa mentioned the lack of cities or the Guanches' failure to live in fixed communities, only to contradict his statement later. He went on to emphasize how the Guanches either lived in natural caves or carefully constructed cave-like homes in those lands given to them. The males respected the boundaries of their farms and did not allow weeds to grow. Although they did not have metals, they cultivated the land with wooden sticks or goat horns. The process was then taken over by the females, who did everything else including the harvesting and storage of the grains. During the month of August, the Guanches celebrated the harvest season, in Espinosa's words, "as if they were expressing gratitude for the goodness received" ("como en agradecimiento del bien recibido") — a statement meant to bridge the Guanche ritual with Christian religious practices of thanksgiving (*Historia*, 39 [bk. 1, chap. 7]). Espinosa chose to juxtapose the absence of elaborate architecture on the islands with the civilizing practice of farming, indicating, as Las Casas had done, that the latter was a more convincing sign for identifying a civil society than the former. In the *Apologética*, Las Casas (ed. O'Gorman, 1: 240 [bk. 3, chap. 45]) had stated, for example, that the true city was made not of dead walls and stones, but of living men who cohabited in love and peace.

When Espinosa described matrimonial practices, he began by enumerating all the possible negative aspects, with which he immediately juxtaposed the positive ones. His affirmation, for example, that all men could have as many wives as they could support, and that the institution of marriage could be as easily dissolved as it was established, was followed by his important comment to the effect that the natives made a clear distinction between legitimate and illegitimate descendants (Espinosa, *Historia*, 40 [bk. 1, chap. 7]). When he described the Guanches' sexual practices, a similar strategy emerged:

> En el uso de la generación, no tenían respeto más que a madre y hermana, porque las demás, tías, primas, y sobrinas, cuñadas, todos las llevaban por un rasero, sin diferencia alguna: pero aunque eran dados a este vicio, abominaban en extremo el pecado nefando.

> [In their procreative practice, they respected only their moth-
> ers and sisters, because all other women, aunts, cousins,
> nieces and sisters-in-law, were equally eligible without making
> any differences among them; but although they were given to
> this particular vice, they abominated in the extreme the sin of
> sodomy.]

The monarchs, however, were occasionally allowed to marry their sisters as a desirable means of ensuring the preservation of the noble lineage.

Espinosa's strategy is transparent: to confess or acknowledge the Guanches' lesser sins only to demonstrate repeatedly that idolatry and sodomy, the pillars of eternal condemnation, were absolutely absent from the practices of the Atlantic islanders. A few years later, Abreu y Galindo (*Historia de la conquista*, ed. Cioranescu, 114 [bk. 1, chap. 23]) would affirm the same: "There has not been any native tempted by heresy, which is something worth pondering, nor has sodomy been found among them, neither as infidels nor after having become Catholics" ("no ha habido ningún natural tocado en especial de heregía, que es mucho de ponderar; ni el pecado nefando se sintió, cuando infieles ni después de católicos").

Like Las Casas before him, Espinosa presented the non-European subject, in this case Guanche society, in terms of European concepts that served not only as common points of reference, but also as signs of exemplary dignity. In the *Apologética*, for example, Las Casas (ed. O'Gorman, 1: 350–53 [bk. 3, chap. 67]) had depicted Aztec military training in terms of the rules and procedures of the medieval chivalric orders, and in this way elevated his subject matter to the level of religious and social prestige that such European institutions had carried throughout the centuries. With the intention of casting Guanche social structure in a favorable light, Espinosa (*Historia*, 42 [bk. 1, chap. 9]) likewise divided social classes into "noblemen" (*hidalgos*), "squires" (*escuderos*), and "peasants" (*villanos*). In addition, his presentation of the ceremony of royal succession evokes the initiation into Christian knighthood insofar as the new native king, like a knight, is initiated by being tapped on the shoulder, not with a sword, but with the bone of one of his illustrious ancestors (Espinosa, *Historia*, 41–42 [bk. 1, chap. 8]). When moving from his summer residence in the mountains to the winter one on the coast, the king took the elders of the community with him, and he had a spear or *banot* that he placed in front of him as a symbol of his royal presence. Upon encountering the king, his subjects knelt down, cleansed the king's feet with their gowns, and kissed them (Espinosa, *Historia*, 42 [bk. 1, chap. 8]).

Many other analogous practices are also described by Espinosa. All the natives, although dressed in animal skins, fabricated this clothing with "much subtlety and sophistication" ("mucha sutileza y primor"), while the Guanche women had a dress code that closely resembled the European one; they wore,

underneath the *tamarco* or short gown, a suede skirt because "it is quite immod-
est to reveal breasts and feet" ("es cosa deshonesta a las mujeres descubrir
pechos y pies") (*Historia*, 37 [bk. 1, chap. 6]). The sewing of clothes also served
to indicate the existence, if not the conscience, of an artisan class which took
care of certain necessities of life. In addition, Espinosa (*Historia*, 38–39 [bk. 1,
chap. 6]) listed the curative practice of bleeding (*sangría*) among the natives'
medical achievements.

A funeral ritual, said Las Casas (*Apologética*, ed. O'Gorman, 2: 527–28 [bk.
3, chap. 240]), following the Aristotelian model, "is sign and proof of good
reason and also of an orderly and well governed republic; the better the ceremonies are and the more exquisite the rituals ... the greater the respect for the
rules of reason and the greater the capacity for civility" ("es señal y argumento
de buena razón y también de ordenada y regida república y tanto más y mejores
ceremonias y exquisitos ritos en ellas se guardaban ... era mayor de seguir las
reglas de razón y tener mayor policía"). Thus Espinosa's project is never more
revealing than in his introductory paragraph to the chapter that describes the
natives' simple burial rituals. Although cannibalism was never attributed to the
islanders in ancient or recent histories, Espinosa categorically stated in his introduction to his account of the natives' funeral practices that an anthropopha-
gous act as part of a funeral ritual was legitimate and admirable as the ultimate
sign of respect that a nation could pay to its dead — a comment that seems
totally out of place. This textual strategy implies that if the practice of cannibalistic burial was valid in one culture, then the rituals of another (the Guanches in
this case) which were not cannibalistic in any way were even more desirable,
civil, and valid. Las Casas's *Apologética* once again seems to filter through the
pages of Espinosa's history. The latter seems to echo Las Casas's well-known
attitude towards the act of ingesting human flesh. With respect to the natives of
New Spain, Las Casas (*Apologética*, ed. O'Gorman, 2: 354 [bk. 3, chap. 205]) had
remarked: "I understand that they did not eat it on purpose; they only ate [it]
... as a sacred thing, more out of religious piety than for any other reason"
("no la comían tan de propósito, según tengo entendido, sino ... como cosa
sagrada, más por religión que por otra causa"). Whereas Las Casas explicitly
justified ritual cannibalism in the proper context, Espinosa imitated him even in
spite of the fact that the subject matter of his history did not require such an
effort because the Guanches followed a quite conventional rite of mourning
and burial. During the fifteen days of the Guanche funeral ritual, the body of
the deceased was anointed with a preservative mixture, dried in the sun, and
carefully embalmed before being buried in a cave or other site (Espinosa, *Historia*, 44–45 [bk. 1, chap. 9]).[89]

---

[89] In Herodotus's *Histories* (trans. Godley, 2: 307 [bk. 4, chap. 106]; 1: 271 [bk. 1, chap.
216]), although the historian points out that the Massagetae (who were like the Scythians)
considered the killing and ingesting of their elders the most blessed death, the description of

To close his first book and its general ethnographic description of the Guanches, Espinosa restated his main point. He asserted once more that the natives of Tenerife, as well as those of the other islands who had a common origin, were gentiles uncontaminated by demonic persuasion who did not in any way idolize false gods or have dealings with the devil as was common among other pagan nations. Espinosa ultimately praised the honorable descendants of the Guanches who had served the Spanish king, been exempted from jurisdiction by the Inquisition because of their purity of blood, become prominent members of society, and occupied the highest places within the Church during his own lifetime (Espinosa, *Historia*, 46 [bk. 1, chap. 10]).

In his second book, after offering the available information about the Guanche culture, Espinosa narrated how, in approximately 1400, the Virgin appeared to two native shepherds and worked miracles on them (*Historia*, 51–53 [bk. 2, chap. 2]). The narration of how the cult began forcefully demonstrates further Espinosa's view that the Guanches had a natural inclination to follow the true religion which made them identify the miraculous icon as a divine sign. The king of Güímar asked the nobles of his kingdom to carry the Virgin in their arms (Espinosa, *Historia*, 55 [bk. 2, chap. 3]), and they created a primitive altar to adore the image, despite having no experience with religious rituals (Espinosa, *Historia*, 58 [bk. 2, chap. 5]). They adored the Virgin's image and presented offerings to her in the form of animals which were then considered to belong to her sacred herd (Espinosa, *Historia*, 61 [bk. 2, chap. 7]). Within thirty or forty years after the appearance of the Virgin, Antón Guanche, whom the Spaniards had captured, baptized, and instructed in the faith, returned to Tenerife and began evangelizing his people. Through him the Guanches gained the knowledge of the source of the miraculous image, and they named her "Achmayex, guayaxerax, achoron, achaman," in other words,

---

the Anthropophagi does not carry positive comments. Neither do the descriptions of Strabo in his *Geography* (with regard to the Scythians, trans. Jones, 3: 195–97 [bk. 7, chap. 3]) or Aristotle in his *Nicomachean Ethics*, 7.5 (ed. Barnes, 2: 1814–15). The same can be said about Roman literature in which cannibalism is a familiar theme although mostly used as a satirical device. However, in John Mandeville's *Travels*, an interesting medieval reworking of the Greeks' "monstrous races" in coexistence with religious miracles, the story of ritual cannibalism is described as a careful and rational structure and therefore as a civil practice (A. Grafton, *New Worlds, Ancient Texts* [Cambridge, MA: Harvard University Press, 1992], 71–73). Aside from the previous example, only Las Casas in his times seemed to explain cannibalism without condemning its practitioners (later J. de Léry and M. de Montaigne showed a similar relativist perspective on the Tupinamba of Brazil). In the case of the New World, Las Casas (*Apologética*, ed. O'Gorman, 2: 352–56 [bk. 3, chap. 205]) rejected Aristotle's explanation of cannibalism, which had to do with a natural inclination given the climate and conditions of the land or some kind of perversion or madness from birth. Instead, Las Casas claimed that cannibalism, especialy in Mesoamerica, was part of religious practices or responded to specific circumstances (*Apologética*, ed. O'Gorman, 2: 356 [bk. 3, chap. 205]). Thus, Espinosa's remarks once again coincide with Las Casas's views.

"the mother of the one who sustains heaven and earth" (Espinosa, *Historia*, 61–62 [bk. 2, chap. 7]). By the time the Guanches received formal religious instruction, they had already been directly evangelized by divine intervention and they exercised their human reason and intellect in order to understand it as such. Thus Espinosa's final portrayal of the Guanches not only reflected the model of a civil society, but it also coincided fully with the picture of a proto-Christian society.

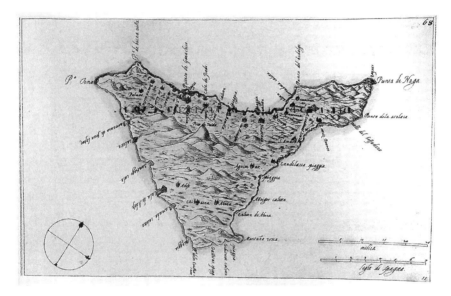

Fig. 4. Map of Tenerife in Leonardo Torriani's *Descrittione et historia del regno del Isole Canarie gia dette le Fortunate con il parere delle loro fortificationi.* The original is housed at the General Library of the University of Coimbra (Codex 314).

4. The Conquest of Tenerife Revisited: Las Casas Returns

The other necessary digression in Espinosa's history of the appearance of the Virgin of Candelaria was his account of the conquest and colonization of Tenerife, which began in the third book. Espinosa (*Historia*, 87 [bk. 3, chap. 1]) recognized that such an endeavor might expose him, as a historian, to the danger of public attack, as indeed ultimately happened. As the reader later discovers, Espinosa was engaged in criticizing the war of conquest, denouncing the numerous slave raids conducted on the islands by the Europeans, and demonstrating that the Guanches had been ruled by legitimate and wise authorities and were thus entitled to self-governance or dominion over their own affairs.

Espinosa's brief yet harsh remarks about the conquest have generated among critics the recognition of an explicit connection with Lascasian thought. Before discussing Alonso de Lugo's final offensive attack, Espinosa referred to the first battle of Acentejo between the Spanish and Guanche armies. He introduced the subject with a categorical statement (*Historia*, 96–97 [bk. 3, chap. 5]):

> Cosa averiguada es, por derecho divino y humano, que la guerra que los españoles hicieron, así a los naturales destas islas, como a los indios de las occidentales regiones, fue injusta sin tener razón alguna de bien en que estribar; porque ni ellos poseían tierras de cristianos, ni salían de sus límites y términos para infestar ni molestar las ajenas. Pues decir que les traían el Evangelio, había de ser con predicación y amonestación, y no con tambor y bandera, rogados y no forzados; pero esta materia ya está ventilada en otras partes; pase ahora.

> [It is an acknowledged fact, by virtue of both divine and human law, that the wars waged by the Spaniards against the natives of these islands, as well as against the Indians in the western regions, were unjust and without any reason to support them. For the natives had not taken the lands of Christians, nor had they gone beyond their own frontiers to infringe upon or invade the lands of their neighbors. If it is said that the Spaniards brought the Gospel, this should have been done by admonition and preaching, not by drum and banner; by persuasion, not by force. But this subject has been discussed elsewhere, so I pass on.]

Once again, Espinosa passed over the name of Las Casas and his source, but not the ideas.[90]

---

[90] The theory of just war is linked to Augustinian thought and Pope Innocent IV's commentaries although, in this case, it is more immediately mediated by Las Casas, who elaborated on the tradition. Las Casas disagreed with both Juan Ginés de Sepúlveda and Francisco de Vitoria. Sepúlveda stated in *Demócrates segundo* (1547) that a just war could be conducted against those who were obligated by nature to obey others superior to them but who refused to display such obedience. Vitoria in his *Relectio de Indis* (1538) stated eight principles upon which just wars could be waged against the Indians, including insufficient rational capacity. Las Casas disagreed openly with Sepúlveda's reasons, which included the natural servitude of the Amerindians, and their crimes "against nature" and against the innocent; he also disagreed in a more subtle way with Vitoria regarding the insufficient rational capacity of the Amerindians that justified a war against them. For a detailed recreation of the arguments among the three, based on all their writings and up-to-date criticism on the fa-

Espinosa espoused what Las Casas had clearly stated and extensively argued. The war against the Guanches had been unjust because it did not meet the three conditions stipulated by Las Casas in the *Historia de las Indias*.[91] The Guanches had not persecuted any Christians, nor had they maliciously prevented the spread of the Christian religion; they had not occupied any Christian kingdoms, stolen any property, nor refused to make restitution; and of course they had not declared war on any Christian nation (Las Casas, *Historia de las Indias*, ed. Millares Carlo, 1: 134–35 [bk. 1, chap. 25]). By contrast, Espinosa's claims of Castile's unlawful actions, which he introduced in a chapter that narrated how the Spaniards were brutally defeated by the natives in Acentejo, implies exactly the reverse: only the natives had the right to wage war on the Spaniards who had invaded their land and disposed of their persons and properties. As the above quotation proves, Espinosa also clearly subscribed to the principle of peaceful evangelization, a project to which Las Casas dedicated most of his life. What Espinosa proposes is precisely the substitution of military force by a peaceful apostolic mission as the only admissible way of bringing the Guanches to Christianity; this was the same argument Las Casas had proposed in his *De unico vocationis modo* for Amerindian societies (see Las Casas, *The Only Way*).

The nature of a just war is connected to one of its most debated consequences: slavery. Espinosa addressed this problem with critical coherence. Once his condemnation of the war of conquest against the Guanches became evident, Espinosa's condemnation of slavery as it was practiced by the Spanish conquistadors logically followed. Throughout his work he referred to several historical injustices suffered by the islanders, even though they did not pertain specifically to the natives of Tenerife. Taking as his point of departure one of the sporadic raids launched by the Spaniards on Tenerife before the final conquest, Espinosa (*Historia*, 91–92 [bk. 3, chap. 3]) narrated the cruelties of Pedro de Vera in his attempt to sell the strongest of the natives of Gran Canaria as slaves. The history of Gran Canaria is not a history which Espinosa had set out to tell; nevertheless, he presented sufficient examples regarding the cruelties of the conquest of the Canaries to validate his critique. Espinosa's denouncement of slavery reveals as well the influence of the Bishop of Chiapas, who had dared to implement anti-slavery laws in the confessional with his controversial guide for confessors that denied absolution to any *encomendero*.

---

mous debates, see the comprehensive summary and comparison of R. Adorno, "Los debates sobre la naturaleza del indio en el siglo XVI: textos y contextos," *Revista de estudios hispánicos* 19 (1992): 47–66, which also reveals the traditionally unseen affiliation between the ideas of Sepúlveda and Vitoria which were both very much in conflict with Las Casas's opinions about the relationship of dominion among nations.

[91] See R. Adorno, "The Intellectual Life of Bartolomé de las Casas" (New Orleans: Tulane University, 1992), 7.

Slavery was indeed one of the issues which concerned Las Casas as a missionary, as a canon lawyer, and as a historian (see Adorno, "Intellectual Life"). He not only argued constantly against the system of *encomienda* as a disguised form of slavery, but also left a great number of invaluable pages which questioned the Aristotelian concept of "natural slavery" and its connection to just wars.[92] As individuals and as a nation, the Guanches, like the Amerindians, could not be subjugated to the Europeans or be taken as slaves because neither the practice of idolatry alone nor the arguments about the degree of rational capacity they presumably possessed were sufficient cause to wage war against them. Furthermore, Las Casas (*Historia de las Indias*, ed. Millares Carlo, 1: 134–35 [bk. 1, chap. 25]) categorically warned that without provocation:

> a ningún infiel, sea moro, alárabe, turco, tártaro o indio o de otra cualquiera especie, ley o secta que fuere, no se le puede ni es lícito al pueblo cristiano hacerle la guerra, ni molestarle, ni agraviarle con daño alguno en su persona ni en cosa suya, sin cometer grandísimos pecados mortales.[93]

> [it is not licit for a Christian nation to wage war on any infidels, whether they are Moors, Arabs, Turks, Tartars, Indians or of any other race, law or sect; neither it is permissible to aggravate them in any way resulting in harm to their persons or possessions without committing grave mortal sins.]

This quotation shows Las Casas's awareness of the categories within the umbrella label of "infidels" or "barbarians"; in fact, Las Casas argued in the *Apologética* for distinct subdivisions within the category of "barbarians" which classified Indians and Turks, for example, very differently.[94]

---

[92] See the pioneering work of Lewis Hanke, *Aristotle and the American Indian* (Chicago: Henry Regnery, 1959), 13–116. See also Adorno, "Los debates," 47–66.

[93] In his *Historia de las Indias*, Las Casas developed these arguments in the context of the Portuguese explorations along the Atlantic coast of Africa and the resulting origins of African slave trade in Europe. He also commented harshly on the occupation of the Canary Islands by French settlers in the fourteenth century (*Historia de las Indias*, ed. Millares Carlo, 1: 108–09, 111 [bk. 1, chap. 19]) and the slave trade in Africa and the Canaries (see *Historia de las Indias*, bk. 1, chaps. 17–27). Despite having proposed in 1516 the substitution of Amerindian forced labor by the importation of a limited number of black and white African slaves, Las Casas retracted from such proposals as soon as he found out that black slaves were unlawfully obtained (*Historia de las Indias*, 3: 177 [bk. 3, chap. 102]; Adorno, "Intellectual Life," 6–9). The general ideas on the nature of just wars were also displayed in other writings of Las Casas that could have been more accessible to Espinosa.

[94] In the last chapters of the *Apologética* (ed. O'Gorman, 2: 637–54 [chaps. 264–67, epílogo]), Las Casas addressed the meanings of the word "barbarian" by expanding the distinctions among three different types to include a fourth. The first type included those who

The battle of Acentejo, which occurred in Tenerife in May 1494 and re-sulted in the defeat of the Spanish troops, provided Espinosa with the oppor-tunity to restate Las Casas's critique. When Espinosa referred to the unjust war conducted by Spain in the New World as equivalent to the one in Tenerife, he showed his awareness of Las Casas's concept of the "barbarian" that allowed Amerindians and Guanches to share a category very different from that of the enemies of the Christian faith. After reflecting on the battle of Acentejo, in which fortune favored the Guanches, Espinosa went on to narrate how the Spaniards tricked the natives of Güímar into visiting the ships, only to capture them aboard in order to sell them and make profit from the human trade (Espinosa, *Historia*, 103 [bk. 3, chap. 5]). Furthermore, Espinosa (*Historia*, 104 [bk. 3, chap. 7]) ended the story of the Spanish defeat in Acentejo by categori-cally stating that all enterprises not guided by God or destined to His praise and service rarely succeeded, and that trying to enslave friends rather than enemies was a clear indication that the Spaniards served only their personal interest and not the promulgation of the evangelical message.

One final episode in the history of the conquest of Tenerife that sheds light on Espinosa's larger project is the narration of the surviving Spaniards' struggle after their defeat at Acentejo.[95] Espinosa (*Historia*, 103 [bk. 3, chap. 7]) described the debacle at Acentejo in great detail in order to demonstrate the magnanimity of the natives' ruler. The king of Taoro exhibited the most civil diplomacy when he forgave the Spaniards, who had been captured in a cave, and allowed them to return without harm to their vessels. Torriani (*Die Kanarischen Inseln*, ed. Wölfel, 170 [chap. 52]; *Descripción*, ed. Cioranescu, 184 [chap. 52]) and Abreu y Galindo (*Historia de la conquista*, ed. Cioranescu, 318 [bk. 3, chap. 18]), on the other hand, would affirm that those who escaped the Guanches' defensive forces rushed to the ships and sailed away. Espinosa's

---

were nature's freaks. The second included those who did not have a writing system and spoke a foreign language (this coincides in part with the classical Greek definition). The third pertained to the so-called *simpliciter*, whom Las Casas argued Aristotle had had in mind when he spoke of natural slaves. The fourth type included all those who lacked the true Christian religion; they in turn could fall into two different categories, that of negative infidelity if they never heard the word of God, or that of contrary infidelity if they had resisted the spread of the true faith and became enemies of it (i.e., Moors, Turks, etc.). For Las Casas, Amerindians could belong only to the second and the fourth types (negative infidelity) insofar as they had no letters, spoke foreign, strange languages, and had never been instructed in the Christian religion. By the same token, argued Las Casas (*Apologética*, ed. O'Gorman, 2: 637–54 [chaps. 264–67, epílogo]), Europeans seemed as barbarous to Amerindians because they too spoke a language that could not be understood by the latter.

[95] After describing the Spanish defeat in the battle of Acentejo (May 1494), Espinosa recounted two other battles that resulted in the defeat of the Guanches: these were the battle of La Laguna (November 1495) and the decisive battle of Victory, also waged in Acentejo (December 1495). The precise dates have been established by Rumeu de Armas (*La conquista*, 185, 247–48, 274).

account of this occurrence seems to be an obvious attempt to present the Guanche rulers as legitimate, as monarchs who were supported by their subjects and who exercised their power with generosity and justice.[96]

The above incident echoes another episode, which Espinosa narrated as having taken place years before, when the Virgin of Candelaria had first appeared among the Guanches in Güímar. Out of respect, the king of Güímar proposed to the most powerful monarch of the island, the king of Taoro, that the image be housed half a year in Güímar and the other half in the kingdom of Taoro. In Espinosa's words (*Historia*, 59–60 [bk. 2, chap. 6]), the king of Taoro refused the proposition because, being a man of sophisticated intellect, he understood that it was his duty and the duty of his subjects to visit the celestial icon rather than having the Virgin visit his kingdom. As lord of the neighboring islands of Lanzarote and Fuerteventura many years later, Sancho de Herrera, on the other hand, stole the statue from the Guanches. To the Christians' surprise, the Virgin returned to her cave in Tenerife. Herrera's subjects stole the image once more and brought it to Lanzarote, only to be forced to return the image after they had been divinely punished by a plague that claimed many victims among them (Espinosa, *Historia*, 70–75 [bk. 2, chaps. 11–12]). Espinosa's account (*Historia*, 60 [bk. 2, chap. 6]) of the miraculous works of the Virgin established in this case a clear contrast between the Guanche monarch and the Spanish nobleman: the first showed the behavior and judgment expected of a "king among kings" ("dicho digno de rey, y para entre reyes"), while the Spaniard behaved dishonorably despite the prominent position he occupied and had to be shown his wrongdoing by the intervention of supernatural powers.

On another occasion, the king of Anaga showed clemency to a Spaniard accused of theft, while in contrast Sancho de Herrera, the Spanish official, condemned some Guanches to death for the same crime (Espinosa, *Historia*, 88–89 [bk. 3, chap. 1]). In fact, when Benchomo was approached in friendly terms by Alonso de Lugo's men upon their first landing on Tenerife in 1494, the Guanche king responded in the same peaceful manner. Espinosa claimed that Benchomo responded not as a barbarian, but as a discreet man, because discretion and royal dignity, the author added, went hand in hand (Espinosa, *Historia*, 96 [bk. 3, chap. 4]). Benchomo willingly accepted Lugo's peace treaty because it

---

[96] Espinosa spoke of an ancient time in which Tenerife was ruled only by the king of Adeje, but that each of his nine children later claimed a piece of the kingdom for themselves. The most important monarch was Betzenuhya or Quebehí, king of Taoro, whose successor was Benchomo; Acaymo was king of Güímar; Atguaxoña and Atbitocazpe were the kings of Abona and Adeje respectively. The kings of Anaga, Tegueste, Tacoronte, Icod, and Daute are not named in the text (*Historia*, 40–41 [bk. 1, chap. 8]). According to Rumeu de Armas (*La conquista*, 169–71, 250–52, 280), archival sources have identified by name two important kings (*menceyes*) of Taoro, Benitomo and Bentor; the first died in the battle of La Laguna in November 1495, while his successor Bentor committed suicide by jumping off a cliff in 1496.

was for the "common good" and war could not be waged without provocation. The Guanche monarch further responded to Lugo's proposal of conversion with a very wise statement. He asserted that the Guanches did not know what Christianity was, but that he was going to look into it, gather information, and respond to the proposal about Christian instruction as soon as he and his advisers reached a decision on the matter. With regard to the demand for their political subjugation to Spain, Benchomo disagreed categorically, declaring that he had never been subjected to another man just like him (Espinosa, *Historia*, 96 [bk. 3, chap. 4]). Espinosa's portrayal of Guanche kings corresponded, not accidentally, to the ideal of a Christian monarch. In this manner he asserted the legitimacy of Guanche self-governance.

Espinosa's affiliation to Lascasian ideas made him ultimately embrace, in a very modern way, the principle of *jure gentium*, as employed by Las Casas, which upheld the legal doctrine of *quod omnes tangit debet ab omnibus approbari* (or *quod omnes similiter tangit ab omnibus comprobetur*, Cod. Just. 5.59.5.2), by which a new prince could not be imposed upon the people of a nation without their common consent.[97] Thus, according to this argument, civil order would exist only in those societies whose rulers were accepted by the voluntary consent of their subjects. The same argument that José Rabasa has made to describe Las Casas's project in the *Apologética* can serve to describe Espinosa's text. That is, insofar as Las Casas attempted to construct an image of the "noble savage" aimed at critiquing representations of the Other "in terms of political, economic, linguistic, and cultural deficiencies" (Rabasa, "Utopian Ethnology," 276), so too Espinosa elaborated his defense of the Guanches.[98] Just as Las Casas claimed

---

[97] See Kenneth J. Pennington, Jr., "Bartolomé de las Casas and the Tradition of Medieval Law," *Church History* 39 (1970): 149–61, here 150; Adorno, "Los debates," 62–63; cf. G. Post, *Studies in Medieval Legal Thought* (Princeton: Princeton University Press, 1964), 163–238.

[98] I follow here R. Adorno's assessment ("Nuevas perspectivas en los estudios literarios coloniales hispanoamericanos," *Revista de crítica literaria latinoamericana* 14 [1988]: 11–27, here 19) of the "Other" as a "category of analysis occupied by all subjects except the European" (my translation). Since the term "Other" was capitalized in Jacques Lacan's works, it has been used in a wide variety of disciplines, including colonial literary studies in which the primary texts self-proclaim the authorization to speak in the name of the Other, the defeated ones. Tzvetan Todorov was one of the first contemporary scholars to call attention to the European construction of the Amerindian (as the Other, in an anthropological rather than psychoanalytical dimension) in the Spanish historical-narrative texts of the sixteenth century (see *The Conquest of America*); however, his attempt proves insufficient, as Adorno points out. The latter privileges the approach of Michel de Certeau to the writings of Montaigne and Léry because it offers a psychoanalytic view that allows the voice of the Other, not the silence, to be heard within the dominant discourse (R. Adorno, "Todorov y de Certeau: La alteridad y la contemplación del sujeto," *Revista de crítica literaria latinoamericana* 17 [1991]: 51–58).

Although in the 1980s and 1990s the term "subaltern" has been used to replace or add nuances to the term "Other," I prefer to use the latter in the case of Latin American texts of

that the need for the imposition of an outside order, a European order, in the New World became an unjustifiable enterprise (Rabasa, "Utopian Ethnology," 274), Espinosa likewise offered the same argument. Ultimately, for both Las Casas and Espinosa, the conquest of the New World and Tenerife should have been, at most, a persuasive spiritual endeavor rather than a violent military affair.

Ironically, Espinosa's text found many detractors, not among those who in principle and in general opposed the vision of Las Casas, but among the interested members and friends of the powerful Guerra family who had participated in the final conquest of the island and enjoyed the fruits of those labors.[99] In Espinosa's work, the contemporary descendants of the illustrious Lope de la Guerra are cast as illegitimate heirs who inherited the family's estate only because of the dishonorable conduct of the legitimate heir (*Historia*, 116 [bk. 3, chap. 10]). This claim somewhat determined the immediate reception of the book, which was subjected to condemnation by the Guerra family who in turn financed another historico-literary project, Antonio de Viana's epic poem *Antigüedades de las Islas Afortunadas*. Espinosa, who had intelligently utilized historiographic models to challenge previous historical assumptions about the Canaries, fell victim to a minor precept that, according to theorists of history writing, any historian should have taken into account.

Espinosa did not conform to historiographical custom or prescription regarding the interests of the living and the recently dead. When the potential criticism of historical actors was at stake, the preceptist Luis Cabrera de Córdoba advised: "he who writes history should not relay all the particularities, on the contrary, only that which will be beneficial to the descendants" ("el que escribe historia no ha de decir todas las particularidades, sino lo que ha de ser

---

the early Colonial period. Since the Indian Subaltern Group (Ranajit Guha, and more peripherally Gayatri C. Spivak, Homi Bhabha, and R. Radhakrishnan, among others) revised Antonio Gramsci's notion of the subaltern to criticize Indian historiographies, many Latin American cultural historians have followed a similar path with less and more felicitous results (see *Dispositio* 19.46 [1994]). What has remained clear, however, is the impossibility to measure the Spanish, Portuguese, and British colonial experiences by the same theoretical apparatus. The term "subaltern" seems to me to be more rigid than fluid, not allowing resistant narratives to be as copresent and interactive as they have been in the cultural tradition of Latin America.

[99] The primary source for this information comes from Viana's prologue, where it is evident that his epic poem was financed by the Guerra family (see Viana, *Antigüedades*, ed. M. R. Alonso, 2 vols. [Islas Canarias: Biblioteca Básica, 1991], 1: 3). Bonnet ("El p[adre] Alonso de Espinosa," 44–45), echoing what Núñez de la Peña had written in 1676, attributed the lack of surviving volumes of Espinosa's history to the work's fierce persecution by the Guerra family. Years later, Cioranescu (in Espinosa, *Historia*, ed. Cioranescu, xxxiii–xxxvi) rejected the idea of an efficient persecution since, at the present time, six of the first-edition volumes are known to have survived — a number quite normal for books dating from the period.

de provecho a los descendientes"). This is so, he adds, because "to speak the truth, even with modesty, the living will not allow it of themselves or of the recently dead" ("decir la verdad, aun con modestia en esto, ni lo permiten los vivos de sí, ni de los recién muertos") (Cabrera de Córdoba, *De historia*, ed. Montero Díaz, 92–93). Espinosa's "mistake" worked to his advantage, since the exposure of the Guerras' dubious territorial acquisitions distracted the attention of readers in such a way that they overlooked the fact that the vision of Las Casas profoundly marked the formulation of the cultural history of the Canary Islands as postulated in Espinosa's work. Espinosa's use of Las Casas's works gives this pioneering historiographical text an ideological cohesion which has been insufficiently explored, despite its importance. In fact, this perspective transcends this period and becomes the basis for histories that follow, mainly those of Juan de Abreu y Galindo and Juan Nuñez de la Peña.[100]

The most important factor regarding the reception of Espinosa's work, however, was the immediate reaction on the part of Antonio de Viana, who in the prologue to his epic poem *Antigüedades de las Islas Afortunadas* attempted to justify the creation of his own text as a way to satisfy the need to undo the history narrated by Espinosa. When Viana explicitly stated that his text constituted the only just and rightful answer to Espinosa's impugning the cultural tradition of the islanders as well as the honor of one of the most prominent conquistadors, he was implicitly reacting to the firm lines of Lascasian thought that are present in Espinosa's history and which offered an image of Tenerife as conflicted and victimized as that of the New World.

Espinosa's study of the historical past of the islanders set out to unveil a subject greatly unexplored before the 1590s. Espinosa utilized the Virgin of Candelaria as the pretext for writing a work which reveals at its core the historical and historiographical paradigm of the New World, as well as Las Casas's anthropological theories and political ideas. Espinosa did not hide the primitivism of the Guanches, but rather introduced subtle distinctions to prove that there were more similarities than differences between a primitive pagan society and European societies. His narrative, in other words, emphasized the familiar

---

[100] Abreu y Galindo (*Historia de la conquista*, ed. Cioranescu, 313 [bk. 3, chap. 16]) explicitly mentioned Espinosa's work as the source of documentation about the miracles attributed to the Virgin, and he also, as I have discussed, closely followed Espinosa's text with respect to the representation of the natives of Tenerife. Juan Núñez de la Peña, who published his *Conquista y antigüedades de las islas de la Gran Canaria y su descripción* in 1676, praised Espinosa's history by stating that it should be given much credibility ("se le debe dar mucho crédito") (quoted in Bonnet, "El p[adre]Alonso de Espinosa," 42). In fact, the first of these historians was somewhat influenced, as was Espinosa, by Las Casas's views on Spanish imperial history. The most important historian of the island during the eighteenth century, José de Viera y Clavijo, commented about Espinosa's text: "This is one of the best public memoirs that we have" ("ésta es una de las mejores memorias públicas que tenemos") (quoted in Bonnet, "El p[adre] Alonso de Espinosa," 42).

and granted equal value to the other culture, while rejecting the notions of strangeness which might have led to the consolidation of an image of cultural inferiority. Espinosa's portrait of the islands and their inhabitants set the stage for his critique of the war of conquest in the Canaries. The historian condemned not only the injustice of the war waged by the Spaniards and the violation of the Guanches' human rights but also the ultimate violation of their nation's sovereignty.

Espinosa's revision of history can be read as a nostalgic gesture before a *fait accompli* hardly remembered one hundred years later, but his text, like Las Casas's writings, voiced concerns and tensions derived from the discovery and colonization of the New World, which continued to be unresolved. Espinosa's work negotiated a contested space, this time in the Old World, and constructed identities not easily assimilated to Spain. The construction of history fostered by Espinosa denies the smooth entrance of the Canary Islands into an integrated and harmonious Spanish imperial identity. Not by virtue of their otherness or difference (the existence of which Espinosa denied), but rather by means of the Europeans' unlawful entry, the inhabitants of the islands located in the Atlantic Ocean clearly shared, along with those of the New World, the space of the colonized.

CHAPTER THREE

AN EPIC REVISION OF HISTORY: ANTONIO DE VIANA AND HIS ANSWER TO "THE CARELESSNESS WITH WHICH THE TRUTH OF HISTORY WAS INVESTIGATED"

> agora … quitaré la tiniebla que a la verdad tenía ofuscada; y así se manifestará lo que antes de agora fuera justo que se manifestase, y con menos ficciones que algunos escritores han añadido, informados de autores que por ventura soñaban en el Parnaso.
>
> (Abreu y Galindo, *Historia de la conquista*, ed. Cioranescu, 3)

> [now … I will remove the shadows which have obscured the truth so that what has been previously obscured can now manifest itself with less fictions ("lies") than have been added by some writers who were informed by authors who, perchance, were dreaming of Parnassus.]

WHO ARE THE AUTHORS DREAMING OF PARNASSUS against whom Abreu y Galindo constructed his history? What tradition resembling fiction was this historian rejecting? If Antonio de Viana's epic poem *Antigüedades de las Islas Afortunadas de la Gran Canaria, conquista de Tenerife y aparecimiento de la Santa Imagen de Candelaria* is not the immediate reference here, it certainly stands as the most evident example of a poetic reformulation of the history of the Canary Islands. Since its publication in Seville by Bartolomé Gomes in 1604, the authenticity of Viana's work as a historical document has been the subject of continuous debate.[101] What Viana claimed, somewhat in keeping with Abreu's cited com-

---

[101] María Rosa Alonso and Alejandro Cioranescu, who have studied Viana's poem comprehensively, have addressed the important issue of the poem's historical accuracy given its early publication date. In her study, *El poema de Viana* (Madrid: CSIC, 1952), 440, Alonso argues that the reception of the poem as a historical text has been used as the measure by which to determine its literary value. She supports her point (*El poema*, 440–61) by surveying

ment, was precisely that his epic poem emerged as a necessary revision of the particular historical account written by the Dominican friar Alonso de Espinosa. Unlike Abreu, however, the prevalence of competing truths for Viana lay more with poetry and less with history.

Viana consequently constructed a poetic text that aimed at the direct revision of history, while shielding himself behind the creation of an ambivalent vehicle that combined fiction and historical material; that is, the epic.[102] In his prologue, Viana writes (*Antigüedades*, ed. M. R. Alonso, 54):

---

a long list of authors who cited Viana's work, including Pedro Alzola Vergara (1604), Juan Núñez de la Peña (1676), Nicolás Antonio (1696), Fernando de la Guerra, José de Viera y Clavijo (1772–1783), Graciliano Afonso (1838), Fernando del Busto y Blanco (1864), Agustín Millares Torres (1872), Gregorio Chil y Naranjo (1879–1899), Francisco María Pinto (1879), Sabin Berthelot (1880), Franz von Lörer (1883), Marcelino Menéndez y Pelayo (1900), José Rodríguez Moure (1905), Ernest Merimée (1922), Angel Balbuena Prat (1929–1937), Ludwig Pfandl (1933), Juan Manuel Trujillo (1932), Andrés Lorenzo Cáceres (1935–1942), and Dominik Joseph Wölfel (1940). Alonso, in turn, offers a complete analysis of the poem and documents its borrowings from historical sources and its reliance on general literary conventions.

    Years later, Alejandro Cioranescu undertook the task of editing the poem and offered an additional comprehensive study of the poem that uses Alonso's work as its point of departure (Viana, *Conquista de Tenerife*, ed. A. Cioranescu, 2 vols. [Tenerife: Aula de Cultura, 1971]). The encyclopedic work of these two important critics, as J. M. García Ramos has observed ("Viana entre la historia y la literatura," *Revista de historia canaria* 37 [1980]: 267–72, here 264), has discouraged others from offering further readings of the poem. García Ramos ("Viana," 265) takes up the challenge and proposes to "rescue" some of the poem's literary elements in order to please the contemporary reader; he fails, however, to do so in his brief article.

    My study, on the other hand, operates on the basis of a proposition that will prove, I hope, more fruitful. In positioning my own reading of Viana's poem on this critical spectrum, I am indebted to all of those who have tried to elucidate the poem's history-literature equation, but I believe that moving beyond this dichotomy may yield reflections that would truly interest the contemporary reader. The most enticing aspect of Viana's epic is precisely his subordination of both historical information and literary forms to an ideological project that provides a preliminary sketch of the identity of the Canary Islands within the purview of Spanish imperialism.

    [102] During the Renaissance and Baroque, the epic genre encompassed a few variants which ultimately held Virgil's *Aeneid* as the perfect model, rejected Lucan's *Pharsalia*, and accepted the Italian romance, first introduced in Boiardo's *Orlando inamorato* and later developed in Ariosto's *Orlando furioso* (see D. Quint, *Epic and Empire* [Princeton: Princeton University Press, 1993]; see also H. D. Brumble, *Classical Myths and Legends in the Middle Ages and Renaissance* [Westport, CT: Greenwood Press, 1998], 106–14 s.v. "Epic Conventions"). This is certainly the opinion of the sixteenth-century Spanish preceptist Alonso López Pinciano (*Philosophía antigua poética*, 3 vols. [Madrid: CSIC, 1953], 3: 143–225), who in the eleventh epistle of his work delineates the precepts of the genre in the late fifteen-hundreds. In more recent times, Frank Pierce (*La poesía épica del Siglo de Oro* [Madrid: Gredos, 1961], 10 n. 1) has pointed out that the poetic theory in Golden Age Spain must accommodate literary practices

lector discreto … el porte que te ofrezco no es el tesoro de
Orlando, las perlas de las lágrimas de Angélica, ni el esmalte
maravilloso de su hermosura, no los frutos del labrador que
glorifica a la Madrid insigne, el Dragón de oro, las grandezas
de Arcadia, las margaritas, diamantes y preciosas piedras del
Templo Militante, ni las riquezas que a tu gusto ofrece el que
en todo es peregrino, sino la verdad (desnuda por mi po-
breza) de una agradable historia.

[discreet reader … what I offer you is not the treasure of Orlando, nor the pearls of Angelica's tears nor the marvelous
sheen of her beauty nor the fruits of the farmer who glorifies
illustrious Madrid, nor the Golden Dragon, the grandeur of
Arcadia nor the pearls, diamonds or precious stones of the
Militant Temple, nor the riches offered up for your pleasure
by him who is a pilgrim in everything. Instead I give you the
truth, naked because of my poverty, of a pleasant
story/history.][103]

This fragment, in which the Canarian poet presented the reader with his epic
poem *Antigüedades de las Islas Afortunadas*, set out to describe Viana's affiliations

---

and that an attempt to define the epic genre in its purest form would result in too many
exclusions. For an overview of the criticism surrounding the most prominent Spanish epic
poems in the sixteenth and seventeenth centuries, see Pierce, *La poesía épica*, 18–27.

[103] All quotes come from Viana, *Antigüedades de las Islas Afortunadas*, ed. M. R. Alonso
(Islas Canarias: Biblioteca Básica Canaria, 1991). The poem has also been edited several
times since the last century. The second edition dates from 1854 and is based on the sections
of the poem published as part of a newspaper entitled *Noticioso de Canarias*. In 1881, another
newspaper, *La Democracia*, re-issued the poem serially. In 1882, the third edition was published by the José Benítez Press in Santa Cruz. The fourth appeared in 1883 in Tübingen,
published by Sociedad Literaria de Stuttgart and edited by Franz von Lörer. The fifth was
published in fragments in the journal *La Candelaria* in 1889. The sixth, edited by José
Rodríguez Moure, appeared in La Laguna in 1905, and was based on a 1904 version of the
poem published in the newspaper *El Noticiero Canario* (Alonso, *El poema*, 28–32; Cioranescu
in Viana, *Conquista*, ed. idem, 2: 47–50). The seventh edition was the two-volume *Conquista de
Tenerife* edited by Alejandro Cioranescu, which appeared in Tenerife in 1968 and 1971. Cioranescu's edition was reprinted in two volumes by Editorial Interinsular Canaria in 1986. The
eighth is the first mentioned above (by Alonso of 1991), from which I quote, and the ninth
is a facsimile edition of the *editio princeps* with a brief introduction by M. R. Alonso which has
recently been published by the Ayuntamiento de La Laguna Press (1996). The *editio princeps*,
according to M. R. Alonso in her preface to the facsimile edition (12–14), was not carefully
done; therefore either Viana himself or someone instructed by him corrected the *editio princeps* adding by hand 3 verses in the fifth canto and 24 verses in the eighth canto.

within the genre. Viana's self-confessed humility and inexperience regarding his epic project forced the poet to place his own text within the conventions of the epic in the different modalities of the Renaissance literary tradition. Viana needed to present his poem as part of the epic tradition by apparently dismissing, yet recognizing, his most immediate influential sources and two of his most important future receptors, Cairasco de Figueroa and Lope de Vega. While he modestly denied the resemblance of his poem to Ludovico Ariosto's *Orlando furioso* (1532), Luis Barahona de Soto's *Las lágrimas de Angélica* (1586), Lope de Vega's *La hermosura de Angélica* (1602), *El Isidro* (1599), *La Dragontea* (1598), and the pastoral romance *La Arcadia* (1598) as well as to Bartolomé Cairasco de Figueroa's *El templo militante* (1602, 1603) (Alonso, *El poema*, 25), he nevertheless proceeded to reproduce, to a lesser or greater degree, the well-established conventions of the genre in the context of the Canaries. Viana was bound to reworking the same literary elements used time and again by epic writers; as the above quotation shows, he appealed to a common rhetorical statement of humility and claimed, as convention required, the non-fictional nature of his poetic history.

What Viana announces in the above passage is his response to the Renaissance epic storyteller's dilemma of choosing between models — between the extreme "fictionality" of Ariosto and what can be called the "historicity" of Tasso.[104] Viana explicitly subscribed to the model of the latter. His readers were made to believe that such an epic project would constitute a chronicle in verse, although the poet's choice of the adjective *agradable* (pleasant) to qualify his history calls to mind the Horatian juxtaposition of *docere* and *delectare* (cf. *Ars Poetica* 333, 344). Since Viana was primarily interested in the entertaining function of poetry, he relegated its instructional function — history's main concern — to a secondary role. By presenting his text in direct contrast to Espinosa's

---

[104] I draw on William Nelson's terminology and argument. With regard to the nuances between lies and fiction, Nelson (*Fact or Fiction: The Dilemma of the Renaissance Storyteller* [Cambridge, MA: Harvard University Press, 1978], 8) states that the Renaissance storyteller had to avoid being accused of lying by resorting to two strategies: "insisting that his fiction was not fiction" or tacitly admitting that "the story was indeed fiction" (cf. Brumble, *Classical Myths and Legends*, 107). Ariosto represented the assumed "wholly fictional" epic poem, while Tasso navigated in more "historic substance" which did not deny the poet the freedom to experiment with fictional material, as long as the epic could uphold an intrinsic truth (Nelson, *Fact or Fiction*, 94). For a complete overview of the "quarrel over Ariosto and Tasso," see B. Weinberg, *A History of Literary Criticism in the Italian Renaissance*, 2 vols. [Chicago: University of Chicago Press, 1961], 2: 991–1073. Regardless of what percentage of fiction or history was used in the formula, Nelson (*Fact or Fiction*, 105) concludes that it was clear that "the status of fictionalized secular history was becoming [increasingly] dubious." For López Pinciano (*Philosophía antigua poética*, 3: 166, 172), the essential conditions for a perfect epic required that the poem preferably have a historical basis and that such a history be made brief so it could be mixed with extensive episodes of fiction. Viana's epic poem follows these general precepts.

historiographical model, Viana further strengthened the historical basis of his text which, in turn, legitimized his fiction. For Viana, as I will demonstrate, history provided the perfect cushion upon which to weave a teleological plot of cultural and political homogeneity in the model provided by the Spanish conquest of Tenerife.

At first, the poem's structure seems to follow the pattern of an historical account. The first canto addresses the geographical location and natural setting of the Canary Islands, the different denominations by which the islands were known from antiquity to contemporary times, and the historico-etymological explanation of their various names as well as the origins of all the islands' inhabitants and the general customs of the Guanches. The second canto briefly tells the medieval history of the islands: the different European raids and settlements up to the time of the final conquest by the Spaniards. In the third canto, any pretension to factual knowledge and historical circumstances yields to the structure of romance, and the arrival of the Spaniards in Tenerife is framed by the conflicts among Tenerife's nine kingdoms, and by the introduction of several native characters and situations, most of which are products of Viana's imagination. Viana introduces King Bencomo of the Kingdom of Taoro, and his two daughters, Dacil and Rosalba; his son, Ruymán; and the king's brother, Tinguaro. Viana also introduces Bencomo's rivals: Anaterve, King of Güímar, and his son Guetón, as well as Beneharo, King of Anaga, and his daughter Guacimara. The poet sets the stage for the tormented love stories (Guetón/Rosalba and Ruymán/Guacimara) that are developed later in the epic. Dacil, in turn, is told by the soothsayer (*agorero*) Guañameñe that her future husband will come from the sea.

Viana's fiction continues, and the fourth canto narrates how Ruymán and Guacimara fall in love with each other's pictures, while the fifth canto narrates the encounter between the Guanche princess Dacil and Captain Gonzalo del Castillo of the Spanish army. Tinguaro has been promised Guacimara's hand, so he forgets his previous beloved Guajara and prepares to fight off the Spanish intruders in the sixth canto, which otherwise deals with the history of the appearance of the Virgin of Candelaria, as narrated by Antón, a Christianized Guanche. The seventh canto, in which several allegorical figures appear, serves as the prelude for the battle of Acentejo, narrated in the eighth canto, which results in the defeat of the foreigners. The triumphant Tinguaro asks for Guacimara's hand, and she refuses him in the ninth canto; she runs away dressed up as a young shepherd and meets Ruymán who had also run away in despair after hearing that his beloved had been promised to his uncle. Meanwhile, Guetón and Rosalba, who are very much in love against her brother's wishes, have been accused of Ruymán's presumed death and have consequently been imprisoned on Bencomo's orders. The Spaniards send a desperate cry for financial help to Spain and they receive it in the tenth canto, while Anaterve tries to liberate his son Guetón, who refuses to be freed, fearing that his innocence will be called into question.

The second Spanish entry into Tenerife occurs in the eleventh canto, while the natives are suffering the evils of a destructive plague. Most of the verses of this canto tediously enumerate the names of all the conquistadors who had arrived on the island (cf. Brumble, *Classical Myths and Legends*, 112 s. v. "Epic Conventions: Catalogue of Participants"). In the twelfth canto, the battle of La Laguna takes place and ends in victory for the Spanish army. Bencomo is forced to flee the battlefield, leaving behind the dead body of his brother Tinguaro. Later, Beneharo is similarly defeated by the Spaniards who have been aided throughout by the natives of the kingdom of Güímar. In the thirteenth canto, the victorious Spanish army delivers the head of Tinguaro to the natives, who professedly grieve together with his widow Guajara; another battle erupts and the Spaniards win once again, but this time Captain Castillo is taken prisoner by the natives.

To Dacil's great pleasure, Castillo is brought to her kingdom in the fourteenth canto. The lovers share a royal meal, a few words, a lot of glances, and an occasional touch, and Castillo is later graciously freed by Bencomo. The second battle of Acentejo or the Battle of Victory, as it is known, takes place and the Spanish forces finally make their triumphant entrance into the powerful Kingdom of Taoro. In the fifteenth canto, Bencomo relinquishes his power and decides to convert to Christianity, while Castillo officially makes peace with the natives and agrees to their continued enjoyment of freedom. The final canto brings the intricate plot lines that form the romance to a closure. During Bencomo and Beneharo's final pacification of the islands' scattered rebels, Ruymán and Guacimara are captured and condemned to death along with the alleged assassins Guetón and Rosalba. A final *anagnorisis* results from the encounter of the four convicted native royal heirs with a subsequent pardon and multiple marriages. Meanwhile, the new governor, Alonso de Lugo, visits the cave of the miraculous Virgin of Candelaria and the makings of a colonial society begin with the settlement and the politico-judicial structuring of the city of La Laguna.

The above plot summary seems to undermine Viana's initial claims of a strict affiliation to true history, reflecting instead the entertaining and meandering fictional strategies of romance. The poem proves, however, throughout its sixteen cantos and almost fifteen thousand verses to be a typical Renaissance epic whose definition springs precisely from blurring the elusive distinctions between history and fiction. The history of the conquest of Tenerife as conceived by Viana makes use of the epic as the most efficient vehicle of literary mediation in order to construct his version of poetic truth which, after all, was held up by Aristotle (*Poetics* 54) as a "more philosophical and a higher thing than history." Viana chose a genre which had been since its origins and was in the sixteenth and seventeenth centuries an imperial political instrument in order to create eventually the ideal project of cultural unification. The fictional strategies of the epic poem may resemble the mocking of literary models and romancing of history that was characteristic of the genre at the turn of the sixteenth century, yet the clear ideological *telos* of the victors prevails, as set forth by the powerful classical model of Virgil's *Aeneid*.[105] Thus, I argue that Viana's text ultimately aims at the revision of the history of Spain in Tenerife and the history of the Guanches in order to offer an alternative and opposing image to the history of Spain in the New World. In fulfilling his mission, Viana is forced to dialogue openly with Alonso de Espinosa, tacitly with Alonso de Ercilla y Zúñiga, and above all, intrinsically with any dissenting voices among which Bartolomé de las Casas was one of the most visible exponents.

1. ON THE TRAIL OF ESPINOSA: THE CANARIES ARE NOT AMERICA

Viana's obsession with history responded not only to the conventions of epic poetry as it was practiced at the turn of the seventeenth century, but also to particular texts and to a specific ideological scheme. His poem directly answered to another model, that of historiography. He engaged in an intertextual play with a historical text, Alonso de Espinosa's *Del origen y milagros de la santa imagen de Nuestra Señora de Candelaria*, published a decade before the epic poem. Viana's interest in exploring Tenerife's historical past evolved from what he and his patrons considered a violation of historical truth. In the prologue, Viana (*Antigüedades*, 53) fervently complained:

> que en los años pasados Fray Alonso de Espinosa del Orden
> de Predicadores, imprimiese un Tratado, digno de que se de-
> trate, escribió en el los milagros de la Candelaria, más sin luz

---

[105] For the most recent and comprehensive study of the "politicization of epic poetry" see Quint, *Epic and Empire*, 3–426, which successfully traces the political and ideological dimensions of the epic from Virgil to Milton. Quint's useful study concentrates on the two prevailing classical models that continue to coexist in epic texts. Virgil's *Aeneid* stands as the epic of the victors, as a coherent story with a linear teleology, as a quest, which ultimately reaches the proposed goal with a closed end. Lucan's *Pharsalia* represents the opposite, the epic of the losers, a shapeless adventure, a circular wandering, and a powerless quest towards an open end (Quint, *Epic and Empire*, 9). For Quint (*Epic and Empire*, 120) the model of the first "ensures the possibility of narrative" while the second "embod[ies] a principle of non-narratable repetition"; thus Quint concludes that the model provided by Lucan constitutes "a rival narrative of resistance," and "other histories" to Virgil's model of "triumphalist history." The first, however, has ideological contradictions that keep it tied to the second, which persists as the stronger tradition (Quint, *Epic and Empire*, 11). Quint provides an intelligent reading of Alonso de Ercilla's poem, *La Araucana*, through this optic. However, Quint's approach may, in the end, unfairly level too much the resistance narrative in Ercilla or the critical/subversive nature of such an original and influential text.

quiso hacerlo en lo poco que le tocó de conquista, que pro-
mete accidental cuidado con que inquirió la verdad de la historia; pues no sólo lo demostró en lo obscuro e indetermin-
able, sino en lo público, cierto y no dudoso ... sentí ... las
injurias que a mi patria hizo el extranjero a título de cele-
brarla, agravió a los antiguos naturales ... obscureciendo su
clara descendencia, y afeando la compostura de sus costumbres y república; y en una no menos injusta y con evidencia
detestable a los descendientes de Hernando Esteban Guerra,
conquistador ....

[that in the preceding years Fr. Alonso de Espinosa of the
Dominican Order published a treatise that merits its refuta-
tion. He wrote about the miracles of the Virgin of Candelaria,
but when it came to the conquest of the island his brief account was uninformed, exhibiting the carelessness with
which he investigated the truth of history. Not only did he
show his carelessness in that which is obscure and cannot be
determined, but also in that which is publicly known, true
and beyond any doubt .... I resented the affronts that the
foreigner inflicted on my homeland under pretext of celebrating it. He offended the ancient inhabitants, ... darkening
their illustrious lineage and belittling the structures of their
customs and government. In a manner no less unjust, he de-
famed the descendants of Hernando Esteban Guerra, the conquistador ....]

Viana's epic poem, the first written about the conquest of the islands, represented, according to the poet, the attempt of a native from Tenerife to rescue
his history from the foreign eye, in this case Espinosa's, a native of Spain who
had been educated in Guatemala. In other words, Viana was positioning himself as the source of cultural authority, not by virtue of being the source of poetic truth in the Aristotelian sense, but by virtue of his place of birth since he,
unlike Espinosa, was born in La Laguna.[106] Along with this cultural construc-

---

[106] According to Cioranescu (Viana, ed. Cioranescu, *Conquista*, 2: 9–47), who offers the
most up-to-date detailed biography of the poet, Antonio de Viana was born in the city of La
Laguna in 1578. His family, or at least his mother María de Viana, whose name the poet took
on, was of Portuguese origin. He studied on the island from 1584 to 1594 with the well-
known Flemish humanist Levino Apolonio, and seemed to develop a vocation for the
priesthood. In 1595, Viana left Tenerife for the University of Seville, where he continued his
studies for the next three years. Personal matters would briefly bring him back to Gran Canaria and Tenerife in 1596 and 1598. By 1598, Viana had married Francisca de Vera and the
couple would later have two children. He returned to Seville to continue his studies in 1599.

tion of his own authority, Viana proceeded to attack Espinosa's historical account on two grounds. Viana's first accusation pertained to Espinosa's representation of the Guanches, but it was quite evident that Viana made the Dominican the target of his criticism unjustly because in actuality Espinosa's portrayal of the Guanches was indeed a favorable one. The second accusation pertained to Espinosa's comment about the heirs of the Guerra family. Although the Dominican's comment was not accurate and even offensive, it reflected certain genealogical uncertainties that Viana also reconstructed falsely in order to please his patron.[107] The whole poem, however, exudes the undeniable influence of Espinosa's account of events as well as his descriptions of the natives' customs and practices (Alonso, *El poema*, 137–94).[108] Once again, Viana's explicit position seemed to contradict his implicit practice since he followed Espinosa's text rather faithfully. Nevertheless, the poet's ideological position was profoundly antagonistic to that of an author who had been so deeply marked by the thought and teachings of Bartolomé de las Casas.

Viana's accusations and his careful revision of Espinosa's text call for further analysis, which I will now pursue by focusing on the issue of misrepresentation of the islanders' culture. Espinosa's text, as I have previously argued in Chapter Two, used the frame of ecclesiastical history to offer the first ethnographic history of the Guanches and their conquest by the Europeans. As we

---

In 1604, while still a *bachiller* (holder of the lowest university degree), he published his epic poem; the following year he took a *licenciatura* and became a surgeon (*licenciado, médico cirujano*). From 1605 to 1610, Viana practiced medicine in La Laguna. Little is known of his whereabouts from 1611 to 1631, but in 1613 he published a sonnet in praise of Cairasco's *Templo Militante.* Throughout this time, he is believed to have lived in Seville where he won himself a reputation as a good surgeon. In 1631, he published *Espejo de chirugía* in Lisbon. This treatise on tumors (*apostemas* or *flegmones*) was reprinted several times. In the same year Viana returned to La Laguna, and two years later he moved to Las Palmas de Gran Canaria. In 1634, he is thought to have left the islands again. In Seville, in 1637, he wrote another medical treatise, *Discurso en la herida que padeció Juan Bautista Silman*, which was instrumental in the treatment of victims of the 1649 plague. His presence in Seville is last documented in 1650, so his death occurred sometime after that date.

[107] Cioranescu made an exhaustive study of the Guerra lineage and discovered two wills signed by Lope Fernández de la Guerra, in 1510 and 1512 respectively. In the first Fernández de la Guerra named his wife as his universal heir, and in the second he left his estate to his cousin Hernán Guerra and his nephew Fernando Esteban. Cioranescu (Viana, *Conquista*, ed. Cioranescu, 2: 54–58) concluded that the situation was sufficiently odd to provoke Espinosa's confused claim that the Guerra estate was inherited by the son of Lope Fernández's wife.

[108] See Viana, *Antigüedades*, ed. M. R. Alonso, whose rudimentary critical apparatus traces Viana's references to Espinosa's history. Cioranescu's more academic edition has a careful and prolific set of notes that includes all of Viana's borrowings, an explanation of the lexicon, and historical information (Viana, *Conquista*, ed. Cioranescu, 2: 117–95). Critics agree that Viana learned most of what he knew about Guanche culture and the history of Tenerife from Espinosa's account.

have seen, Espinosa's vision of history exhibited an ideological consistency that dealt with the same human and political concerns expressed years before by Bartolomé de las Casas about the New World. As the controversial Dominican had shown with Amerindian societies, Espinosa's apparently primitive Guanches exhibited the elements that were considered to truly represent civil society in the tradition of Las Casas's apologetic view. Espinosa's portrayal of Guanche society stressed its similarities to his own but did not recognize its differences as signs of political, economic, or cultural deficiencies. By voicing Las Casas's condemnation of the Spanish war of conquest as unjust, Espinosa also denied the need for the imposition of a European order on the Guanches. Viana, then, engaged in a reconstruction of Guanche society that would serve as the counter-image of the one proposed by Espinosa. The poet's version of history ultimately demarcated the identity of the islands and sought to secure a clear sense of them as belonging to Spain.

Viana did not demonize or infantilize the native islanders as many had the Amerindians; on the contrary, Viana's Guanches became idealized projections of forgotten Christians who were totally assimilated to the ideal of the Christian and civilized European or were simply literary types. If Espinosa, in the spirit of Lascasian ideas, had recognized and valued the Guanches by upholding their cultural and political rights, Viana recognized the Guanches only in their re-semblance to the Spaniards. In fact, his Guanches aspired to embody the forgotten half which could not be complete until it was reunited with the Spanish paragon of civilization. Viana's project set out to cancel a model of history that had proven to be critically divisive because it delimited the realm of the colonizer and the victim of colonization and had a destabilizing effect within the Spanish empire. Instead, Viana's proposed model intended to stabilize and mend that divisive dichotomy by removing the boundary line between the outsiders and the native islanders. He enhanced certain aspects and silenced others in Espinosa's account ultimately to create an idealized image of the Guanches, a flattering elegy to the Spaniards who conquered Tenerife, and, above all, a utopian colonial space where there was little possibility for injustice or abusive treatment.

Viana's reworking of Espinosa's account of Guanche history included the manipulation of some basic information about which Espinosa, Abreu, and Torriani agreed. Viana also distorted some important elements that would eventually lead to the dismantling of the Dominican's critical stance on Spanish colonial history. In the first canto the points about which Viana dissented with Espinosa are particularly revealing. Viana (*Antigüedades*, 1.205–236) began by addressing the etymology of the word "Canarias," tracing it to a corruption of the word "Cranaria," which in turn came from the names of Italian monarchs descended from Noah, "Crano" and "Crana." Critics have not been able to determine the source of this imaginative etymology. Nonetheless, it is obvious that Viana, as many chroniclers of the Indies had sought to do in the *cuarta ter-*

rae, was attributing to the Canaries a direct connection with sacred history, and he went so far as to claim that La Gomera was named after "Gomer," the nephew of "Crana" and "Crano." Viana proceeded to trace different origins for the different populations of the islands, qualifying Espinosa's opinion that all islanders originally came from Africa. He restated that the natives (*mahoratas*) who inhabited Fuerteventura and Lanzarote, the closest islands to the African coast, had been exiled from the continent before Muslim rule ("muy semejantes a los africanos, / Mas no tuvieron rastro de su secta") (Viana, *Antigüedades*, 1.329–330). For Viana, Palma and Tenerife had been inhabited by a group of the most ancient occupants of the Iberian Peninsula — I will discuss this important point later when I attempt to explicate Viana's ultimate project. These ideas further qualify and round out Viana's categorical denial of the islands' possible geographical dismembering from the African continent (*Antigüedades*, 1.168–78):

> unos dicen que descienden de Mallorca;
> otros, que de Numancia; otros, que de Africa,
> y que con ella fueron estas islas
> confines, cual Sicilia con Italia;
> y que pudo el tiempo el largo curso
> en tantas como vemos separarlas;
> ...
> Pero repugna a esta razón dudosa
> la diferencia de sus varias lenguas,
> de costumbres y modos de república.

> [some say that the islanders descend from Majorca, / others say from Numancia; others still from Africa, / whose outer most parts were / the Canaries, as Sicily was of Italy, / and that with time the islands / separated from the continent, ... / But the differences in languages, / customs and manners of organizing the body politic / deny such a doubtful descendance.]

Here he openly denies any cultural connection with Africa and contradicts Espinosa's view that the proximity of Africa and the similarities in customs, language, and diet were clear evidence of the islands' link to the African continent. Whereas Espinosa ultimately urges his reader to make up his own mind ("Destas opiniones puede seguir el lector la que le pareciere y más le cuadrare" [*Historia*, 33 [bk. 1, chap. 4]]), Viana's statements do not allow for much breadth of interpretation.

This is the beginning of a process of deliberate assimilation between Guanches and Spaniards that would serve to exaggerate Espinosa's ethno-historical arguments. Viana's Guanches also accepted religion in its purest form of monotheism, and they did so freely and willingly. Their merit was so great that Viana (*Antigüedades*, 1.383–442) interpreted the presence of the Virgin of Candelaria among the islanders as a reward from God. Not only were the Guanches the perfect Christians without benefit of indoctrination, but their society brought up its citizens to reject the seven deadly sins (Viana, *Antigüedades*, 1.527–537), respect the ten commandments (1.545–551), and obey and serve kings as civil authorities (1.554–556). Before the young men learned the arts of war, they had to prove their purity of blood (1.559–563) and their merits in battle would enhance their lineage (1.690–699). Furthermore, Viana (1.677–699) makes direct reference to some of those classes that Aristotle deemed an indispensable part of a well-governed civil state. He also (1. 656–679) considerably increased the repertoire of curative methods employed by the "Galenos" and "Avicenas" who lived among the Guanches. Viana's Guanche Republic, unlike Espinosa's, did not need to resort to elaborate arguments to disguise primitivism, because it ceased to be bound to idolatrous practices or any possible violations of natural laws.

Those liberal heterosexual practices that had been reported by Espinosa became in Viana's epic poem the most civilized monogamous embodiment of the sacrament of matrimony (*Antigüedades*, 1.740–745):

> Lícito fue a una hembra un varón sólo,
> y al varón una hembra permitido,
> y en matrimonio entre ellos dependía
> de solo voluntad que los ligaba,
> durando el sí otorgado hasta la muerte,
> sin que se permitiese haber divorcio.[109]

> [It was legal for a woman to have only one man, / and a man was allowed to have only one woman. / Marriage between them depended solely / on the free will that bound them together, / and the "I do" lasted until death / without divorce being permitted.]

Viana also insisted on the distinction between legitimate and illegitimate children, and he explicitly added that all illegitimate children were excluded from

---

[109] In Viana's strategies, M. R. Alonso has seen the poet's counter-reformist zeal as well as an indication that the poet might have had Guanche origins (Viana, *Antigüedades*, ed. Alonso, 95 n. 66; Alonso, *El poema*, 72). Years later, Cioranescu would make clear that Viana descended neither from Guanches nor from the first conquistadors (Viana, *Conquista*, ed. Cioranescu, 2: 17). Although the speculations over this aspect of Viana's personal history have been laid to rest, I see in this type of strategy more of an ideological leaning than personal pride; that is, the poet constructs the cultural and religious identity of the Atlantic islands as conforming to the dominant imperial ideology.

inheriting. Any transgression between social classes was strictly forbidden, and contrary to what Espinosa had said, the royal succession was carried out from father to son and not from brother to brother (Viana, *Antigüedades*, 1.746–756).

Viana also advances a class argument that touches on all spheres of Guanche life. The social classes, as reported by Espinosa, became more distinguishable in Viana's poem since nobles wore *tamarcos* with sleeves as well as some manner of stockings, *huirmas*, and sandals called *xercos* (*Antigüedades*, 1.599–605) (Espinosa had not documented these last two native garments and their denominations). When Viana offered a physical portrayal of Bencomo, he insisted that his *tamarco* was refined and delicate, that his arms were covered by sleeves or *huirmas* and his legs by stockings or *guaycas* (*Antigüedades*, 3.122–125); apparently he was not very consistent in his use of the Guanche lexicon, as M. R. Alonso has noted (Viana, *Antigüedades*, ed. Alonso, 1: 146 n. 15). Funeral rituals also varied according to the class to which the deceased belonged. Nobles were buried in durable wooden coffins instead of mere animal skins (Viana, *Antigüedades*, 1.832–840, 863–866). Following Espinosa, Viana added (*Antigüedades*, 1.870–877) that the caste who took care of the preparation and burial of corpses kept to themselves and never mixed with the rest of the population because their lineage was considered impure. Viana also stated (*Antigüedades*, 1.632–635) that the *gofio* eaten by the Guanches was prepared with milk, honey, and lard but that the poor only used water and salt. Furthermore, Viana's noble class, that is, those who governed the nation, as well as the artisans, did not engage in the natives' main source of livelihood, the tending of flocks (*Antigüedades*, 1.680–695). Differing from Espinosa's more rudimentary model, Viana reconstructed a perfectly stratified society that was very much like a mirror image of Spain — "fueron muy parecidos a españoles" (*Antigüedades*, 1.379).

After the defeat of Acentejo, Espinosa narrated the Spaniards' entrapment of their allies, the Guanches of Güímar, and their subsequent sale into slavery (*Historia*, 103 [bk. 3, chap. 5]); Viana, on the other hand, chose not to include this episode in his poem. As M. R. Alonso (*El poema*, 161) has pointed out, Viana's purposeful silence was part of his general exaltation of the Spanish contingent, and particularly of Alonso de Lugo and his men.[110] Viana was nonethe-

---

[110] Rumeu de Armas (*La conquista*, 200–5) has reconsidered this episode in the history of the conquest of Tenerife and has concluded that reasonable doubt can be cast on its historical accuracy; thus in a way he agrees with Viana's version. Rumeu de Armas speculates that Espinosa must have been confused by Alonso de Lugo's actions during the conquest of Palma, in which he captured and sold his native allies from the region of Gazmira. Rumeu de Armas finds it improbable that Lugo would have betrayed his only allies in Tenerife when he would need their support in the near future. Interestingly enough, the German traveler J. Münzer in his *Itinerarium Hispanicum* reports that in 1494 he saw men and women from Tenerife being sold as slaves in Valencia. Rumeu de Armas does not see sufficient evidence in this corroboration to support Espinosa's claim, although it is very clear that during the next two years Lugo captured and sold a great number of Guanches. I would venture to say here that

less quick to blame the French colonists of the early fifteenth century for en-slaving the natives of Lanzarote and Fuerteventura (*Antigüedades*, 2.64–79, 92–97). He also echoed Espinosa's denouncement of Pedro de Vera's and his son Hernando's dishonorable actions in Gran Canaria (*Antigüedades*, 2.782–763, 969–971). Viana could not censor this last episode because it was a well-documented fact; nonetheless, the poet consistently disassociated Alonso de Lugo from any wrongdoing upon his arrival at Gran Canaria as well as on his expedition to conquer Tenerife.[111] Partial concessions aside, it remains clear that Viana's ultimate purpose was to justify and praise the Spanish occupation of the Canaries.

If Espinosa's history had used the legend of the appearance of the Virgin of Candelaria as both a pretext and a justification for his ethnographic apology of the Guanches, Viana seems at first to have had a similar purpose. The poet specifically uses the Virgin of Candelaria's rewarding appearance to frame his history of the Guanches (Viana, *Antigüedades*, 1.425–440) — an appearance that created a new nation, indeed a "blessed nation" ("nación dichosa" [Viana, *Antigüedades*, 1.500]) very much like the one that his poem aspired to create. Viana imagined a fortunate space for a cultural re-encounter where violence would be played down and harmony would forever reign. Viana stated (*Antigüedades*, 6.649–650; 16.742–843) that there were two festivities in honor of the Virgin, and he echoed some of the miracles that Espinosa had recorded. Espinosa (*Historia*, 65 [bk. 2, chap. 9]) had on one occasion lent a greater authority to his account of the miracles by stating that he himself had found some miraculous wax near the Virgin's site. Viana, in a similar strategy, affirmed that he had been present during a procession on the beach when numerous fish swam alongside the human procession as it made its way to the Virgin's cave (*Antigüedades*, 16.820–841). Despite the apparent centrality of the Virgin in the title of the

---

Rumeu de Armas's speculation is somewhat academic, given the abundant evidence for Lugo's ruthlessness. It is worth noting here that both Espinosa and Viana considered only the natives of Güímar as allies of the Spaniards, but archival materials show that other native groups (known as the "bandos de paces") had negotiated for peace with Vera and Lugo. Among these groups were the natives of Adeje, Abona, and possibly Anaga, according to the summary offered by Cioranescu (in Viana, *Conquista*, ed. Cioranescu, 2: 163–64 n 726).

[111] According to M. R. Alonso (Viana, *Antigüedades*, ed. Alonso, 129 n. 42), Alonso de Lugo was the Major of Agaete in Gran Canaria after the expedition of Juan Rejón settled there in 1478. Lugo was the brother-in-law of Pedro del Algaba's wife; Algaba was executed by Juan Rejón and Lugo denounced this execution to the Catholic monarchs. Rejón was made prisoner and sent to Spain by Pedro de Vera in 1480. Espinosa and Viana both indi-cated that an injustice had been done to Pedro del Algaba. Viana further exalted Lugo's rightful actions, but the local chroniclers of Gran Canaria are all in agreement that Algaba was hardly innocent, since he was attempting to sell the island to the Portuguese. For a lengthy discussion and transcription of these local chronicles, see Morales Padrón, *Canarias*, 9–468.

epic, Viana's references to the Virgin in the first and last cantos serve only to frame the complex plot of the poem.

The history of the advent of the Virgin of Candelaria, however, makes an additional appearance in the sixth canto of Viana's text. It is narrated in a canto that is seemingly disjointed from the rest of the poem. Not only is the Virgin left on the margins of the main plot, but the historical appearance of the icon is narrated not by the poet but by Antón, an indoctrinated Guanche who had returned to the island. By voicing the story of the miraculous appearance, Antón, not the Virgin of Candelaria, becomes the mediator between the Christian and the non-Christian world. With this narrative strategy, Viana took away the validation of the Guanches' religious experience before they understood the significance of the icon. The evangelizing mission of the Virgin could acquire meaning only if it was explained and codified by a Christian, in this case, Antón. Viana (*Antigüedades*, 6.293–348) went so far as to reproduce the whole catechism lesson that Antón allegedly preached to the Guanches — from Genesis to the birth of Christ. Espinosa, on the other hand, had put more emphasis on the instinctive reverence felt by the Guanches for a long time prior to the return of Antón, whose role is diminished considerably in the historical account. Moreover, in Viana's poem (*Antigüedades*, 16.702–721), the name by which the Virgin would be known — "of Candelaria" — originated only after Alonso de Lugo and his men witnessed the light that emanated from the statue. Viana's poetic license reflects his conscious attempt at rewriting history to help support the unifying model that he tried to create. The Virgin of Candelaria thus embodies another justification for the inevitability of the European conquest and colonization of the Guanches.

Other issues surface when one turns to Viana's second accusation against Espinosa; that is, Espinosa's misconstruction of the inheritance of the Guerra estate. He directly attacked Espinosa in the prologue and at the end of the sixteenth canto (*Antigüedades*, 16:1010–1031); but above all, Viana carefully crafted the historical role of the conquistador Lope Hernández de la Guerra — the poet's patron's ancestor — throughout the poem. In Viana's poem, Lope Hernández, whose economic position was higher than his social rank, became a nobleman (*Antigüedades*, 3.570–572) and a *Maestre de campo*, second-in-command officer in charge of tactics and supply (8.288).[112]

His heroic deeds were exalted when he would kill (with astonishing agility) four natives, one after the other (*Antigüedades*, 8.288–304), and the integrity of

---

112 Viana also narrates (*Antigüedades*, 16.1011–1039) how Lope Hernández became *regidor* of the island (one of the six first appointed *regidores* in 1496), as confirmed by Cioranescu's research. Cioranescu also states that the conquistador became Major of the island in 1498 and in charge of land distribution in 1505 (Viana, *Conquista*, ed. Cioranescu, 2: 53), thus emphasizing Lope Hernández's rank as a prominent member of the early colonial society of Tenerife.

Fig. 5. False family tree of the Guerras that appeared in Antonio de Viana's *Antigüedades de las Islas Afortunadas de la Gran Canaria, conquista de Tenerife y aparecimiento de la Santa Imagen de Candelaria* (Seville, 1604). From Facsimile Edition. Courtesy of the Excmo. Ayuntamiento de San Cristóbal de la Laguna.

his character was overly praised when, after the defeat of Acentejo, he offered
to sell his properties in Gran Canaria to help Alonso de Lugo's next expedition
(Viana, *Antigüedades*, 8.1386–1402, 1415–1416). Lope's deeds and character
were, of course, seconded by those of his two nephews, Hernán Guerra and
Hernando Esteban Guerra — the latter being Viana's patron's great-
grandfather. In the fifteenth canto, the allegorical figure of Eternity shows
Alonso de Lugo the future, in other words, Viana's present. The vision included an overview of the Castilian royal succession, which Viana used to
honor the Guerras and provide a drawing of their family's (false) genealogical
tree (*Antigüedades*, 15.327–82).[113]

One of Cioranescu's main contributions to the study of the poem has been
precisely the unveiling of Viana's relation to the Guerras (Viana, *Conquista*, ed.
Cioranescu, 2: 50–63). Viana made Hernando Esteban Guerra a conquistador
along with his uncle, Lope Hernández: this famous uncle was in reality his father's cousin, not his brother. Furthermore, Hernando Esteban was only a
small child at the time of the conquest and came to Tenerife only in 1504. Cioranescu emphasizes the relationship between the poet and his patron, Juan
Guerra de Ayala, to highlight the epic celebration of the prominent family and
the false reconstruction of the family tree as a self-motivated enterprise on the
part of Guerra de Ayala. Viana's fiction connected Guerra de Ayala to nobility
and presented him as a patron of the arts. Most importantly, Guerra de Ayala
became Captain General of Honduras one year after the appearance of the epic
poem, in which the Guerra family lineage had been cleared and honored. Although Cioranescu's argument is historically accurate and valid, Viana's epic
project transcended such personal issues and became instrumental in the colonial history of Tenerife and the Canaries as well as that of the New World.[114]

As M. R. Alonso (*El poema*, 163) has rightfully stated, Viana's text became
crucial for the legitimization of the islands' aristocratic elite. Not only did the
Guerras see their own lineage exalted in Viana's poem, but also many other
families could trace their beginnings to the moment of the conquest thanks to
Viana's text, which elaborated considerably on Espinosa's list of the first conquistadors.[115] Above all, however, Viana's apparent attempt to vindicate the

---

[113] The diagram of the genealogical tree is reproduced on the previous page; see also
Viana, *Antigüedades*, ed. facsímil (San Cristóbal de La Laguna: Ayuntamiento, 1996), 301; or
Antigüedades, ed. Alonso, 2: 217. For a historically accurate and complete genealogy of the
Guerras, see Cioranescu's family tree (Viana, *Conquista*, ed. Cioranescu, 2: 53–54).

[114] M. R. Alonso (*El poema*, 313, 450) presented a crucial model for the cultural understanding of the text and the colonial history of Tenerife when she drew initial attention to
the importance of the symbolic union of Spain and Tenerife in the poetic text. This model
was later elaborated by Cioranescu (Viana, *Conquista*, ed. Cioranescu, 2: 88–89).

[115] Cioranescu (Viana, *Conquista*, ed. Cioranescu, 2: 199–368) has searched in the archives for any extant information about the first conquistadors and settlers of the island. He

honor of the Guerras was indeed justifying the rights exercised by the Spanish crown in conquering Tenerife and the rights of all conquistadors to claim lands and possessions which had been connected to their ancestors. The family history of the Guerras is only one of the elements used by Viana to legitimize the colonial history of Spain in Tenerife. I will further develop this point below when I address Viana's other strategies in constructing his project.

Antonio de Viana's premise in writing an epic that would contradict Espinosa's controversial historical text proposes instead a fictional reconstruction of the past disguised as history. When Viana explicitly stated that his text constituted the only just and rightful answer to Espinosa's blemishing of the cultural tradition of the islanders as well as the honor of prominent conquistadors, he was implicitly reacting to the resonances of Lascasian thought that were present in Espinosa's history. Whereas Espinosa had offered an image of Tenerife that was as victimized as that of the New World, Viana instead envisioned the colonial experience of the Canary Islands as clearly distinct from that of America.

2. DIALOGUING WITH ERCILLA: IS THE EPIC FROM MARS OR FROM VENUS?

Viana's position in favor of including more historical than fictional material in his epic also points in the direction of one of the most popular and influential texts of the time: Alonso de Ercilla's epic poem *La Araucana* (1569, 1578, 1589). Although Viana never explicitly mentioned Ercilla, Viana's epic portrayal of the Guanches, the natives of Tenerife, as well as the history of the conquest of the island is in part a dialogue with Ercilla's portrayal of the Araucanians and his reflections on the war of conquest in Arauco.

Some critics, in fact, have explored how Ercilla's epic poem served as a formal model for Viana's poem.[116] Ercilla presents the geographic and general cultural background of the Araucanians as the point of departure for his epic

---

has made a comprehensive inventory and established possible correspondences between historical figures and the lists provided by both Espinosa and Viana.

[116] Angel Valbuena Prat (*Historia de la poesía canaria* [Barcelona: Universidad de Barcelona, 1937], 1: 15), contradicting Marcelino Menéndez y Pelayo (introduction to *Obras de Lope de Vega* [Madrid: Atlas, 1968], 91), affirms that Viana's poem showed little resemblance to Ercilla's. M. R. Alonso's scant remarks about Ercilla's poem suggest only that Viana must have read it and occasionally borrowed elements. For Alonso (*El poema*, 258–62), Ercilla's is only one more poem in which, as in Viana's, all classical and Renaissance epic models meet. Cioranescu, on the other hand, enumerates those passages in Viana that more or less resemble Ercilla's poem as well as some similarities in stylistic traits (Viana, *Conquista*, ed. Cioranescu, 2: 84–86). I have borrowed from his list those examples whose similarities appear to support the case for a more clear influence. I am, however, more interested in those aspects that appear to contradict Ercilla's epic.

poem; Viana follows this strategy, substituting the Guanches for the Araucanians. Ercilla's epic upholds a single central chronological plot, as does Viana's. In the second canto of *La Araucana*, the Araucanians meet in a general assembly to dispute who should lead the community. Viana (*Antigüedades*, 5.741–864) reproduces a similar quest for power among the nine *menceyes* of Tenerife who were enraged by Bencomo's supremacy. Just as in Ercilla's text, in which the soothsayer Puchecalco was killed by Tucapel after he had augured misfortune (canto 8), in Viana's poem the soothsayer Guañameñe foresaw the arrival of the Spaniards and the end of Guanche rule, a vision for which he would be subsequently condemned to death by Bencomo (*Antigüedades*, 3.250–325). Viana introduces the *lucha canaria* or wrestling matches between natives, which could have come from Ercilla's descriptions (cantos 10 and 11) of Araucanians' wrestling games.[117] Lautaro, in Ercilla's text, could have been the model for Tinguaro in Viana's. In addition, the triumphant vision that Alonso de Lugo experienced when seven maidens took him to the peak of Mount Teide resembles Ercilla's contemplation of the battle of San Quintín from the vantage point of a flowery field to which he was taken by Bellona, the Roman goddess of war (canto 17). Another rhetorical element that appears to point to the immediate influence of Ercilla is, according to Cioranescu (Viana, *Conquista*, ed. Cioranescu, 2: 84–86), the convention of closing one canto by announcing its immediate continuation in the next one.

Although the aforementioned critics have explored the structural similarities between the two texts, the points of comparison or contrast between Ercilla and Viana can yield more fruitful reflections at the conceptual level. The contradictions and complexities of Ercilla's text have posed several problems for the Renaissance epic and its critics who have tried to deal with the absence of certain traditional elements in the structure of his epic, such as the praising of one central hero and the ultimate celebration of a triumphant party.[118] Viana

---

[117] Cioranescu has noted that the *lucha canaria* (Canarian wrestling) was only mentioned in historical accounts in the context of Gran Canaria prior to Viana who attributed the custom to Tenerife as well. Thus there is a possibility that he is imitating Ercilla's depiction of wrestling contests (Viana, *Conquista*, ed. Cioranescu, 2: 85).

[118] See Pierce (*La poesía épica*, 24; idem, *Alonso de Ercilla y Zúñiga* [Amsterdam: Rodopi, 1984], 70–71) and Beatriz Pastor, "Alonso de Ercilla y la emergencia de una conciencia hispanoamericana," in *Discurso narrativo de la conquista de América* [Habana: Casa de las Américas, 1983], 451–570, here 470. William Melczer ("Ercilla's Divided Heroic Vision: A Re-Evaluation of the Epic Hero in *La Araucana*," *Hispania* 56 [1973]: 216–21, here 217) has rejected the notion that the poet himself is the hero of his poem (as first set forth by Voltaire), and he also departs from the notion that the individual hero is always undermined by the collective. Melczer ("Ercilla's Divided Heroic Vision," 218, 220) proposes a "dual solution" in which Ercilla's loyalties are divided between the ideological righteousness of the Spaniards on one hand and the moral righteousness of the Araucanians on the other insofar as he "felt committed to both sides and to neither." Several critics have explained the duality of Ercilla's text by the poet's use of Lucan's *Pharsalia*. On one side of the critical spectrum,

seems to share such an unconventional approach with Ercilla. He claimed, at least in his prologue, that his epic would tell the heroic struggle of the Guanches against the Spaniards in the conquest of the last Canary Island, which would be incorporated into the crown of Castile by 1497.

In the case of Ercilla, however, Beatriz Pastor ("Alonso de Ercilla," 563) has commented that *La Araucana* constituted the beginnings of a critical Hispanic-American conscience in which the unresolved conflict between cultures, rather than its fusion, is presented. Viana's epic deviates from Ercilla's in this important aspect, since the former poet is dealing not with an ongoing war of conquest, but with a *fait accompli* that took place more than one hundred years earlier. By Viana's times, Tenerife's colonial society was largely in place, thereby allowing him to reconstruct the history of the island as a perfect fusion of cultures. If there was a space within the Spanish empire at that moment in which such fusion could have occurred, it was the Canary Islands. Thus Viana took advantage of this potentially utopian locus to challenge the image of colonial violence as depicted in Ercilla's poem about Arauco, as representative of the New World.

Above all and at the very least, Viana claimed, like Ercilla, that he too was invested in depicting the side of the defeated. He justified his gesture by (falsely) building his epic poem in direct opposition to Espinosa's history, while Ercilla (*La Araucana*, ed. Morínigo and Lerner, 1: 122) warned his reader in the prologue:

> Y si alguno le pareciere que me muestro algo inclinado a la parte de los araucanos, tratando sus cosas y valentías más estendidamente de lo que para bárbaros se requiere ... veremos ... que son pocos los que con tan gran constancia y firmeza han defendido su tierra contra tan fieros enemigos como son los españoles.
>
> [If I seem somewhat inclined to the side of the Araucanians by treating their affairs and their bravery at greater length than barbarians deserve ... we shall see ... that few have shown, as they have, such great perseverance and strength when they defended their lands against such fierce enemies as the Spaniards.]

Quint (*Epic and Empire*, 157–90) has explored Lucan as a failed ideological model for Ercilla, while Isaías Lerner ("Ercilla y Lucano," in *Hommage à Robert Jammes*, ed. F. Cerdan [Toulouse: Mirail, 1994], 2: 683–85) has emphasized the presence of Lucan in Ercilla's poem as a predominantly formal strategy and as the result of the poet's humanist education.

Both Ercilla and Viana seem to coincide in a writing project that addressed —
as Pastor ("Alonso de Ercilla," 568) has pointed out in the case of Ercilla —
the fragmentation of a reality of violence, and the exploitation and injustices in
the conquest and colonization of America. Nonetheless, both Ercilla and Viana
adopted different ideological positions in dealing with the issue.

Ercilla, in fact, has often been considered sympathetic to anti-conquest
ideas generally associated with Las Casas. A recent study by William Mejías-
López ("Relación ideológica," 197–217), for example, has explored the connections between Ercilla and the ideas of Vitoria and Las Casas — mainly the indigenous rights to self-government and property.[119] The novelty of this study
("Relación ideológica," 199) is the evidence of an actual encounter between
Ercilla and Fray Gil González de San Nicolás, a disciple of Vitoria and a corre-
spondent of Las Casas, during a fifty-eight-day-long maritime trip from Chile
to Peru. This physical evidence of a possible intellectual exchange only con-
firms the extensively argued textual evidence of the influence of Las Casas in
Ercilla's text, summarized by José Durand as follows ("Caupolicán," 373):

> La actitud fundamental de honrar a unos héroes bárbaros se
> nutre de los grandes debates lascasianos sobre la dignidad
> humana de esos indios y la justicia de esas guerras: ideas res-
> piradas a diario en la vida chilena, o en Lima, o en la Corte.[120]

---

[119] Perhaps one shortcoming of this article ("La relación ideológica de Alonso de Ercilla
con Francisco de Vitoria y Fray Bartolomé de las Casas," *Revista iberoamericana* 61 [1995]:
197–217) is the similarity that Mejías-López attributes to the ideas of Vitoria and Las Casas,
although this error has little effect on his argument with respect to Ercilla's poem. As it has
been argued, the theoretical differences between Vitoria and Las Casas are far greater and
those between Vitoria and Sepúlveda, much less so than has traditionally been thought
(Henry Méchoulan, *El honor de Dios*, trans. Enrique Sordo [Barcelona: Argos Vergara, 1981],
64–65; Adorno, "Los debates," 47–66).

[120] Durand ("El chapetón Ercilla y la honra araucana," *Filología* 10 [1964]: 113–34) has
studied the figure and ideas of Ercilla more as a soldier than as a colonist, thereby allowing
the poet to expose the heroism of the Araucanians and the ideas of Vitoria and Las Casas.
See also Ciriaco Pérez Bustamante, "El lascasismo en La Araucana," *Revista de estudios políticos*
64 (1952): 157–68, on Las Casas and *La Araucana*. While some critics have agreed with these
ideas and offered further evidence for Ercilla's positive view of the Araucanians and critical
outlook on the war (Pastor, "Alonso de Ercilla," 523; Mejías-López, "Relación ideológica,"
198–217), still others insist that Ercilla did not have a totally positive image of the Amerindians and that the poem cannot help being shaped by Spanish imperial ideology (F. J. Cevallos,
"Don Alonso de Ercilla and the American Indian: History and Myth," *Revista de estudios
hispánicos* 23 [1989]: 1–20). If the contradictions or ambivalence in Ercilla's text cannot be
denied, there is not such a thing either as one monolithic "Spanish ideology" that can group
Las Casas, Ercilla, and Sepúlveda, for example, in the same category. The legal and moral
issues debated during the sixteenth century reflected a critical dynamism that was complex
and subversive enough to shake and influence the institutions of empire as well as to filter
into literary works such as Ercilla's.

Paraphrasing the above quote, Ercilla, like any man of his times and social position, was exposed either at court or in the colonies to the widespread reformist ideas put forth by Las Casas and his supporters. His moral concerns with the Araucanians and the war waged against them proved to go beyond the conventional demands of the epic. Ercilla and his poem became indirect participants in a debate that questioned the justice of the military conquest of the New World. In fact, one of the digressive paths that Ercilla takes in his poem exemplifies his critical position. The story of Dido, inserted in an epic about the conquest of Chile (cantos 32 and 33), served the poet's aims openly to contradict Virgil's "slandering" of the queen, while offering instead an alternative model of conquest and colonization in the founding of the ancient city of Carthage.[121] Ercilla emphasized how Dido, a newcomer on the North African coast, ingeniously managed to acquire enough land to build the new city using her intelligence to trick the local residents, but also displaying a great sense of justice by remunerating them, and thus gaining their respect and acceptance.

Ercilla's critical remarks and strategies do not find a replica in Viana's text; on the contrary, the latter takes a different direction.[122] Viana's response to the violence inherent in conquering and colonizing was the creation of a text that reformulated the history of Tenerife, to propose the Atlantic Islands as an alternative textual space in which to negotiate Spanish history in the New World. Tenerife was constructed in Viana's epic as the space of cultural union and harmony rather than of violence and division. Viana's model of syncretism, however, needed to find a way to negotiate the demands of the epic as a genre and

---

[121] On Dido, see Brumble, *Classical Myths and Legends*, 101–3 (cf. María Rosa Lida de Malkiel, *Dido en la literatura española: su retrato y defensa* [London: Tamesis, 1974]).

[122] I fervently disagree with Cioranescu's reading of Ercilla and Viana with respect to their representation of the natives. Cioranescu (in Viana, *Conquista*, ed. Cioranescu, 2: 86–87) affirms that:

Viana parece situarse en la continuación de la tradición lascasiana y considera al guanche, no solo con la simpatía artística, sino también con la humana, mientras que Ercilla representa al indio de modo realista y en general desprovisto de poesía y de idealización como no sean las que se derivan de la retórica y el manierismo.

[Viana seems to be in the line of Lascasian thought and depicts the Guanches with not only artistic but also human sympathy. Meanwhile, Ercilla depicts the Indians in a realistic way and in general lacking that lyricism or idealization unless when following rhetorical or mannerist practices.]

With respect to Cioranescu's assessment of Ercilla's representation of Arauco and the Araucanians, there have been many critical studies which rightfully contradict this critic's opinion (see above, note 120). With respect to Viana's poem, my study sets out to prove that Viana's poem is ideologically antagonistic to Las Casas's ideas.

of his implicit model (Ercilla), which emphasized division and war, in order to project the ultimate triumph of one party over the other.

Although Ercilla has been accused of failing to comply with his openly stated epic objectives — of depicting only war — by including several love stories among the Araucanians, his conflicted or dual position with respect to his heroes has hardly been put into question. Viana's failure to comply with his apparent goals, however, is profoundly tied to his ideological commitment to the Spanish imperial conquest. Viana consistently undermines his position as champion of the native Guanches. If there are heroes in Viana's epic, they are ultimately on the Spanish side. In several military encounters that are depicted in the poem, the violent deaths of the natives may take center stage, but only as a pretext to set off the valor of the Spanish soldiers. An illustrative example of Viana's heroic portrayal of the Spaniards at the expense of the natives occurs when Lugo gets rid of a Guanche — who had dared to jump on Lugo's horse — by skillfully using a rope to suspend the native by his hands from a tree before chopping his arms off (*Antigüedades*, 8.240–269). Viana's depiction of this cruel act serves to emphasize the strength and ingenuity of a proud General Lugo who remains unbeaten.

The natives as well as the epic violence of war are also exploited in a gallery of conventional exotics. Viana's use of the figure of the giant, which appears as a literary device throughout medieval and Renaissance literature, is particularly illustrative of his ideological appropriation of the marvel.[123] Most natives in Viana's poem are not metaphorical giants as in Ercilla's epic, but literal giants — "todos medio-gigantes" (Viana, *Antigüedades*, 8.360); here, Viana used the information that Espinosa had reluctantly reported in his history — the true existence of giants among the ancient Guanches — to compose his epic. Rucadén, a fierce giant ("gigantazo fiero," Viana, *Antigüedades*, 8.345–352), dies in

---

[123] In mapping the literary traditions that influenced Cervantes and other Golden Age writers at the turn of the seventeenth century, Francisco Márquez Villanueva (*Fuentes literarias cervantinas* [Madrid: Gredos, 1973], 264–357) has analyzed the literary device of giants as primarily derived from the Italian epic and the *ars macaronica*. Although the theme of the giants dates from classical literature and later spreads throughout medieval legends, the *Historia Turpini* or *De Vita Caroli Magni et Rolandi* (1140) directly influenced Renaissance writers (e.g., Dante, Ariosto, Rodríguez de Montalvo). The giant, as the *homo deformis et pravus*, mostly became the target of derogatory representations as part of a typology of human deformities. The benevolent giant was rare in medieval literature but became prominent in the Italian epic (e.g., L. Pulci's *Morgante*, T. Folengo's *Baldus*).

In the context of the Renaissance epic, the treatment of the giant was both heroic and at the same time burlesque. This approach passed into the macaronic poetry that took root in Spain among intellectual and university circles during the last quarter of the sixteenth century and the first decade of the seventeenth. Viana's characterization of giants fits well into this picture, as he was a university student in Seville at the time. Furthermore, he had access to historiographic information on the Guanches' mythical gigantism, which allowed him to integrate both historical and literary models.

battle with his thighs pierced, while the death of Guadafret, another giant, serves the gruesome spectacle of the spoils of war (*Antigüedades*, 12.444–463):

> andaba Guadafret, gigante fiero,
> muy grueso, egdematoso, barrigudo,
> como torre de carne, aunque pesado,
> valiente, suelto, diestro y animoso
> encarnizado en española gente,
> encuéntrale Albornoz, que sin caballo
> con la adarga y la espada combatía,
> cierra con el gigante valeroso,
> …
> llega la espada por la recta línea
> del invencible brazo gobernada,
> y por el grueso ombligo, palpitando,
> salen los intestinos con la sangre;
> desmaya luego el cuerpo gigánteo,
> …
> y al fin con el mal parto movedizo
> de la hinchada preñez, perdió la vida.

[There he was, the fierce giant Guadafret, / fat, bloated, big-bellied, / like a tower of flesh; although heavy / he was agile, skillful, vigorous / in the slaughtering of Spanish troops. / Without a horse, Albornoz found him, / and with shield and sword / he attacked the brave giant … / the sword, governed by the insuperable arm, / reached the belly in a straight line. / Out of the navel, palpitating / and bloodied the intestines emerged. / The enormous body faints right away … / and at last with this wobbly miscarriage, / in a bulging pregnancy he lost his life.]

Unlike Ercilla, who used the gore of war to expose the unnecessary cruelty and violence of Spanish warfare while effectively praising the heroism of Araucanians (for example in the case of Galvarino [canto 22], whose hands are cut off), Viana was more concerned with the spectacle *per se*. Galvarino is given a voice in Ercilla's poem (canto 26), and when he fights to the end with his mutilated arms it is to teach a lesson of courage and resistance to the Spaniards.

In Viana's poem, Guadafret and later Sigoñe (another native whose slow death is graphically described as he bites off the flesh of his attacker) are voiceless and appear in vignettes of mocking fictions. The comparison of Guadafret's death to a miscarriage is more ludicrous than it is an occasion for commiseration. Perhaps the only exception — aside from King Bencomo, who does not die in the poem — is Tinguaro, the gigantic brother of the king, who finds his death towards the poem's end. Tinguaro is an important character who is truly developed in the course of the poem, but whose mangled and mutilated corpse is displayed as a warning to the natives by the Spaniards. Tinguaro's heroism only served to teach the natives a lesson that would result in their final decision to relinquish power. Above all, Viana's giants and their gruesome yet mostly humorous depictions reflect the poet's insertion into the tradition of the mock epic. These giants are predominantly redeemable but ambiguously heroic.

The pronounced mythic quality of some of the native characters like King Bencomo also undermines the heroic acclamations of war. The king is less a mythical hero and more a ridiculous monster when he is portrayed by Viana (*Antigüedades*, 3.99–113) as

> robusto, corpulento cual gigante,
> de altor de siete codos[124] y aun se dice
> tenía ochenta muelas y otros dientes
> ...
> rostro alegre, y feroz color Moreno,
> negros los ojos, vivos y veloces,
> pestañas grandes, de las cejas junto,
> nariz en proporción, ventanas anchas,
> largo y grueso el bigote retorcido,
> que descubría en proporción los labrios
> encubridores del monstruoso número
> de diamantinos dientes; larga, espesa
> la barba, cana de color de nieve,
> que le llegaba casi a la cintura.

[robust and corpulent like a giant, his height / of about twelve feet, and it is still said / that he had eighty molars and other teeth ... / bright face with a fierce dark coloring, / his eyes black, sharp and quick, / long eyelashes and a joined eyebrow, / a well-proportioned nose, its nostrils wide. / His mustache, long and crooked, / uncovered the well-proportioned lips / which covered the monstrosity of / the

---

[124] Cioranescu (Viana, *Conquista*, ed. Cioranescu, 2: 151 n. 100) comments that one *codo* is equivalent to 574 mm, so seven *codos* is 3.62 meters, that is, almost twelve feet. Cioranescu sees in this portrait only the poet's failed attempt of creating the fantastic and magic ambiance of the epic.

numerous shiny teeth; his beard, / long, thick and white like
the snow, / fell almost to his waist.]

This portrait of King Bencomo inspires little fear, and his role as a protagonist
in armed confrontations occurs only towards the end. Bencomo is bluntly in-
sulted by a Spanish soldier, Trujillo, who treats the king as his equal when he
tries to recover his stolen sword; when Bencomo fights in the decisive battles,
he is injured first by Lope Fernández de la Guerra and then by Trujillo until the
king finds himself forced to leave the Spanish sword behind (Viana, *Antigüedades*, 5.571–685; 12.423; 14.635–648). His "twin" brother Tinguaro ("pues
dicen ser los dos de un parto mismo" [*Antigüedades*, 13.179]), however, is depicted as the fiercest warrior of all. In a clear Manichean classification of "the
enemy," Bencomo eventually becomes the wise one, unthreatening and ultimately quick to compromise and convert to Christianity. Meanwhile, his
brother Tinguaro becomes the bad, the fierce, the threatening force directly
propelled by Alecto and Mars but, naturally, destined to die.[125] Bencomo's
physical portrayal shows an ambiguous heroism, but not incidentally the only
physical portrait of Tinguaro given in the text occurs after his death at the
hands of the Spaniards (*Antigüedades*, 13.130–168). In Viana's text, only dead
could the enemy temporarily embody the space of the hero (see Adorno, "Literary Production," 4–8).

Although Viana's insistence on painting physical portraits of individual
Guanches with words — which is not the case with the Spaniards — may indicate an effort on the poet's part to affiliate himself with the loser's cause, each
portrait has a flaw.[126] The singling out of Guanches does not feed a heroic portrayal of the adversary, as in the case of Ercilla, but rather Viana's affiliation to
the mock epic. As in the case of Bencomo's less than flattering picture, Viana
will paint Bencomo's daughters, Dacil and Rosalba, as well as Princess Guacimara, the daughter of King Beneharo of Anaga, with a brush that distorts,
exaggerates, and blemishes. Dacil's apparently perfect physiognomy is marred
by freckles, while Rosalba's exaggerated eyelashes reached up to her eyebrows;
and although her physical beauty was not inferior to her sister's, she suffered
the disadvantage of not being her father's favorite (Viana, *Antigüedades*, 3.631–
651; 4.420–470).[127] Guacimara's portrait further illustrates Viana's (*Antigüedades*,
3.768–802) mocking constructions of the natives:

---

[125] Viana changed the correct historical information provided by Espinosa. Bencomo
(or Benitomo, according to legal documents), not his brother Tinguaro — whose name was
invented by Viana — died in the battle of La Laguna.

[126] In a way, Viana's epic perfectly suits Quint's argument (*Epic and Empire*, 11) that in
the epic poetry of the period "losers are born losers — monstrous, demonic, subhuman,"
thus conditioning their story of "self-defeat."

[127] It is worth noting in Dacil's case that M. R. Alonso (*El poema*, 315), although aware
of the imperfections common to Viana's portraits, still considers the poet's gaze a sympa-

Era en extremo Guacimara hermosa,
tenía partes dignas de loarse,
aunque robusto cuerpo giganteo:
cabellos rubios, claros, rutilantes,
...
alta la frente, y encarnadas cejas
negras, y negro en medio un lunar bello,
que con lustrosos pelos las juntaba
...
era dotada: pero estuvo a punto
cuando en su concepción obró natura,
de declinar al masculino género,
que dello daba verdadero indicio
su gran persona y valerosos hechos,
mas por la falta del calor innato
quedóse femenina en grado altivo.

[Guacimara was extremely beautiful, / she had parts that
were praiseworthy. / Although her robust body was gigantic:
/ her hair was light blond and shiny ... / her forehead high
and her eyebrows / black; black was also a lovely mole / that
with lustrous hairs united her eyebrows ... / she was gifted,
but at conception / nature almost made her / of the mascu-
line gender / which was quite evident in her / stature and
brave deeds, / but lacking the innate heat / she remained
feminine to a greater degree.]

Guacimara is not the conventional literary type of the virile female (*mujer varonil*).[128] Her body instead becomes the playful locus of exotic contrasts and
gender confusions that were fashionable in the biological theories (e.g., *calor
innato*, an Aristotelian concept) and the scientific discourse of the day (cf.
Huarte de San Juan, *Examen de ingenios para las ciencias* [Baeza, 1575]). This

---

thetic gesture that rejects the classical model in favor of a more human or realistic one. Cioranescu has claimed the same, stating that Viana's characterization of the natives was more
developed and sympathetic (Viana, *Conquista*, ed. Cioranescu, 2: 86). It becomes practically
impossible to sustain this point of view if the other textual portraits (e.g., Guacimara's) and
the overall objective of Viana's poem are taken into consideration.

128 Although M. McKendrick's typology of women primarily concerns dramatic representations, her study on the *mujer varonil* is still very useful (*Woman and Society in the Spanish
Drama of the Golden Age: A Study of the mujer varonil* [Cambridge: Cambridge University Press,
1974]).

Guanche princess could have been exhibited as a rare piece in the "curiosity cabinet" (*Kunstkammer* or *Wunderkammer*) of any European court.[129]

In comparison, the only instance in which Viana uses an element of mockery to target the Spaniards occurs when invading troops, weakened by hunger, land in Tenerife and reach down to the ground to gather what they take to be edible *mocanes* (*Visnes mocanera*), only to find out that the black, small, rounded fruits were in actuality the excrement of goats! This incident does little to undermine the poetic characterization of the foreigners. Viana introduces this humorous scene at the expense of the conquistadors, and perhaps also attempts to lend verisimilitude to the portrayal of his native Tenerife.

By ridiculing or showing the monstrosity of the enemies or their executions, however, the poem disengages from any significant discussion of Guanche culture and sublimates or exploits epic violence for aesthetic experience. Viana makes use of the traditional conventions of both the epic destined to produce a legitimate marvel and the mock epic, which introduces burlesque elements, in order consistently to undermine any cathartic experience of the war of conquest.

Although the greater part of Viana's poem explores the most notorious battles between Guanches and Spaniards, the poet was concerned with past wars principally to enhance his portrayal of the present peace. In Viana's poem, Mars functions according to a conventional formula; his name is invoked throughout, and the pagan god becomes an allegorical figure who, lobbied by Fortune on behalf of Nivaria/Tenerife, makes a one-time appearance to grant a single military victory to the natives (*Antigüedades*, 7.575–582). Mars is part of the repertoire of classical references through which the paganism of the Guanches is constructed in the poem. If Viana insists on depicting the "fury of Mars" — a mechanically repeated phrase throughout the poem — it is only to make the achievements of his syncretic symbol more powerful in the end.

Anchored in the historical information that the natives of Güímar had repeatedly signed peace treaties with the Christians, Viana in fact engages in another polarization of the enemy's image: Guanches are then split into wild, savage fighters on the one hand and peaceful, friendly natives on the other. Thus, war scenes of brutal struggle alternate with gracious encounters. For example, King Anaterve of Güímar and his noblemen visit Alonso de Lugo and the

---

[129] Natives of Tenerife were indeed exhibited, painted, and exchanged as gifts in European courts as in the case of the Gonzalez family. As Christiane Hertel ("'Der rauch man zu München'," in *Sammler-Bibliophile-Exzentriker*, ed. A. Assmann et al. [Tübingen: Gunter Narr, 1998], 163–91) has shown in a very interesting article about the Kunstkammer of Archduke Ferdinand II of the Tyrol, the Gonzalezes, who originated on the paternal side from Tenerife, suffered from a rare hirsute condition that made them the object of European exotic collections. Hertel studies a series of portraits made between 1580 and 1610 which shows Pedro Gonzalez and his children as pseudo-werewolves. Viana's literary brush, in a way, contributed to the exotization of the natives of Tenerife that already circulated in Europe.

Spanish troops in Santa Cruz to declare their subjection to the Catholic monarchs. Amazed by the display of sophisticated weapons and the etiquette of a
civilized meal, the Guanches embrace the Spaniards (Viana, *Antigüedades*, 6.42–
141). This scene foretells the final outcome of Viana's poem in which Kings
Bencomo and Beneharo will also embrace Lugo and recognize the military and
cultural supremacy of Spain.

Furthermore, the several love stories in the poem — Guacimara and
Ruimán, Rosalba and Guetón, Tinguaro and Guajara, and Dacil and Castillo —
seem to overshadow the historical encounters of the armies.[130] The asymmetri-
cal increase of additional or secondary materials results in shifting the emphasis
of the epic away from Mars to Venus, in keeping with Viana's objective of
crafting the perfect blending of the two cultures. Ercilla's famous verses opposing Ariosto and announcing the objective of his epic as the depiction of not
love but war — "No damas, no amor, no gentilezas … / mas el valor, los
hechos, las proezas …" (*La Araucana*, 1.1.1, 5) … "Venus y Amón aquí no tie-
nen parte / sólo domina el iracundo Marte" (1.10.7–8) — find in Viana their
opposite. If in Ercilla's epic love stories among the natives served as peripheral
material to the heroic deeds of Araucanians and Europeans, in Viana any heroic
deeds were largely diminished by the love union between Dacil, the daughter of
King Bencomo, and Castillo, a Spanish captain in the army of the *adelantado*
Alonso de Lugo — in other words, by the peaceful and symbolic connection
between Spain and the Canaries.

This insistence on harmony seems to be, if not in direct contradiction with
the genre's thematic link to Mars and the arts of war, at least a strategy that
displaces war from the center of the epic. Viana's ultimate ideological project
rejects the disorder and violence of war to make pure and harmonious love the
core of his epic. This evolution becomes evident (Viana, *Antigüedades*, 14.151–
152) when at first Castillo, as a prisoner of the Guanches, embodies the dilemma of the poem:

> los [triunfos] del amor y del Dios Marte
> andaban con rigor en competencia.
>
> [the triumphs of love and of the God Mars / were in rigor-
> ous competition.]

---

[130] Cioranescu has noted, approvingly, that Viana's interweaving of heroic and lyrical
elements in imitation of Tasso makes the epic poem refreshing although inferior to Tasso
(Viana, *Conquista*, ed. Cioranescu, 1: 82). It is also worth mentioning here Nilo Palenzuela,
"El arte del retrato en el poema de Viana," in *Homenaje al profesor Sebastián de la Nuez* (La Laguna: Universidad de La Laguna, 1991), 79–91, a study that focuses as well on Viana's appropriation of lyrical conventions for his epic poem, such as the portrait motif — seen only
in its literary dimension and not its ideological one. Putting aside these aesthetic judgments,
Viana's choices in this matter become more revealing if read instead in the context of Ercilla.

At the end of the epic poem, however, after the relinquishment of the Guanches and the union of the lovers, Viana's formulaic depiction of war becomes easily replaced by peace (*Antigüedades*, 15.613–619):

> celebran todos con placer inmenso
> las paces y amistades deseadas,
> júntanse luego todos los soldados
> nivarios y españoles como amigos,
> piden perdón los unos a los otros
> por tantas inquietudes y trabajos,
> y daños ordinarios en la guerra.

> [All of them, with immense pleasure / celebrated the long-wished-for peace, / Guanche and Spanish soldiers / came together as friends and / asked each other for forgiveness / for the uneasiness, the many hardships / and the common wreckage of wartime.][131]

At last the project that Viana had been staging becomes explicit: the dismantling of the violence of war to lay the foundation of a colonial society. The poet borrows the "magic girdle" of the goddess of love to ultimately turn the reader's thoughts away from war and towards love — the vehicle to achieve his imagined patterns of domination, and one which differed considerably from Ercilla's and the New World immortalized in *La Araucana*.

3. WHEN IDEOLOGICAL TELOS MEETS LITERARY CONVENTION

At first glance, Viana's revision of the historical material that he inherited primarily from Espinosa seems to be limited to a few changes. At the same time,

---

[131] In the next canto, after the *anagnorisis* of Guacimara and Ruimán, Viana repeats practically the same words in a scene set among Guanches (*Antigüedades*, 16.493–497):

> Juntos se ven los dos firmes amantes,
> Juntos los enemigos ya conformes,
> y todos satisfechos de constancia,
> de leal amistad y desengaños,
> se piden el perdón de las ofensas.

> [Together the two faithful lovers are seen, / together all enemies now agreeable, / and being satisfied with the loyalty / and the friendship, they saw the truth / and asked forgiveness of each other's offenses.]

his affiliation to Ercilla's heroic portrayal of the enemy seemed more than nominal. However, as I have argued above, Viana is engaged in a far more radical process of antagonism; his epic project is in direct opposition to Espinosa's vision of Canarian history and Ercilla's depiction of the war of conquest overseas. Viana's position is profoundly supportive of an imperial ideology destined to homogenize and annul any troubled voices like that of Ercilla, or any dissenting views like those of Espinosa, and above all, of Las Casas, his colleagues and his followers.

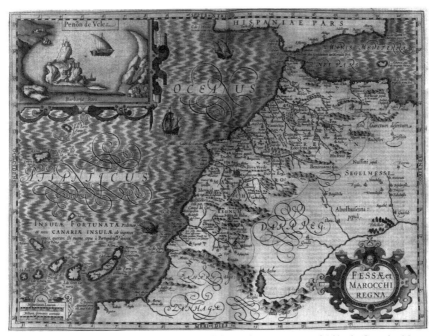

Fig. 6. Map of the Canary or Fortunate Islands and the northwestern coast of Africa in Gerardus Mercator's *Atlas* of 1607. Courtesy of the General Library at Salamanca University.

Viana's epic poem aims at the creation of a perfect utopian model of cultural integration. He achieves such blending by revisiting the origins of both cultures as sprouting from the same source, by conflating Guanches and conquistadors into a single ethnic identity, and by ultimately proposing the symbolic union of the two in the individual union of a Guanche princess and a Spanish conquistador — a union that is reinforced by the allegorical joining of Alonso de Lugo and the figure of the island/woman, Nivaria. In so doing, Viana makes the literary conventions of the epic fit his ideological *telos*.

First, the poet reconstructs the cultural origins of the Guanches to create the mold that will later be fitted with all the pieces of his harmonizing view at the moment of the encounter between Spaniards and Guanches in the late fifteenth century. The most interesting claim that Viana makes in his epic poem, one which has puzzled critics and remained unexplained, comes early in the poem.[132] When he artificially constructed the historical beginnings of Tenerife and La Palma as distinct from those of the rest of the islands, Viana bluntly wrote (*Antigüedades*, 1.333–365):

> Cuando reinaba en la vandalia Bética
> Abis, antiguo rey, y tantos años
> negó a la tierra el cielo el agua y pluvias,
> con la notable perdición de España,
> los que escaparon a oportuno tiempo
> . . .
> Pasábanse a provincias diferentes
> . . .
> de aquéstos, aportaron ciertas naves
> a la que se llamaba Pintuaria,
> y diéronle de Palma el justo título
> . . .
> De aquesta misma gente antigua y noble
> entonces se pobló también Nivaria
> . . .
> Consta destas razones verdaderas,
> que de españoles nobles andaluces
> fueron pobladas por grandeza insigne
> La Palma y Tenerife, ilustres islas.

> [When in the Vandalian Betis / reigned Abis, ancient king, and for so many years / the sky denied water and rains to the earth / with the noticeable loss to Spain; / Those who escaped on time ... / left for different provinces ... / Some arrived by ship / to the island then called Pintuaria / and rightfully gave it the just title of Palma. / Of such old and noble people / was also populated Nivaria ... / This truthful reason proves / that noble Andalusians from Spain / populated with great pride / Palma and Tenerife, noble isles.]

---

[132] M. R. Alonso has repeatedly attributed the many mistakes that run through the poet's account of historical information to Viana's youth or carelessness. Viana's imaginative etymologies and other inventions have been widely dismissed by critics who have failed to see the ideological relevance behind many of the poet's choices.

According to the poet, these two islands, like the southern parts of the Iberian peninsula, were populated by pre-Roman peoples, while the other islands were populated by Africans exiled from their continent before Islamic rule. Viana makes his argument by linking the inhabitants of Tenerife to the rule of Abis or Abiddis, who was considered in the Hispanic tradition the last legendary king of Tartessus. The poet also reinforces this idea by pointedly choosing the Germanic and Latin denominations to describe Andalusia ("vandalia Bética") and avoiding any connections to the Muslim world.

By making such a distinction between the different islands, the past of Tenerife and Palma, the last two islands to be conquered by the Spaniards, is closely united to Spain, thereby erasing Espinosa's model of the colonized as illegally devoured by the colonizer. In his epic poem, Viana does not directly address the question of whether the war against the Guanches was just or unjust, but by constructing this common origin he becomes indirectly involved in the debate. What he has done here is implicitly establish the legal basis by which the Spaniards had the right to conquer and colonize those islands that had been occupied, in his account, by the ancient inhabitants of Spain. Viana is loosely reformulating a legal argument that had been ingeniously used before by the jurist Alonso de Cartagena in the context of the Canary Islands and by the royal chronicler Fernández de Oviedo in the context of the New World. Viana's argument resembles the famous sophism developed by Cartagena in 1435, in which he made the Canary Islands part of the Visigothic African kingdom to defend Castile's claims to the islands in a dispute against the Portuguese crown (Cartagena, *Diplomacia y humanismo*, 57–163; Pérez Voituriez, *Problemas jurídicos*, 95–96).[133] Cartagena's legal strategy was quite effective at the time, since the Canaries were eventually occupied by Castilian forces. Viana's similar strategy becomes quite effective when revisiting the history of Spain in the Canaries.

Viana's paradigm serves two clear purposes. One feeds his heroic literary model by establishing a separation between worthy adversaries, that is, between the islanders who posed the most difficult conquest, and the others who gradually surrendered to the Europeans much earlier and joined forces with the Spaniards in the conquest of Tenerife. By incorporating the islands into the pre-Roman world of the Iberian peninsula, he above all annuls Espinosa's denunciation of an unjust war, because the Spanish conquest of the islands was tantamount to the recovery of territories over which the Spanish crown could have legitimate rights dating from ancient times, even before the Visigothic occupation. Thus, for Viana, the war of conquest did not carry the unlawfulness openly denounced by Espinosa or the disturbing violence that concerned Ercilla; it was constructed instead as a necessary step for a Spanish colonial project of smooth integration.

---

[133] For a discussion of Cartagena's arguments, see Chapter One of this study.

Such quasi-legal justification is simultaneously complemented by the announcement of an ethnic homogeneity which erases any traces of the composite and seeks an ancestral purity, a totalizing sameness.[134] Ultimately, Viana's main proposition is the restoration of a symbiosis that had previously been achieved. By claiming the same cultural background for Spaniards and Guanches, he foreshadows the matrimonial synthesis that will later take place in the text and in his model of the colonial history of Tenerife.

The final union in matrimony of the two is carefully built up throughout the poem.[135] At first the poetic picture of Princess Dacil reveals that her physiognomy corresponds fully to the ideal European standard of beauty. Viana wrote (*Antigüedades*, 3.631–651):

> Es de muy poca edad, gallardo brío,
> tiene donaire, gracia, gentileza,
> frente espaciosa, grave, a quien circuye
> largo cabello más que el sol dorado,
> cejas sutiles, que del color mismo
> parecen arcos de oro y corresponden
> crecidas las pestañas a sus visos,
> los ojos bellos son como esmeraldas
> cercadas de cristales transparentes,
> entreveradas de celosos círculos;

---

[134] Diana de Armas Wilson ("'Vuela por alta mar, isleño esquife': Antonio de Viana's *Conquista de Tenerife* (1604)," *Calíope* 3 [1997]: 24–36), who has given the poem a good introduction among Hispanists in the United States, shows a critical sensibility which mirrors very much my own; however, she concludes, in the tradition of Cioranescu and Alonso, that Viana "literalizes and celebrates [a] bi-cultural marriage" (33). Other critics perpetuate the same argument. Luis Alemany ("Antonio de Viana: una postura literaria ante la historia," *Revista de historia canaria* 37 [1980]: 267–72, here 271), for example, identifies in Viana's text a cultural *mestizaje* while at the same time recognizing the implicit justification of colonialism inherent in it. I, on the other hand, believe that it is hard to reconcile both observations. Viana builds his model not as the hybrid product of two cultures but as one culture with a single ethnic origin. The justification of colonialism is much more than implicit, as I have attempted to explain in this chapter.

[135] In the margins of Espinosa's history, a note appears to the effect that a certain gentleman named Gonzalo Castillo married the daughter of the King of Taoro, from whom the canon Pedro Mártir del Castillo descended (Espinosa, *Historia*, 107 [bk. 3, chap. 7]). The name Dacil is Viana's invention. There are discrepancies in the use of the written accent mark: Dácil vs. Dacil. Wölfel (*Monumenta*, 2: 916–17) registers the name without accent, while Francisco Navarro Artiles (*Teberite* [Las Palmas: Edirca, 1981], 125) documents both versions. Although the use of Dácil has been more generalized, I prefer to use Dacil. In fact, I found one instance in Lope de Vega's play ("Los guanches de Tenerife," 1.906) in which the stress of the word must fall on the last syllable to fit the meter; the name of the princess can also echo or rhyme with the name of another character, Manil.

cual bello rosicler las dos mejillas
y afilada nariz proporcionada,
graciosa boca, cuyos gruesos labrios
parecen hechos de coral purísimo
donde a su tiempo la templada risa
descubre y cubre los ebúrneos dientes,
cual ricas perlas, o diamantes finos;
largo el hermoso rostro, en color nieve
con fuego y sangre mixturado a partes
y como a cielo claro lo estrellan
algunas pecas como flores de oro.

[She is very young and has / elegance, grace and gentility. / Her broad, serious forehead is circled by / hair more golden than the sun. / Subtle eyebrows of the same color / like golden arches match / the long eyelashes underneath. / Her beautiful eyes like emeralds / are rounded by transparent crystals. / Delineated by zealous circles, stand / her two rosy and heavenly cheeks, / sharp and well-proportioned nose, / graceful mouth whose full lips / seem made of the purest coral, / where at the right time, her tempered laugh / covers and uncovers white teeth / like rich pearls or fine diamonds. / Her face is long and snow-like / mixed with fire and blood, and / like the stars in the sky, it is sprinkled / with freckles like golden flowers.]

Viana here makes use of the traditional medieval and Renaissance convention of feminine blond beauty — not without resisting as well the temptation to mock the Petrarchian model in the final image of the freckled or imperfect beauty.[136] Viana also used Espinosa's historical information which indicated that the northern region of Tenerife was inhabited by blond and blue-eyed Guanches while in the south the population seemed to have darker skin. As Viana did in the case of the giants, he once more fused literary traditions and historical narratives, this time for the purpose of setting the stage for the conflation of two supposedly different cultures that actually mirrored each other

---

[136] See Marlene K. Smith, *The Beautiful Woman in the Theater of Lope de Vega: Ideology and Mythology of Female Beauty in Seventeenth-Century Spain* (New York: Peter Lang, 1998) for a comprehensive summary of the canons of female beauty in medieval European *artes poeticae* and in Renaissance arts, as practiced in Spain (30–36, 37–50, 61–62). A poetic portrayal of women usually involved a description in "descending order from forehead to toes" or a "grouping of three," for example, three fair features: hair, hands and throat; three dark; three rosy; three long; three short; three round; and so on" (Smith, *The Beautiful Woman*, 30–31).

historically as well as physically. His polarized classification of the Guanche image operates at the ethnic level as well. In fact, when Castillo encounters Dacil for the first time near a pond where the princess had been taking a stroll (alluding perhaps to the meeting of Ulysses and Nausicaä), he can only see her shadow reflected on the water next to his own shadow. Surprised, he wonders (Viana, *Antigüedades*, 5.169–171):

> Un bulto solo soy, pero dos sombras
> veo en el agua, aquesta cierto es mía,
> mas ¿tú quién eres, sombra que me asombras?

> [I have one body only, but two shadows / I see on the water, this is certainly mine, / but, who are you, shadow that overshadows me?]

This strange image of a body with two shadows is immediately surpassed when, continuing to question himself, Castillo asks (Viana, *Antigüedades*, 5.185–186):

> Loco debo de estar, ¿qué es esto? ¿Acaso
> es Narciso a sí mismo aficionado?

> [I must be mad, what is this?
> Perhaps Narcissus loving himself?]

The allusion to the myth of Narcissus points to an exact correspondence between the body and its reflection on the water. Narcissus becomes Viana's instrument for denying the native Other and affirming the European self.[137] Viana intelligently binds "reality" and "fiction" to further support his claim of a pre-existing bond between the two, which is materialized here in the physical and symbolic resemblance. This episode is the most overt foreshadowing of the total fusion of Self and Other which the poem advocates. Castillo further exemplifies Viana's (*Antigüedades*, 5.246–248) integrating project by alluding to love as a powerful unifying force:

> Es poderoso amor como la muerte,

---

[137] See Chapter Two, note 98 on the definition of "Other" in colonial literary criticism. With regard to literary genres such as the epic, for example Ercilla's *La Araucana*, the image of the Other has been extracted throughout in terms of Renaissance rhetorical practices to the extent to which they broke formulaic constructions and embraced more innovative approaches. Whereas Ercilla seems to give a dignified place to the Other, Viana fully conforms to the dominant ideology and does not acknowledge or entertain any moral or cultural notions of Spain's Others within the context of imperial expansion.

que si la muerte aparta lo muy junto,
él junta lo apartado en unión fuerte,

[Love is as powerful as death / if death unbinds what is
united / love unites in a strong bond what is unbound,]

Although the lovers speak different languages, love becomes their common
language, the most effective vehicle for returning to that ancestral unity, to the
proper order, to the beginning. At the end of the poem, the wedding of Castillo
and Dacil becomes "the fortunate beginning of new lineage" ("principio di-
choso de linajes"), which constituted the foundation of a colonial identity aspir-
ing to be inseparably joined to Spain.[138]

The symbolic marriage of Dacil and Castillo is replicated in the allegorical
dream that Alonso de Lugo has immediately before the final victory over the
Guanches. In this apotheosis of the hero, the conquistador is taken to Mount
Teide by seven maidens — the seven Canary Islands — to marry the one who
remains single and untamed, Nivaria, one of the mythical names of Tenerife. In
a complete inversion of Guanche mythology, Mount Teide, which for the natives was the site of hell, as Viana reported in the first canto, becomes at the
end a kind of conflation of classical paganism and Christian symbology, for it
becomes Mt. Olympus or the heavens. At the majestic peak, the allegorical figure of Eternity officiates the marriage (Viana, *Antigüedades*, 15.211–213):

Nivaria se te rinde, en nombre suyo
te doy de paz la mano, que reprueba
las guerras, y la quiero hacer tu esposa.

[Nivaria surrenders to you, in her name

---

[138] The *égloga* of Dacil and Castillo, as Valbuena Prat has called it (*Historia de la poesía canaria*, 1: 20), had its homologue in the story of Tenesoya and Maciot de Béthencourt, as Cioranescu has noted (Viana, *Conquista*, ed. Cioranescu, 2: 88). Apparently Tenesoya, while bath-
ing with her ladies-in-waiting, was kidnapped by Maciot. They married out of free will and
had numerous descendants who also symbolized the union of two cultures. Cioranescu (Viana, *Conquista*, ed. idem, 2: 114 n. 164) attributes the episode, narrated in two *octavas reales*
which circulated anonymously in the Canaries since the eighteenth century, to Cairasco de
Figueroa, Viana's counterpart poet and likely mentor in Gran Canaria. If this is the case, then
both Viana and Cairasco were involved in a similar process of demarcation and self-
definition that involved a syncretic model of natives and Europeans. This early romancing of
history could be considered a "foundational fiction" that served in this case "regionalist" as
well as imperialist agendas. See Doris Sommer's comprehensive and masterful study of nineteenth-century Latin-American novels as "foundational romances" of emerging modern
nations (*Foundational Fictions: The National Romances of Latin America* [Berkeley: University of
California Press, 1991]).

I give you the hand of peace that repudiates
all wars, and I make her your wife.]

From this point on, Eternity takes Lugo and the reader on a journey made possible by the panoramic and strategic position of Mount Teide. Eternity serves
to map colonial Tenerife and to define every district, main cities, and their inhabitants. This spatial map is complemented by a temporal one in which Tenerife is forever connected to Spanish history. The poem offers a triumphant vision of the Catholic monarchs yielding to their future successor, Philip III, and
to the noble Guerra de Ayala and his poet, Antonio de Viana, whose epic will
ensure the preservation of that history.

Confronted with the image of the New World in which the Spanish enterprise had been problematized by Ercilla and openly criticized by Las Casas and
his followers, among whom Espinosa figured, Viana proposed an alternative
model. Tenerife and the Canaries became the utopian space of a harmonious
cultural encounter that was legally sound, ethnically homogeneous, and finally a
complete and perfect cultural "match." Viana used both historical narratives
and literary models to construct a history of Tenerife that conforms to the
dominant ideology of empire. In his poetic revision of history, the identity of
the Canaries ceased to be associated with the colonial space of victimization
and violence. Instead, Tenerife joined the center.

Viana's utopia, unlike More's, attempted to reject the notion of "no place"
to embrace the notion of the "place of happiness," perpetuating the mythical
image of the Canary Islands from antiquity onward. From the periphery, Viana's dream helped to shape the identity of the islands with respect to Spain
and the New World, and it continues to be the dream of many islanders, or the
dominant story. Viana was successful in appropriating the island and its inhabitants for his ideological project; however, his utopia remains a "no place," for
his elimination of the basic equation of colonialism was only partially recognized by the imperial center, as Lope de Vega's reformulation of Viana's model
would prove. The appropriation of Tenerife and the Canaries for a utopian
dream is doomed to fail, because the history of the conquest and colonization
of Tenerife was marked by the sign of violence. However, in its time, Viana's
utopian model allowed for an alternative textual space of negotiation in which
to imaginatively mitigate and perfect the unsettling colonial history of the Canary Islands and, by extension, of the New World.

CHAPTER FOUR

HISTORY AND UTOPIA: LOPE DE VEGA'S REMAKING OF THE CANARY ISLANDS AND THE SPANISH ENTERPRISE IN AMERICA

> ¿qué causa legítima o que justicia tuvieron esos Betancores de ir a inquietar, guerrear, matar y hacer esclavos a aquellos canarios, estando en sus tierras seguros y pacíficos, sin ir a Francia ni venir a Castilla ni a otra parte a molestar ni hacer injuria, violencia ni daño alguno a viviente persona del mundo? ...
>
> (Las Casas, *Historia de Indias*, 1: 108 [bk. 1, chap. 19])

> [What legitimate or just cause did the Béthencourts have to disturb, wage war, kill or enslave those Canarians who lived safe and peacefully in their land, without having gone to France or come to Castile or any other place to bother, injure, bring violence nor harm to any other living person in the world? ...]

LEONARDO TORRIANI, an engineer commissioned by Philip II of Spain to build new fortifications and inspect existing ones in the Canary Islands between 1584 and 1593, wrote one of the most valuable works about the Canary Islands in its long history. Not only did he offer a geographical and historical description of the islands and their fortifications, but he also compiled the first and only surviving drawings of the natives and several poetic compositions in the native tongue of the islanders. Following the pattern of a historical account, he first enumerated all writers from antiquity to more recent times who described the islands before him, and concluded: "but such writers, one after another, repeated the false stories which lying Fame dictated to the first who wrote the fables" ("ma essi scrittori togliendo l'un da l'altro, seguirono quello che la bugiarda fama dettò à i primi che d'esse fabulosamente scrissero") (*Die Kanarischen Inseln*, ed. Wölfel, 44–46 [chap. 1]; *Descripción*, ed. Cioranescu, 4 [chap. 1]). Torriani was indeed voicing the same opinions that Petrarch had already uttered about the disparity between the literary image and the geographical reality of the islands.[139] As the name indicates, however, the Fortunate Islands were never divorced from myth: at first, they were the "makárôn nēsoi" for the Greeks, then became the Homeric idea of the Elysian Fields or the "Fortunatae Insulae," and later the Platonic Atlantis or one of the six earthly paradises — the eastern one — as described by Felipe Bergomense.[140]

The mythical image of the islands extends beyond a location, a particular landscape, or a desirable natural abundance of wealth to include a reformulation of the historical account of their conquest and colonization in the literary production of the late sixteenth century and early seventeenth century. That is the case of Lope de Vega's play *Los guanches de Tenerife y conquista de Canaria* (1604–1606), based on Antonio de Viana's epic poem *Antigüedades de las Islas Afortunadas de la Gran Canaria, conquista de Tenerife y aparición de la santa imagen de Candelaria en verso suelto y octava rima* (Seville, 1604), which is in turn based on the historical text *Del origen y milagros de la imagen de nuestra señora de la Candelaria, que apareció en Tenerife, con la descripción de esta isla* (Seville, 1594) written by the Dominican friar Alonso de Espinosa. Lope's drama emerges, as Viana's epic poem had emerged, from the need to reformulate the historical past of the Fortunate Islands within the framework of a utopian model of cross-cultural integration and harmony. Such a reformulation responded directly to the critical view expressed by Espinosa's chronicle in 1594 and ultimately by the writings of Bartolomé de las Casas from the 1540s and 1550s, which had condemned the islands' war of conquest along with the entire Spanish enterprise in America.[141]

---

[139] See M. Martínez Hernández, *Las Islas Canarias de la Antigüedad al Renacimiento* for a survey of the textual allusions to the islands from antiquity to the Renaissance. See also A. Cioranescu, *Colón humanista: estudios de humanismo atlántico* (Madrid: Prensa Española, 1967), 211–30 for an overview of the islands' images throughout the Renaissance, and T. Cachey's works ("Petrarch," 45–59; *Le Isole Fortunate*, 11–283) for an insightful reading of Dante, Petrarch, Boccaccio, Tasso, and several historians of the *Cinquecento*.

[140] Jacobo Filippo Foresti or Felipe Bergomense, *Supplementum Chronicarum* (Brescia, 1485), as quoted by Torriani and discussed by Cioranescu (Torriani, *Descripción*, ed. Cioranescu, 140 n. 2). See also Delumeau, *History of Paradise*, for a broader context. For a description of the Canary Islands as presented in classical literature, see Antonio Cabrera Perera, *Las Islas Canarias en el mundo clásico* (Las Palmas: Gobierno Canario, 1988), 53–78, whose bilingual Spanish-English edition also offers reproductions of several world maps and Greek texts in the original language. For a more accessible and comprehensive study of the historical development of the myths associated with the islands and a complete bibliography, see Martínez Hernández, *Canarias en la mitología* and *Las Islas Canarias*.

[141] The influence of Las Casas's ideas in Alonso de Espinosa's chronicle was demonstrated in Chapter Two of this study. It is worth mentioning here that the resonances of Lascasian thought were not confined to historical accounts but also reached the dramatic genre rather early. The *Brevísima*, for instance, is thought to be the basis for another critical text, the theater piece *Auto de las Cortes de la Muerte* by Micael de Carvajal and Luis Hurtado de Toledo, written between 1552 and 1557 and published in Toledo in 1557 (Marcos

Lope's drama nonetheless exhibits a critical position, which sheds light on the role of the Canary Islands and the New World in the cultural imagination of Spain.

1. THE HISTORY PLAY: OLD AND NEW READINGS

Before exploring Lope's dramatic recreation of the history of the conquest of Tenerife, it is necessary to establish the dramatist's relationship to history and the historical drama. Lope's biographical information, as well as his dramatic corpus, show a long-standing interest in history (Shannon, *Visions of the New World*, 188–95). This interest not only included Lope's own personal pursuit of a position as Royal Chronicler (Bershas, "Lope de Vega and the Post of Royal Chronicler," 109–17; Weiner, "Puesto de cronista," 727), but it also determined the composition of a great many of his dramatic works. In keeping with a practice common at the time, Lope found inspiration for the fictional world of his theatrical pieces in historical events, texts, and personalities, and such was the case of *Los guanches de Tenerife*. A good starting point for the analysis of a historical play is the examination of the theoretical issues generated by the inclusion of historical material in a work of fiction. These issues address the problems of definition and classification within the aesthetic demands of the genre, as well as the conceptual functions of the different manipulations of history as contemporary critics have explored them.

"It is evident that the poet's function is not to report things that have happened, but rather to tell of such things as might happen, things that are possibilities by virtue of being in themselves inevitable or probable," stated Aristotle (*Poetics* 54) in his attempt to define the poet in contrast to the historian. Alonso López Pinciano in the sixteenth century took up the paradigm in his monumental *Philosophía antigua poética*, and further explored the difference between history and fiction only to show, as the writing practices of the time demon-

---

Morínigo, *América en el teatro de Lope de Vega* [Buenos Aires: Instituto de Filología, 1946], 42–47; Francisco Ruiz Ramón, "El Nuevo Mundo en el teatro clásico," in *Celebración y catársis (leer el teatro español)* [Murcia: Nogués, 1988], 69–137, here 74–82). In scene nineteen of the play, a group of Amerindians appears in a court, presided over by Death, to voice their protest against abuses committed by the Spaniards. Death is assisted by a jury whose members are the following six characters: three friars from three different religious orders, a Dominican, a Franciscan, and an Augustinian (who sympathize with and console the Indians, lamenting the outcome of the discovery of the New World), and the other three, Satan, the Flesh and the World (who act as defense lawyers for the accused Spaniards). The Amerindians' denunciation echoes that of Las Casas, and although Death remains impartial in the final judgement, he admitted the rightness of the Indians' complaint (Ruiz Ramón, "El Nuevo Mundo," 74–82). Since Lope's theatrical production came much later, any potential traces of Las Casas's ideas can have been mediated only through other texts.

strated, that such a dichotomy was more fluid than rigid. In fact, history and fiction were separated by the thin and permeable membrane of rhetoric that allowed a mutual exchange of formal elements (López Pinciano, *Philosophía antigua poética*, 2: 98). The poet could experiment with several combinations of *fábulas* or plots. One plot could be all based on lies, another could be based on a lie but arrive at a truth, while the last could use an historical truth as the inspiration for many fictions. The construction of such plots could in turn be encapsulated in either epic, tragic, or comic modes (López Pinciano, *Philosophía antigua poética*, 2: 12–15). With respect to drama, Torres Naharro, one of Lope's predecessors, distinguished between the *comedia a noticia* and the *comedia a fantasía*; the first upheld the literal truth while the second merely aspired to verisimilitude (Lauer, "Use and Abuse of History," 17–18).[142] Every attempt, however, to trace a fine line between the two was sabotaged by the artifice contained in the making of the *fábula*. Lope's own views on the issue eloquently illustrate the difficulty inherent in separating history from fiction:

> Repartieron entre sí las artes liberales, y cupó á las más famosas la historia y la poesía, que todo puede ser uno, aunque haya opiniones contrarias respecto de la verdad y la licencia: cosas en su género distintas; pero pueden usarse iguales, habiendo historia en verso y poesía en prosa ....
>
> [Among the liberal arts, history and poetry occupied the most prominent places; the two can be one, although there are contrary opinions with respect to what is true or what is not. They belong to different genres, but they can be used indistinctly; thus, history could be in verse and poetry in prose ....][143]

The so-called history play, as it was conceived in the Golden Age of Spanish literature, reflected after all a somewhat elusive classification.

These formal considerations have been complemented with conceptual ones in recent critical studies. Several contemporary critics have attempted to categorize the "national history play" in terms of the functionality or ideological purpose to which the historical material was put. The use of history in the thea-

---

142 For a general overview of dramatic literary theory in Golden Age Spain, see Federico Sánchez Escribano and Alberto Porqueras Mayo, *Preceptiva dramática española: del Renacimiento al Barroco* (Madrid: Gredos, 1972), 57–351, giving selections of texts from Juan de Mena to Bances Candamo. See also Miguel Zugasti's theoretical summary on the relationship between poetry and history in the drama of the Spanish Golden Age and more specifically in the context of Tirso de Molina's plays about the Pizarro brothers (*La "trilogía de los Pizarros" de Tirso de Molina*, 4 vols. [Trujillo: Obra Pía, 1993], 1: 49–60).

143 As quoted by Zugasti (*La "trilogía de los Pizarros,"* 1: 55) from the text of Lope's dedication for the second part of *Don Juan de Castro*.

ter has been generally divided into three main categories by contemporary critics. The first — rejected by some critics as being unworthy of classification —
uses history as background, as a mere excuse for a plot of timeless significance.
The second, inherited from the humanist tradition, uses history as a pastoral
genre; in other words, a manipulation of the past occurs to reflect or fit present
concerns, and this process can take the form of the celebratory, exemplary,
hortatory, or admonitory. The third considers history a subject and is concerned with the past for what it is, the past.[144] These considerations reveal that
the inclusion of historical material in dramas may be part of a greater project in
which dramatists, willingly or not, explore and influence the social-political
sphere.

Critics such as José Antonio Maravall and José María Díez Borque mainly
conceive the *comedia* as one more manifestation of the religious and political
hegemonic power which dominated the whole of society in seventeenth-
century Spain. They argue that dramatic representations are nothing more than
an instrument of manipulation destined to consolidate the political order of a
directed society. The *comedia*, then, has been anachronistically denominated as
propaganda which allowed only a very controlled and inconsequential escapism
from the established social and political order.[145] In a similar way, the model of
subversion/containment, made popular by the "new historicists" who have
studied Elizabethan theater, redefines the political nature of dramas. At first,
the debate suggested that a certain apparent subversion of political and social
order as revealed in many plays was only one of the required mechanisms for
the affirmation of the established power structure. More recently, however,
new-historicist criticism has evolved into a more fluid model, allowing other
negotiations to open more possibilities between the extremes of subversion and
containment.[146] Above all, and despite differences in methodology, these socio-

---

[144] See Walter Cohen, *Drama of a Nation: Public Theater in Renaissance England and Spain*
(Ithaca: Cornell University Press, 1985), 218–32, for a summary of these categories as they
are set forth by several critics of Elizabethan drama. He also examines the outcomes of these
respective manipulations of historical material. History as pastoral runs the risk of distorting
the past to conform to the present, while history as subject can become antiquarianism and
lead to the "belief in the continuity between past and present inherent in the providential[ist]
view" (Cohen, *Drama of a Nation*, 219).

[145] In *La cultura del Barroco* (Barcelona: Ariel, 1989), Maravall deals with the period in
which the Baroque flourished in Spain, and he sees all artistic manifestations (creations and
performances) as tools of the exercise of power by the state, in which any apparent disorder
is always absorbed by order. In *Sociedad y teatro en la España de Lope de Vega* (Barcelona: Antoni
Bosch, 1978), Díez Borque applies Maravall's ideas to theatrical practices. Although this
critical tendency has proven illuminating, it has not done justice to the *comedia* or to its complex artistic devices and functions.

[146] Although the "new historicist" approach emerged on the American academic scene
as a reaction against the New Criticism and more recent formalisms, producing studies primarily about Renaissance England, several Hispanists have successfully adopted this critical

logical and new historicist critical reflections have made the claim that European dramatic production was a political activity and that it addressed the ideological mechanisms of power.

Rejecting the notion of the *comedia* as propaganda (or as instrument for containment), in her article "Lope de Vega: Propagandist?," Charlotte Stern has offered one of the most insightful theoretical guides for the reading of a *comedia*. Stern's reflections on Lope and his works revise the reductive if not incomplete treatment that classical Spanish theater has suffered under the magnifying glass of the dominant criticism from Karl Vossler to Díez Borque. What is most evident in sociological criticism, which otherwise has contributed important readings to the field, is that the dramatic structure of a particular play tends to be read as determined by one economic class or cultural group. Stern proposes instead that Lope's dramas should be read on three levels. The first operates under the assumption that Lope shared social values and set out to promote social cohesion in order to uphold a monarchic political order. However, on a second level, the aesthetic form is "less bound to a particular moment," and dramatic modes introduce ambiguities and contradictions into the possible meanings of the play. A third level reveals, then, that any surface meaning is "filtered out or transmitted into ethical issues of universal significance." For Stern ("Lope de Vega," 1–36) such readings find powerful confirmation when dealing with comic and tragic modes; the pastoral and the historical modes, however, offer more difficulties and can easily be trapped by the label of propaganda.

---

perspective, as it pertains to the historicity of literary texts and the power plays, in order to analyze Spanish Golden Age dramatic production before the emergence of the term "new historicism." This is the case of Margaret Greer, "Constituting Community: A New Historical Perspective on the *Autos* of Calderón," in *New Historicism and the Comedia: Poetics, Politics and Praxis*, ed. José A. Madrigal (Boulder: University of Colorado Press, 1997), 33–60, who not only examines Calderonian *comedias* and *autos* from this perspective, but also offers a useful summary of the theoretical critical approach. The subversion/containment dichotomy, first articulated by Jonathan Dollimore, has then been associated with Stephen Greenblatt, who in "Invisible Bullets" makes a case for subversion insofar as it serves containment. Later, however, in "Shakespearean Negotiations," the model of power becomes less rigid. Greer ("Constituting Community," 33–60) proposes that Calderón does not have one single strategy for addressing authority, but that "he adopts a position of critical support that is nuanced to suit the audience at hand." With respect to Lope de Vega, see the recent study by Elizabeth R. Wright, *Pilgrimage to Patronage: Lope de Vega and the Court of Philip III, 1598–1621* (London: Associated University Presses, 2001), 13–163, who has masterfully disentangled literature and politics in the Court of Philip III using Greenblatt's notion of "self-fashioning" but pointing out and complementing the limitations of new historicism. I bring up the new historicist methodological approach, in its applications to the Golden Age *comedia*, mainly because of the method's concerns with politics. My study is centrally concerned with ideology, which is a category analytically distinct from politics, but always related to it, insofar as ideology can be broadly used to designate a coherent system of political ideas.

In his Marxist approach, Walter Cohen agrees somewhat with the subversive nature of certain modes like tragedy. Cohen (*Drama of a Nation*, 228–29) also considers more innovative those plays in which the historical drama is indistinguishable from tragedy because of "their serious treatment of everyday life, their break with generic, ideological and social convention" at the cost of "eliminating that concern with public affairs which characterizes the history play." Tragedy then becomes "peripheral," because it challenges the established order but is incapable of making any significant changes in its core (Cohen, *Drama of a Nation*, 232). Stern recognizes that plays dealing with the *res historica* leave less space for ambiguous readings so the historical mode remains somewhat intangible — dramatists and critics have less freedom, thus Stern does not give any further suggestions on how to read a historical play. Cohen, when dealing with the historical drama in the context of the New World, sees only a transfer of the Reconquista paradigm to America, based on the reading of only one play, *Arauco domado*. He looks at this play as another exercise in a project of imperial harmony. In his own words, "… the Hispanic nation is internally harmonious; it has exported its problems. The late-sixteenth-century Golden Age national history play … tends to emphasize the struggle between Catholic Spain and its infidel, external foes. When the dramatized events postdate the Reconquest, the structure of the Christian/Moor struggle is simply shipped abroad, for instance to the New World" (Cohen, *Drama of a Nation*, 227).

Despite Cohen's serious comparison between English and Spanish national history plays, his analysis (as in his reading of *Arauco domado*) can be characterized in the same way that Stern criticized Maravall and Díez Borque; that is, the imposition of a cultural paradigm on a dramatic composition that has not been subjected to an analysis of its complex plot structure. Furthermore, the analysis of a play without taking into consideration its relation to its sources (i.e., Ercilla's *La Araucana*) or its place within a much larger thematic corpus (i.e., *El Nuevo Mundo, Los guanches, La Araucana*, etc.) likewise fails to do justice to a drama or a dramatist.

The challenge for today's critic lies in the ability to find in the dramatic use of historical material room for maneuvering, a space where ambiguities and criticism regarding the Spanish colonial enterprise overseas may surface to put such disturbing national issues to the test. The objective of my study is to analyze Lope's historical drama *Los guanches de Tenerife*, as a significant component of both a thematically coherent dramatic corpus and a collective conscience which negotiated the conflicted history of Spain in the New World.

2. LOPE DE VEGA AND THE NEW WORLD: A CRITICAL OVERVIEW

Although *Los guanches de Tenerife* addresses the history of the Canary Islands, I argue that the play also serves as a space of negotiation in which a certain degree of knowledge and level of reflection about the conquest and colonization of the New World take central stage. Thus, the textual analysis of *Los guanches de Tenerife* must first take into consideration its thematic link to the corpus of Spanish Golden Age historical dramas that directly take on the conquest and colonization of the New World.

Los guanches is thematically linked to Lope's *El Nuevo Mundo descubierto por Cristóbal Colón* and *Arauco domado*. All three plays also happened to coincide chronologically, as they were written in the first decade of the seventeenth century. A reading of *Los guanches*, therefore, must take into consideration the many readings of the other two.[147] A review of the criticism points to an early debate

---

[147] *Los guanches* has been seen as part of the Golden Age Americanist dramatic corpus, but only marginally: Morínigo, *América en el teatro de Lope de Vega*; Andrés Lorenzo Cáceres, "Las Canarias en el teatro de Lope de Vega," *El Museo Canario* 3 (1935): 2–32, and idem, "Las Canarias de Lope de Vega," ibid. 4 (1936): 38–40; Jack Weiner, "La guerra y la paz espirituales en tres comedias de Lope de Vega," *Revista de estudios hispánicos* 17 (1983): 65–79; José A. Madrigal, "El discurso primitivista en las obras de colonización de Lope de Vega," *Círculo* 20 (1991): 147–55. Only Sebastián de la Nuez y Caballero ("Las Canarias en la obra de Lope de Vega," *Anuario de estudios atlánticos* 10 [1964]: 11–159) seriously studies the particularities of the play within the local as well as the more universal context of conquests and colonization. See also a more recent article by Carlos Brito Díaz, "Visiones del indígena canario en el teatro del Siglo do Oro," *Revista de literatura* 61 (1999): 225–37. My study is concerned, not only with *El Nuevo Mundo* and *Arauco domado*, but with all the plays that Lope and other dramatists wrote on the topic of imperial expansion, although the plays mentioned above in particular are chronologically closer to *Los guanches*.

El Nuevo Mundo was written in the period between 1598 and 1603 according to Menéndez y Pelayo ("Introduction") and S. Griswold Morley and Courtney Bruerton (*The Chronology of Lope de Vega's Comedias* (New York: Modern Language Association, 1940), or in 1605 according to Entrambasaguas (see J. M. Gárate Córdoba, *La poesía del descubrimiento* [Madrid: Cultura Hispánica, 1977], 57). The date for *Arauco domado* is more disputable. Menéndez y Pelayo affirms that it was written in 1625, Morley and Bruerton suggest a date prior to 1604, and Medina claims 1620 as the date (see R. M. Shannon, *Visions of the New World in the Drama of Lope de Vega* [New York: Peter Lang, 1989], 105–107). Shannon, however, convincingly argues for the period 1604–1618, and more specifically 1607 or 1609, because the title appeared in the 1618 edition of *El peregrino en su patria* but not in the 1604 one. Shannon (*Visions of the New World*, 106–7) further supports his argument contextually by appealing to the significance of these dates in the Hurtado de Mendoza family. It is important to take into consideration the documented fact that Lope had already read by 1598 Pedro de Oña's epic poem *Arauco domado* (1596) (A. Miró Quesada, *América en el teatro de Lope de Vega* [Lima, 1935], 61–62), whereas Ercilla's *La Araucana* circulated constantly from 1569, the date of the publication of the *Primera Parte*.

As Morínigo has established, other plays such as *El arenal de Sevilla* (1603) are thematically connected to the New World. Although this play is chronologically close to the ones I am focusing on, it is not historical and its references to the New World are peripheral. In addition, Lope wrote the *auto sacramental* called *La Araucana*, *El Brasil restituido* which dates from 1625, and a *comedia* about Cortés, now lost. See J. T. Medina, *Dos comedias famosas y un auto sacramental*, 2 vols. (Santiago de Chile: Litografía Barcelona, 1915); W. L. Fichter, "Lope

about these plays which still influences the ways many critics view Lope's dramas. Some adopt a moralistic outlook which is based on the author's biography; others evaluate the plays' aesthetic value, taking into consideration the speed with which Lope exercised his craftsmanship; while still others search for evidence that supports an agenda of imperial propaganda.

The late eighteenth- and turn-of-the-nineteenth-century Spanish playwright Leandro Fernández de Moratín (1760–1828) (*Obras póstumas* 3: 133–35), for example, criticized *El Nuevo Mundo* for its nonsensical and distasteful mixture of theology and lust, and suggested that *Arauco domado* was one of those *comedias* that Lope wrote "after saying mass while his lunch was heating on the stove" ("después de decir misa, mientras le calentaban el almuerzo"). Although Menéndez y Pelayo (101) disagreed with Moratín, he lamented the good fortune of the unworthy play about Columbus, which had been translated into several languages, because of its "treatment of such an important subject in a careless, superficial, and infantile aesthetic manner."[148] In recent years, other

---

de Vega's *La conquista de Cortés* and *El Marqués del Valle*," *Hispanic Review* 3 (1935): 163–65; C. Romero Muñoz, "Lope de Vega y 'Fernando de Zárate': *El Nuevo Mundo* (y *Arauco domado*) en *La Conquista de México*," *Studi di letteratura ispano-americana* 15–16 (1983): 243–64. Other Golden Age dramatists also inspired by the conquest of the New World include Tirso de Molina, who wrote three plays about the Pizarro brothers, *Todo es dar en una cosa*, *La lealtad contra la envidia*, and *Amazonas en las Indias* (1626–1631), and Calderón de la Barca, for his *La aurora en Copacabana* (1653–1661). See Shannon, *Visions of the New World*, 6–7 for a more complete list, which includes plays by other major as well as minor dramatists.

[148] For a brief history of the critical reception of *El Nuevo Mundo* in Spain and France and for excellent annotations in French, see Lope de Vega, *El Nuevo Mundo descubierto por Cristóbal Colón*, ed. J. Lemartinel and C. Minguet (Lille: Presses Universitaires de Lille, 1980), 1–69. Gárate Córdoba in his *Poesía del descubrimiento* also offers a detailed summary of the principal criticism trends from the nineteenth century to the present, but fails to offer any new insights into the play itself. He begins his summary with the negative observations of Moratín and Eugenio de Ochoa and goes on to express the positive evaluation of the French Hispanist M. Damas-Hinard, from whose outlook Gárate Córdoba is not far removed. He also presents a summary of the attacks that the drama has received from Edmund Barry and Calixto Oyuela, and examines the critical views of Menéndez y Pelayo, Lasso de la Vega, and Miró Quesada. He describes the poetic praises of Vossler, followed by a consideration of the historical richness that Rodríguez Casado and Morínigo see in the play. Gárate Córdoba also applauds Valentín de Pedro's protest against the vision of Lope as a critic and detractor of imperialism, and lauds Jorge Campos for his textual comparison between Lope's drama and López de Gómara's chronicle. Gárate Córdoba concludes his review with Joaquín Entrambasaguas, who re-edited the play in 1963 prior to Lemartinel and Minguet's French edition of 1980, and whose comprehensive analysis helpfully contextualizes the production of the play and Lope's historical choices (*Poesía del descubrimiento*, 57–80). For a more contemporary reception of Lope's play, see the recent studies by John Brotherton, "Lope's *El Nuevo Mundo descubierto por Cristóbal Colón*: Convention and Ideology," *Bulletin of the Comediantes* 46 (1994): 33–48, on ideological uses of conventions; and Teresa Soufas, "Rhetorical Appropriation: Lope's New World Play and Canonicity," *Hispanic Review* 67 (1999): 319–31, on the play as

studies have attempted to investigate the theme of the conquest of the Indies as narrated by the historical chronicles and appropriated into Lope's theater. Unfortunately, the great majority of articles produced either fall into the same moral and aesthetic judgments of Moratín and Menéndez y Pelayo (e.g., Miró Quesada, *América*; Leavitt, "Lope de Vega"; Flint, "Colón") or tend to reduce the theme to a laudatory survey of allusions with no further argumentative development (e.g., Fernández Shaw, "América"; Miramón, "El Nuevo Mundo") or devote themselves primarily to the identification of sources (e.g., Campos, "Lope de Vega"; Minian de Alfie, "Lector de cronistas" and "Nombres indígenas").[149] Azorín, however, raised long ago the issue of the dramatist's

---

an "allegory of canonization." See also an interesting article that involves in general Lope's plays about the New World by Teresa J. Kirschner, "Enmascaramiento y desenmascaramiento del discurso sobre el 'indio' en el teatro del 'Nuevo Mundo' de Lope de Vega," in *Relaciones literarias entre España y América en los siglos XVI y XVII*, ed. Ysla Campbell (Ciudad Juárez, México: Universidad Autónoma de Ciudad Juárez, 1992), 47–64.

[149] Miró Quesada (*América*, 91–96) looks for America in Lope's *El Nuevo Mundo*, *La Araucana*, *Arauco domado*, and *El Brasil* only to conclude that Lope's knowledge is limited and superficial and that even though "he alludes to America, he also eludes it." In his analysis of the American plays, Sturgis E. Leavitt ("Lope de Vega y el Nuevo Mundo," *Mapocho* 1 [1963]: 225–30, here 226–27) dismisses *La Araucana* as Miró Quesada and Menéndez y Pelayo had done before him; Leavitt finds Moratín's comments about *El Nuevo Mundo* somewhat severe, but coincides with the latter in his negative aesthetic judgment of *Arauco domado*. In the end, Leavitt ("Lope de Vega," 228) considers Lope a manipulator of the *vulgo* and a loyal servant of his patrons. The only interesting reading that Leavitt offers is that of the role of Terrazas in *El Nuevo Mundo*, as both *pícaro* and preacher of the Catholic faith, which suggests that Lope was criticizing Terrazas' religious mission. The critic ("Lope de Vega," 229) speculates, with no evidence, that for this reason the play must have been a failure in Lope's time.

Weston Flint's criticism ("Colón en el teatro español," *Estudios americanos* 22 [1961]: 165–86, here 181–86) of the figure of Columbus in Lope's play does not offer anything new; on the contrary, in his analysis he isolates the character of Columbus from the dramatic structure of the work and complains about the lack of heroism in the portrayal of the character. Alberto Miramón ("El Nuevo Mundo en el universo dramático de Lope de Vega," *Revista de Indias* 28 [1968]: 169–77) merely offers praise for Lope's love of America. Carlos Fernández Shaw ("América en Lope de Vega," *Cuadernos hispanomericanos* 161–162 [1963]: 678–83, here 682–83) suggests that Lope was very well informed and he rejects Miró Quesada's negative evaluation. On the other hand, Jorge Campos and Raquel Minian de Alfie study the plays in relation to their sources among the chronicles of the Indies. Gómara and his *Historia general de Indias* is for J. Campos ("Lope de Vega y el descubrimiento colombino," *Revista de Indias* 38–39 [1949]: 751–54) the main source for *El Nuevo Mundo*; R. Minián de Alfie ("Lope, lector de cronistas de Indias," *Filología* 11 [1965]: 1–21; "Nombres indígenas en una comedia de Lope," *Filología* 7 [1961]: 173–75) agrees with Campos but rejects his idea of the influence of Cieza de León and attempts to incorporate into her own essay all previous studies of sources (Menéndez y Pelayo, Vossler, Miró Quesada, Rodríguez Casado, Campos, and Medina) in order to conclude that Lope must have used a variety of sources. One of the valuable results of Shannon's more recent study (*Visions of the New World*, 189) is precisely to

political and ideological views. He alluded to Lope's amorality as a response, by and large, to the amorality of his society; above all, he sarcastically referred to the aesthetic condemnation of *El Nuevo Mundo* as a way of condemning the Spanish conquest of America. He made reference to those critics who considered Lope's play an attack on the sixteenth-century conquests, and remarked that, although present-day Spaniards should not be held culpable for the sins of their fathers, there were no excuses that could be offered to justify Spain's past.[150] As Azorín recognized, Lope, along with the dramatic genre in which he practiced, served and continues to serve as the springboard for studies which mainly conceive of the *comedia* as inhabiting a rigid social structure and as a means to reinforce religious values and imperialistic interests. Once again, one confronts the questions: To what degree was Lope informed about and concerned with the conquest and colonization of the New World as he reconstructed the historical past of the Canary Islands? What ideological views prevailed in his plays? What literary mechanisms did he design to reflect on the event?

The limited number of plays that address the conquest of the New World has traditionally served as an indication that this particular silence might have resulted from a lack of interest in the subject on the part of Spanish dramatists.[151] Although much speculation has surrounded the issue, several studies

---

show that Lope never utilized one single source but rather several, and that he followed his sources somewhat closely.

[150] Azorín's ("Retratos de algunos malos españoles y de un español honorario," in idem, *Obras completas* [Madrid: Aguilar, 1947], 2: 651–52) exact words in his "gallery of bad Spaniards" are: "¿Por qué es un mal español Lope? ... Por su comedia El Nuevo Mundo descubierto por Colón ... Un consenso universal ha condenado nuestra conquista americana. Lope marcha en compañia, entre nosotros, de Voltaire, Montaigne, Herder, Andrés Chénier ... No necesitamos, como ahora se hace, que se nos excuse por lo que hicimos en aquellas centurias ... Hombres habrá siempre que condenen la iniquidad y que crean que el haberla cometido ciudadanos antecesores suyos, tres siglos atrás, no es para ellos ningún baldón. El baldón consistiría — puerilmente — en querer paliar lo que no tiene paliativo." See also Gárate Córdoba (*Poesía del descubrimiento*, 73–74).

[151] The issue of why Lope or any of his contemporaries did not write more about America has served as a significant research query for many studies. In fact, one of the indirect undertakings of critics, as they attempted to classify the entire dramatic production of the Golden Age, was to continue enriching the list of plays (and poetry in general) concerned with American themes. This is the case of J. T. Medina's survey (*Dos comedias*, 1: 3–149) and that of W. L. Fichter in his classification of *La conquista de Cortés y El Marqués del Valle* (163–65); Miró Quesada's readings as well as Morínigo's extensive study help definitively to shape the list, and so does Ángel Franco (*El tema de América en los autores del siglo de Oro* [Madrid: n.p., 1954]). The inquiry of C. Romero Muñoz, as he shows in his article about the Cortés drama cycle and further explains in a footnote continues the search ("Lope de Vega," 253, n. 11); while Glen F. Dille's article ("El descubrimiento y la conquista de América en la comedia," *Hispania* 71 [1988]: 492–502, here 493) lists three more plays, and Frederick de Armas ("Fashioning a New World: Lope de Vega and Claramonte's *El nuevo rey gallinato*," in *Critical*

have offered plausible explanations. For example, Marcos Morínigo's pioneering and valuable analysis disclosed that the idea of America, with all its complexities and unconventionality, was already incorporated into the world vision — however fantastic it might be — of Lope and his audience (Morínigo, *América*, 8–9). The critic points out (*América*, 18–19), nevertheless, that insufficient military glory as well as the lack of noble leadership in the enterprise could explain the absence of greater literary praise of both conquistadors and the conquest in Golden Age Spain. Furthermore, Morínigo (*América*, 251) assumes that Lope's ideas reflect the general perception of his audience; therefore, one is led to believe from this study that the theater-going public at large shared Lope's critical position with respect to greed and the imperfect process of evangelization practiced by the Spaniards (Morínigo, *América*, 146–48). Although Morínigo offers little evidence for this conclusion, his arguments might have profited by considering other theatrical works, such as the many *danzas* in the Corpus Christi celebrations of the time, which found inspiration in America.[152]

The analysis of Lope's plays in light of the theoretical frame established by the paradigmatic Sepúlveda-Las Casas debate has shown itself to be much more

---

Essays on the Literature of Spain and Spanish America, ed. L. T. González del Valle and J. Baena [Boulder: University of Colorado Press, 1991] 1–10, here 2) recovers Claramonte's *El nuevo rey gallinato* as the possible first comedy about the New World, although it was apparently dissolved or disguised as a shapeless mass of exotic continents that bore no direct reference to the New World. See also Thomas Benedetti's more recent article ("The Noble Triumph of Cortés: *El valeroso español y primero de su casa*," in *Looking at the "comedia" in the Year of the Quincentennial*, ed. B. Mujica and S. D. Voros [Lanham, MD: University Press of America, 1993], 3–12) about Gaspar de Ávila's *El valeroso español y primero en su casa* that was devoted to Hernán Cortés. The issue remains unresolved and the list of plays keeps growing; I also propose to study in depth *Los guanches de Tenerife* in light of its relationship to the New World.

[152] Jean Sentaurens enumerates and discusses the number of *danzas* in which Amerindians served as the protagonists during the festivities of Corpus Christi in Seville. Ercilla's epic poem, for example, serves as the basis for five *danzas* in 1613, 1633, 1638, 1642, and 1654 (J. Sentaurens, *Seville et le théâtre de la fin du Moyen Age à la fin du XVIIe siècle* [Talence: Presses Universitaires de Bordeaux, 1984], 789). The New World was also the theme of another series of *danzas*: *Los Indios* in 1570, 1593, 1597, and 1608; *Indios e Indias* in 1574 and 1586; *La conquista de las Indias* in 1610, 1613, 1625, 1629 and 1630; and *La sujeción de los reinos de Nueva España* in 1604. Sentaurens (*Seville et le théâtre*, 793–94) also affirms that, contrary to what the modern critic may think, the Spaniards were not the sole protagonists and that, on the contrary, the Indians occupied a central role: Moctezuma, for example, served as the central character in three *danzas* in 1592, 1636, and 1693. I cannot offer any further insights into the importance of these *danzas* in conjunction with the corpus of the *comedias* dealing with the New World, but this is a path worth pursuing. With respect to religious theater, the critical reception of Lope's *La Araucana* has been very similar to that of *Arauco domado*. Regarding Calderón's *Autos sacramentales*, Parker ("The New World," 261–69) has studied the use of the marginal presence of America embodied by an Indian character who represented the allegorical figures of Idolatry or Atheism.

fruitful. In discussing the controversy, Robert Shannon (*Visions of the New World*, 11–42), for example, includes the figure of Vitoria as well to demonstrate how Lope's knowledge of the chronicles of the Indies and the mid-sixteenth-century debates on the conquest of America permeates his American plays. Shannon (*Visions of the New World*, 5, 44, 191) concludes that Lope's attitude, "proud yet troubled," does not ignore the controversy, but rather subordinates the problems emerging from the interpretation of the conquest of the New World to the messianic mission of the Spaniards and the necessity of furthering the teachings of the Roman Catholic Church there. Shannon (*Visions of the New World*, 22) denies an explicit relation between Vitoria and Lope but he states that the widely influential Salamanca professor criticized the ruthless behavior of the Spaniards and had a moderate view which questioned the Spanish enterprise in America (21–42); therefore, one must conclude that Vitoria's position is quite similar to Lope's, although the latter was limited by the demands for entertainment prescribed by the *comedia*. Shannon repeats the commonplace error of Vitoria's opinions being close to those of Las Casas; yet we know that ideologically Vitoria shared the same premises as Sepúlveda, which departed from a reading of Aristotle positing a clear hierarchy between those destined to rule and those destined to be ruled; or, in Sepúlveda's words, the supremacy of perfection over imperfection, of strength over weakness and of virtue over vice (Méchoulan, *El honor de Dios*, 64–65; Adorno, "Los debates," 47–66). La Nuez y Caballero, who has written the most important study about *Los guanches*, in fact makes an explicit connection between the ideas of Vitoria and Lope's creation while pointing to some nuances of Las Casas's powerful denouncements. La Nuez y Caballero ("Las Canarias," 149–59), however, sees the dramatist as somewhat distanced from abstract theories and controversial political debates and concerned mainly with more mundane themes of his time. Within this context, Lope's position — although not coinciding completely in time and agenda with the relevant and subtle differences among the positions of Las Casas, Sepúlveda, and Vitoria — must be as carefully reconsidered at this time for the no less ideological nature of the subject that he has chosen to portray. The fact that Espinosa's history, the main source of Viana's epic poem which Lope appropriated, is unquestionably linked to the debate, demands a reconsideration. Lope's Spain was the product of these legal and moral debates which over the decades continued to be reenacted in one form or another.

Francisco Ruiz Ramón has further developed these issues, taking an even more radical step towards the definition of a "collective consciousness" — shared by Lope and his contemporaries — in which the anguished conscience of a Las Casas coexisted with and undermined the imperialist pride of a Sepúlveda. Such an ambivalence expresses the voice of a divided social consciousness that struggled to express itself in the dramatic genre (Ruiz Ramón, "El Nuevo Mundo," 137). According to Ruiz Ramón's innovative critique of this corpus, Lope's as well as Tirso's "American" plays set themselves a double purpose: the celebration of imperial power and expansion and the simultaneous questioning of the same enterprise. Responding to this thematic grouping, Ruiz Ramón's readings approach these dramas in their complex theatrical functions and demonstrate that, contrary to previous analyses, the authors' critical intentions convincingly prevailed over the celebratory.[153]

By placing in the foreground Lope's *Los guanches de Tenerife* as an essential part of the dramatic corpus that deals with the New World, my study will attempt to answer the question that concerned Morínigo, of why the conquest and colonization of the New World was not as well represented as it might have been in the thematic contents of Golden Age drama. After all, the magnitude of an event that elicited so many political and moral debates must have been influential in the artistic production of its time, as Ruiz Ramón's arguments seem to suggest. I shall argue here that Lope's views on the conquest and colonization of America fifty years after the Valladolid debate find yet another space in which to negotiate his critical gaze within the expected imperial celebration of his times: the dramatic locus of the Canary Islands.

3. LOPE'S *COMEDIAS* AND THE HISTORY OF THE CANARY ISLANDS

Los guanches de Tenerife and the dramatization of the account of the life of *San Diego de Alcalá* are the two plays in which Lope refers to the history of the Canary Islands. The latter, in brief scenes during the second act, tells the story of San Diego as a missionary friar in Gran Canaria where he encounters a barbaric queen and her subjects. The play, following Rivadeneyra's *Flos Sanctorum*, according to Menéndez y Pelayo (Vega, "San Diego," ed. Menéndez y Pelayo, 4–11), offers a generalized exotic view of the natives which is deeply rooted in the stereotype of the savage and has no particular relation to the history or customs of the Canary Islands apart from the episode of the apostle's visit.[154] The

---

[153] Zugasti (*La "trilogía de los Pizarros,"* 1: 98), in his useful study of Tirso's trilogy about the Pizarros, fundamentally agrees with Ruiz Ramón's ideas. The first, nevertheless, is less inclined to accept a Spanish "guilty conscience" and is more in favor of a sort of "duality" that prevails in New World plays of the period.

[154] *San Diego de Alcalá* cannot really be considered illustrative of Lope's interest in the Canary Islands since there are no references to common places in history; on the contrary, the scenes dealing with the natives are completely irrelevant to the main action and show a total disregard for island customs. For these reasons, I prefer, as Lorenzo Cáceres did ("Las Canarias," 30), the date of composition of 1588 (given by Menéndez y Pelayo, who followed Franz Grillparzer) rather than 1613 (see below). It is hard to imagine that Lope, after his encounter with Viana's text and his writing of *Los guanches*, would portray the natives in such a simple stereotype. The early date has been challenged, however, by Morley and Bruerton, who propose 1613 as the year of composition (*Chronology*, 26, 41), and this hypothesis has been accepted by Thomas E. Case ("History and Structural Unity in *San Diego de Alcalá*,"

scenes (*San Diego*, 2.1166–1309) served as an excuse to introduce *el baile canario* (2.1310–57), a dance that was very well known on and off the stage, having been presented at various European courts, such as that of Louis XIV and among the German aristocratic elite; by the end of the sixteenth century, it had entered the realm of the popular spectacle.[155] The *baile*, as well as the feathered costumes of the natives, represented an element of dramatic effectiveness which balanced the seriousness of this particular *comedia de santos*, but it was used in the theater along with a great variety of many *danzas* and *bailes* to exploit its appeal to the popular, the exotic, and the erotic.[156] While *San Diego*'s connection to historical material is weak, that is not the case of *Los guanches de Tenerife*.

Bulletin of the Comediantes 32 [1980]: 55–62) in his (perhaps unsuccessful) attempt to prove that the play deals with the expulsion of the *moriscos*. As author of a valuable study about both *Los guanches* and *San Diego*, La Nuez y Caballero ("Las Canarias," 12–13) identifies two epochs in Lope's writing about the islands: 1588–1600, when he wrote *La Dragontea* and *San Diego*, and 1600–1604/1609, when he wrote *Los guanches*. La Nuez y Caballero ("Las Canarias," 20–25) concludes that the *comedia* about the saint portrays a medieval vision of the islands based on well-known legendary elements. This leads, of course, to the affirmation that *Los guanches* reflects a Renaissance vision. Such a division constitutes a questionable dichotomy mainly because it does not transcend a conventionally rigid reading of the European view of the savage.

[155] Leopoldo de la Rosa ("Bailadores canarios en unas bodas reales europeas en 1451," *Anuario de estudios atlánticos* 23 [1977]: 661–63) documents the presence of "savage men" from "Camaria" and their "very particular dances" in a royal wedding at the Portuguese court as early as 1451, while Boccaccio wrote in the 1340s that the natives danced like Frenchmen (Cachey, "Petrarch," 56). In a contemporary study, Elfidio Alonso (*Tierra canaria* [Madrid: Zacosa, 1981], 15–26) alludes to the later popularity of the *baile* and traces the musical and choreographic changes that *el canario* underwent from its genesis to the present. He also summarizes the different opinions about its origins, which are doubtfully tied to the native population of the Canaries. However, E. Alonso (25), partially following Luis Cobiela and Carlos Vega, has concluded that *el canario* was born due to a double process of ascendance and descendance in which a European dance had come to the islands, mixed with an aboriginal dance, and then returned to Europe. See also E. Alonso, *El canario (Baile del siglo XVI)* (Santa Cruz de Tenerife: Litoten, 1985) for a comparison with other European and transatlantic dances.

[156] The distinction between *baile* (popular) and *danza* (aristocratic) made by Díez Borque (*Sociedad y teatro*, 286–97), who followed Castro Escudero, seems less accurate than the distinction made by Lynn Matluck Brooks (*The Dances of the Processions of Seville in the Spanish Golden Age* [Kassel: Reichenberger, 1988], 155). For the latter, there is a "permeable border between courtly and popular dance forms" in religious festivities, which must have not been much different from secular theater. According to Brooks (*Dances*, 146), the term *danza* applied to "works which stood independent of any text or play" or "were whole theatrical statements in themselves," while the term *baile* applied to those "dance intervals in the *Autos Sacramentales*, bearing little, if any, relation to the main body of the play" (146). With respect to *el baile canario*, as shown in the previous note, and in Gómara's statement, quoted in the body of my exposition, a division in the terminology is not as demonstrably clear.

This play follows rather closely the historical events leading to the conquest of Tenerife by the Spaniards in the late fifteen-hundreds, albeit with a
large fictional component. [157] The first act begins with the arrival at the island
of a ship laden with Spanish troops. The introduction of the Spanish characters
at sea is followed by a meeting of the natives on land and the intervention of
the main characters on the native side. The soothsayer, whom Lope named
Sileno (instead of Viana's Guañameñe), foresees the third arrival (rather than
the second) of the Spaniards to Tenerife in their "black birds with white wings"
(Lope de Vega, *Los guanches*, ed. Menéndez y Pelayo, 1.224–25), much to the
distress of the rest. The Spaniards disembark and Captain Castillo begins his
exploration of the land; at the same time, the Guanche princess Dacil goes to a
lake to bathe. The two meet there and the Spanish captain takes the princess
prisoner. She cleverly breaks her seashell and amber necklace, leaving a trail
behind for her guards to find her. Following the strand of seashells, Siley,
Manil, and Firán, the royal guard, find Castillo and Dacil. Although the natives
try to capture Castillo, Dacil pardons him and sends him to his ship accompa-

---

[157] From here on, all quotations of the play come from *Los guanches de Tenerife y conquista
de Canarias*, in *Obras de Lope de Vega*, ed. Marcelino Menéndez y Pelayo, Biblioteca de autores
españoles 24 (Madrid: Atlas, 1968), 65–119, unless otherwise indicated. A more faithful edition to the *princeps* has appeared recently in *Obras completas de Lope de Vega*, ed. Jesús Gómez y
Paloma Cuenca, *Comedias* 13 (Madrid: Biblioteca Castro, 1997), 803–94. However, I have
collated all the editions and a late manuscript copy of the play to correct the errors with
respect to the *editio princeps*, and also renumbered the verses throughout for a soon-to-appear
critical edition under my care (Newark, DE: Juan de la Cuesta, 2003). See the Bibliography
for a listing of editions. The *editio princeps* of the play appeared as part of the *Décima Parte de
las comedias de Lope de Vega Carpio*, published in Madrid and Barcelona in 1618, and later reprinted in Madrid in 1621. Menéndez y Pelayo modernized the orthography of the play in his
Real Academia 1900 edition, but incurred several errors in the process and made some arbi-
trary changes. The series Biblioteca de Autores Españoles reprinted Menéndez y Pelayo's
edition in 1968, which in turn was reprinted by the Museo de Historia of Tenerife in 1996.
The publisher Aguilar also reproduced the Menéndez y Pelayo edition of 1900 in the collection of *Obras escogidas* in 1955. Besides the above-mentioned editions, there is a copy of the
play in manuscript form at the Biblioteca Palatina in Parma, Italy, probably dating from the
end of the seventeenth or early eighteenth centuries, according to Antonio Restori (*Una
collezione di commedie di Lope de Vega Carpio* [Livorno: Vigo, 1891], 16). In addition, Claudio de
la Torre freely adapted the play for its first known performance, and he then published his
version of the text in Madrid in 1963. Aside from the known editions, there are other issues
concerning the play. An early confusion by the critics caused *Los guanches* to be catalogued
also as *Nuestra Señora de la Candelaria*. M. R. Alonso, however, has made it clear that the latter,
which she edited and published from the original manuscript at the Biblioteca Nacional, is a
different play. She also discusses the impossibility of attributing the authorship of the play to
Lope de Vega. *Nuestra señora* seems to be based on Espinosa's text instead of Viana's, leading
Alonso to suspect that it was written by a Dominican friar who did not visit the Canary Islands. See M. R. Alonso, ed., *Comedia de Nuestra Señora de la Candelaria* (Madrid: CSIC, 1943),
1–28.

nied by Manil. Manil meets the rest of the Spaniards, who decide to send back with him a present for the king of Tenerife: Manil chooses a collar which he values, for it would become the fatal constraint under which the arrogant necks of the enemies were to perish.

The second act begins with King Bencomo's short monologue lamenting the invasion of the foreigners, while Manil describes his encounter with the Spaniards. Dacil and Manil find each other. She confides her love for Castillo to her servant, and he gives her a reassuring love message which Castillo had entrusted to him. Two Spanish soldiers, Trujillo and Valcázar, engage in the courting of the native women Palmira and Erbasia, respectively. Both Spaniards fall asleep, and they are found by Bencomo's brother Tinguaro and Arfino who steal Trujillo's sword — an episode that Lope takes loosely from Viana's poem. The natives meet to discuss the reason for Dacil's sadness, which is echoed by the equally love-sick Palmira and Erbasia. The meeting ends with a dance, *un baile canario*, which is immediately followed by the staging of the first battle of Acentejo. Siley defies the Spaniards in a powerful monologue, while Alonso de Lugo sends a message to Bencomo stating that his mission is more evangelical than military. The drums call all to battle. Tinguaro, holding the stolen sword, encounters Trujillo, who recovers his weapon after being injured. Castillo disappears in the confusion of the struggle. After the battle, the natives celebrate their victory. Desperately, Dacil asks Manil to look for Castillo, but he claims that the captain is dead. Dacil wants to die and join her lover, and Manil proposes a sweet death with a presumed poison that he has taken from the Spaniards — wine. This comic scene is followed by the subsequent happy encounter of the now intoxicated princess and Castillo, who had been injured in battle, but who is nonetheless alive.

In the third and last act, there is a slight change of pace since the appearance of the Virgin of Candelaria now becomes central to the plot. While Manil and Firán are leading their flock, they find the image of the Virgin inside a cave. They try to speak to her but receive no answer. Manil lifts his arm to throw a stone at her only to see his arm immobilized. Firán takes out his knife but cuts his own fingers. The Virgin miraculously cures both of them and they promise to bring offerings to her every afternoon. Meanwhile, the Spaniards plan their final offensive. Castillo promises to marry Dacil and, pointing to a mountain which she takes as her witness, she makes him swear that he will keep his word. The natives observe another miracle when a tree full of birds bows down to within Manil's reach, thereby allowing him to fulfill his wish of offering little canary birds to the Virgin and her child. At this point the final battle between natives and Spaniards occurs. Trujillo encounters Dacil and tries to imprison her, but Castillo comes to her rescue. The two compatriots recognize each other and Dacil is freed. This battle results in the defeat of the natives, which Bencomo dramatizes in his lamentation. Bencomo then receives the visit of Saint Michael who, by threatening the king with his sword, demands his conversion. Alonso de Lugo also receives a visit from the saint, who announces the final subjugation of the islands as well as the existence of an undiscovered treasure. Bencomo capitulates, but Dacil refuses to do so until Castillo marries her. The appearance of the Virgin shows her to be both treasure and witness: thus Castillo offers his hand to Dacil while Trujillo and Valcázar offer theirs to Palmira and Erbasia. The *comedia* ends as expected in a conventional multiple marriage, although the grooms and brides supposedly belong to different cultures.

The ramifications of the dramatic plot call for an analysis of Lope's most important historical and fictional sources and how he deviates from them. Lope's inclusion of historical material in *Los guanches* most probably follows the brief and general vision of the Fortunate Islands given by López de Gómara in three chapters at the end of his *Historia general de Indias* (1552) (314–19 [chaps. 221–23]), and it definitely borrows its main plot from the Canarian epic poem *Antigüedades de las Islas Afortunadas*, written by Antonio de Viana.

Gómara's chronicle, known and used by Lope in other plays on New World themes,[158] is one of many in which the historical account of the conquest and colonization of the Canary Islands is confined to one brief section. Gómara's description was more detailed than Oviedo's passing comment in his *Historia natural y general de las Indias*, which was another of Lope's proven sources for his American plays. Gómara (*Historia general*, 319 [chap. 223]) summarizes the conquest of the islands, and the costumes of the natives, and affirms: "Two things bring honor to these islands in the eyes of the world: the birds called canaries ... and the Canary dance" ("Dos cosas andan por el mundo que ennoblecen estas islas: los pájaros canarios ... y el baile canario, baile gentil y artificioso"). Lope shares with Gómara the briefness of the historical narration pertaining to the period prior to the 1490s and the spelling of Betancor (Betancurt for Gómara [*Historia general*, 315 [chap. 222]; Letancur for Viana [*Antigüedades*, 2.36]). According to Lope (*Los guanches*, 3.2475–2529), the singing canaries

---

[158] See Campos, "Lope de Vega," 751–54; Minian de Alfie, "Lector de cronistas," 1–21; Shannon, *Visions of the New World*.

DE LOPE DE VEGA
Carpio , al Bachiller An-
tonio de Viana.
SONETO.

POr mas q̃ l viēto entre las õdas graues
Montes leuante, y con las velas rife,
Buela por alta mar, Isleño esquife,
A competencia de las grandes naues.
Canta con verfos dulces y fuaues
La hiftoria de Canaria y Tenerife,
Que en ciegos laberintos de Pafife
Da el cielo a la virtud faciles llaues.
Si en tiernos años, atreuido al Polo,
Miras del Sol los rayos Orientales,
En otra edad feras fu Atlante folo:
Islas del Occeano, de Corales
Ceñid fu frente, en tanto q̃ de Apolo
Crece, a las verdes hojas inmortales.

Fig. 7. Laudatory Sonnet written by Lope de Vega in praise of Antonio de Viana's epic poem *Antigüedades de las Islas Afortunadas de la Gran Canaria, conquista de Tenerife y aparecimiento de la Santa Imagen de Candelaria* (Seville, 1604). From Facsimile Edition. Courtesy of the Excmo. Ayuntamiento de San Cristóbal de la Laguna.

and other birds involved directly in one of the play's miracles would make the best gift for the Virgin of Candelaria. As he had done and would do in other *comedias*, he exploits the appeal of *el baile canario* as an active element in the dramatic spectacle (*Los guanches*, 2.1515–66). What Lope possibly copies from Gómara are general descriptive elements which allow him to display a certain basic cultural and historical knowledge to fulfill the functions of atmospheric verisimilitude in the play. What Lope appropriates from the elaborate heroic rhetoric of Viana's poem, however, provides the play with more precise details and a historical vision of the island's European conquest. Lope duplicates such a vision, yet he adds his own twist. Viana's account of the history surrounding the appearance of the Virgin of Candelaria and his fabrication of the fable about the symbolic union of the Spanish Captain Castillo and the Guanche princess Dacil play a crucial role in the dramatic structure of Lope's piece.[159]

Lope takes advantage of Viana's epic poem, the first written about the conquest of the islands, which, as I have shown, represented the attempt of a native of Tenerife to refute the history of an outsider, Alonso de Espinosa, a native Spaniard educated in Guatemala. Viana justified the birth of the epic as the only honorable reaction to the personal affront that Espinosa had inflicted upon one of the most prominent families involved in the conquest of Tenerife as well as on the natives of the islands. His text also responds to the necessity to mend, integrate, and heal the ruptures that Lascasian thought had left in Espinosa's chronicle about the history of the conquest of Tenerife and the Canary Islands. The epic poem, which fluctuates between history and fiction, where winners and losers alike can be praised, becomes the ideal stage on which to orchestrate the blending of two cultures. The ethnic origin of Spaniards and Guanches is united from time immemorial and results in the offspring of noble and brave Andalusians who populated La Palma and Tenerife

---

[159] As Lorenzo Cáceres ("Las Canarias," 28–29) first, and later M. R. Alonso and La Nuez y Caballero, suggested, Lope most probably met Viana in Seville when the latter visited the Andalusian city to arrange the publication of his epic poem. In 1602, the company of Baltasar de Pinedo (*autor*), and the actress Micaela Luján, Lope's mistress, traveled to Seville and Lope followed them with the excuse of visiting his uncle Miguel del Carpio. From that year until 1605, the dramatist moved frequently between Seville, Toledo, and Madrid (Luis Astrana Marín, *Vida azarosa de Lope de Vega* [Barcelona: Juventud, 1935], 192–204). In Seville, Lope had a friend and patron, Juan de Arguijo, who was also a poet and a member of an active literary circle. Juan's uncle, Diego de Arguijo, lived on Tenerife and occupied a position in the government, while Juan's father, Gaspar de Arguijo, was His Majesty's Lieutenant Admiral Treasurer in the Canary Islands. The latter also owned a vessel, Our Lady of Belén, and a frigate, San Bernabé, which sailed to the Canaries, Honduras, and Havana (Celestino López Martínez, *Teatro y comediantes sevillanos del siglo XVI* [Seville: Imprenta Provincial, 1940], 46–49). The Arguijos' relationship to Spain, the Canaries, and the New World must have been very relevant to their social and artistic lives, and thus influential in Lope's as well. See also John W. Hamilton, "Las relaciones personales de Lope de Vega con el Nuevo Mundo," *Romance Notes* 8 (1967): 260–65.

— an offspring that is, therefore, totally indistinct from those Spaniards who finally subdued the islands. Both cultures also symbolically fuse into one in the marital union of the Spaniard Castillo and the blonde, blue-eyed Guanche Dacil, as well as in the one religion in which both profess their faith, thanks to the intervention of the Virgin of Candelaria and the Christian Guanche Antón who had already undertaken the evangelization of the islanders.

These particular elements, among the many other conventions of the epic genre reproduced by Viana, became the beginning of a constructed identity which united the islanders in an undifferentiated bond to the Spaniards. Lope reshaped these elements and produced a drama which reflects less the carelessness that Menéndez y Pelayo ("Introduction," 83, 98) attributed to the use of his main source (Viana's epic poem) than the choices of a dramatist who intends to convey his own vision of the conquest of the islands, or at least one that would acknowledge the blemishes in Viana's perfect model.[160] Lope subscribed to Viana's vision of cultural integration. Unlike Viana, however, Lope never united Spaniards and Guanches in a single ethnic identity, and he exposed the violence contained in an unjustly waged war of conquest. The perfect picture painted by Viana's poem becomes a distorted replica in Lope's drama.

In contrast to Viana's text, the appearance of the Virgin of Candelaria occurs in Lope's play simultaneously with the Spanish offensive in the 1490s, not during the French settlement at the beginning of the same century. Lope's choice seems to support the argument regarding imperial propagandistic intentions that many critics have attributed to his creations.[161] Nonetheless, Lope

---

[160] In his introduction to the edition of Lope's plays, Menéndez y Pelayo ("Introduction," 83, 98) affirms that Lope did not read Viana's poem in its entirety and that he made changes out of laziness. Nevertheless, Menéndez y Pelayo does not give enough weight to the appearance of a laudatory sonnet written by Lope in the 1604 edition of Viana's poem, nor does the Spanish critic give the dramatist enough credit, considering Lope's demonstrated interest in history. See Shannon, *Visions of the New World*, 188–95; H. N. Bershas, "Lope de Vega and the Post of Royal Chronicler," *Hispanic Review* 31 (1963): 109–17; J. Weiner, "Lope de Vega, un puesto de cronista y *La Hermosa Ester*," in *Actas del VIII Congreso de la Asociación Internacional de Hispanistas*, ed. D. Kossoff et al. (Madrid: Ediciones Istmo, 1986), 723–30, here 727; also Elizabeth R. Wright, *Pilgrimage to Patronage*, 16, 18, 30–32. 91–93.

[161] Besides the sociological criticism that Stern contests ("Lope de Vega: Propagandist?" *Bulletin of the Comediantes*, 34 [1982]: 1–36), Américo Castro and Hugo A. Rennert have seen *La Dragontea* (another text which deals indirectly with the Canary Islands) as an embellished reconstruction of the Spanish colonial affair (*Vida de Lope de Vega (1562–1635)* [Salamanca: Anaya, 1969], 132–35). J.-L. Flecniakoska ("Lope de Vega propagandiste nationaliste: *La Dragontea* (1598)," in *Hommage des hispanistes français à Noel Salomon* [Barcelona: LAIA, 1979], 321–33) has also applied the concept of propaganda to the poem in which Lope takes a clear position in favor of the Spanish empire against Sir Francis Drake, the knighted seapirate and emblematic dragon symbolizing England. These readings have solid bases, since Lope defends his own and praises the valor of his kind in a heroic genre against the danger-

keeps the appearance of the Virgin of Candelaria separate from the Spanish presence in the islands; she appears at the same time as, but independently from, Alonso de Lugo's offensive landing in Tenerife. Apart from the play's limitation to the length of three thousand verses, Lope's separation of the two events suggests the incapability of the Spaniards to implement the process of evangelization, for which divine intervention is necessary. Throughout the play, the Virgin is the center of several miraculous occurrences that teach the natives to respect and worship such a symbolic icon, yet at the end the same Virgin teaches a more important lesson to the Spanish conquistadors. Although Viana (*Antigüedades*, 5.400–412, 10.753–757) insisted that Alonso de Lugo had planted a cross in the harbor which later became known as the "Santa Cruz de Tenerife," Lope chooses only to integrate the Virgin of Candelaria into his play's plot as an independent agent of evangelization. Such a use of the Virgin as an exemplary religious icon for the Spaniards contrasts with *El Nuevo Mundo*, where the miraculous icon is a wooden cross brought by the Spaniards to the land of Dulcanquellín and planted on the beach in order to turn the natives away from idolatry and the devil, as would eventually happen (Lope de Vega, *El Nuevo Mundo*, 2.1570–1639, 1844–1882; 3.2795–2811).[162] The appearance of the Virgin in *Los guanches* would prove instrumental in the final resolution of the plot's conflicts, as I will discuss later. Thus Lope repositioned the icon of the Virgin into the central place from which Viana's poem had displaced her.

The dynamics surrounding the encounter between Spaniards and natives are transformed since the inability to communicate with one another disappears. Unlike his technique in *El Nuevo Mundo*, in which a type of miscommunication constitutes the basis for a recurring comic motif, Lope reduces the confusion generated by differences in verbal codes to a single incident in *Los guanches* (1.694–700). He ignores Viana's claims of the lack of interpreters which prevented communication between Castillo and Dacil (*Antigüedades* 5.232–34); instead, he puts the words in Dacil's mouth to confirm that the natives also shared, though imperfectly, the invaders' language, having learned it from the Spaniards' previous visits (Lope de Vega, *Los guanches,* 1.654–661). The dramatist remains loyal, at least in the beginning, to the fictional fable of Castillo and Dacil as fabricated by Viana, who had developed it out of a brief remark in the margins of Espinosa's history. The encounter of these two characters develops into a play of cultural allegiances, based not on the common ethnic origin constructed by Viana, but rather on a vision of the Guanches as being free of

---

ous attacks of another empire. Stern's arguments, however, are still valid for the dramatic genre which, by virtue of being expressed through different modes, such as the tragic, the comic, and so on, offers more possibilities for ambiguities and criticism.

[162] In *Arauco domado*, the emphasis turns away from the supernatural to a more crude description of war among men, following the epic models of Ercilla and Oña. I will discuss Lope's treatment of war below.

idolatry and untainted by any demonic cult. This view was first put forth by Espinosa and reaffirmed by Viana, in contrast to Gómara's earlier argument about diabolic intervention among the Guanche pagans.[163] The fact that Lope (*Los guanches*, 1.295–299, 2.1622) seems to express contradictory ideas about the natives' idolatry — alluding first to human sacrifices by way of the character of a conquistador in the play, but later denying any affiliation to the devil, as expressed by another conquistador — can perhaps be explained by the contradictory nature of his sources, namely Gómara and Viana, or his references, namely the New World and the Canary Islands.[164] Lope provides Gómara's view of the natives only to retract it later, indicating that the Canary Islands provided an alternative model to the New World.

Lope's interest in history serves here not as a mere reconstruction of the past, nor as a picturesque background or excuse for fiction, but rather as a way of contrasting the artificially harmonious encounter of Europeans and Guanches to that of Europeans and Amerindians. While the dramatist reproduces Viana's model of cultural unification, other elements in the play indicate that Lope's proposition, unlike Viana's, renders a critique of the Spanish imperial enterprise overseas.

4. THE IMAGE OF OTHERNESS: CULTURAL ALLEGIANCES

La Nuez y Caballero ("Las Canarias," 70) has pointed out that in the encounter of Dacil and Castillo the cultural differences that separate them seem to blur and fade out. Perhaps this can be explained by a conscious attempt on Lope's part to tone down the conflict and violence common to the representations of wars of conquests without dismissing them altogether. Consequently, his project also involves constructing a different place for rethinking the Other. Although the Spanish classical theater was further away from a more direct American experience than the chronicles and some epic poems written about the natives and their defeats at the hands of the Spanish invaders, any attempts critically to understand the dramatic reconstruction of the Other cannot be limited to the formulas or precepts emerging from such texts as the *Arte nuevo de hacer comedias* and the tradition; instead, such attempts should search for the

---

[163] Gómara (*Historia general*, 319 [chap. 223]) wrote that "they worshipped idols; each one worshipped whom he wanted; and the devil, father of idolatry, frequently appeared to them" ("adoraban ídolos, cada uno al que quería; aparecíaseles mucho el diablo, padre de la idolatría"). The Venetian traveler Alvise Ca' da Mosto had claimed the same in the mid-fifteenth century, but there were plenty of accounts which denied this information.

[164] La Nuez y Caballero ("Las Canarias," 117–18) points out the contradiction, but does not propose to solve it, for perhaps the notion of Lope's quick and thoughtless formulas prevails after all in his reading of the play.

ruptures in those norms so as to avoid a purely monolithic vision of the dramas and the dramatists as well as the represented cultural Others. Lope's *Los guanches de Tenerife* questions the conventional and stereotypical dramatic image of the savage Other by allowing a certain play between the positions of the Spaniards and Guanches in the text. Ultimately, Lope's critical evaluation of the clash between cultures becomes more evident as the complex dramatic mechanisms of *Los Guanches* are explored not only in terms of their own internal coherence but also in comparison to *El Nuevo Mundo* and *Arauco domado*.

Lope (*Los guanches*, 1.458–776) reproduces in fine lyrics Viana's (*Antigüedades*, 5.71–349) scene of the encounter between the Guanche princess Dacil and the Spanish captain Castillo. The Spaniards announce that they have landed for the third time on the island of Tenerife, and, after arguing about who will explore the new territory, Castillo wins the honor. He goes onto the island and arrives at a beautiful lake where Dacil, moments before, has decided to take a bath. The princess is alarmed by the presence of the foreigner and climbs on top of the branch of a tree in such a way that her shadow is projected onto the waters of the lake. Castillo rushes down to the waters to wash his face. Unlike Viana's use of Narcissus, Castillo's allusion to the myth occurs when he contemplates only himself, and becomes an ironic comment (*Los guanches*, 1.557–560):

> Aquí pensara un poeta
> escribir en dulces versos
> la fábula de Narciso
> el príncipe de los necios.

> [Here a poet would think
> of writing in sweet verses
> the fable of Narcissus,
> the prince of the foolish.]

The myth that Viana uses to indicate a mirroring of Castillo and Dacil becomes in Lope's play a metapoetic play of Castillo's self-reflection in solitude. Only after he observes himself in the waters does he discover, to his surprise, another presence (*Los guanches*, 1.577–580):

> ¿Cómo puede ser que haga
> dos sombras mi propio cuerpo,
> como se ven en las aguas
> de este cristalino espejo?

> [How can it be that
> my own body two shadows

does make, seen in the
limpid mirror of these waters?]

Castillo looks up and, in an immediate attempt to classify Dacil within familiar
categories, either human or divine, he wonders (*Los guanches,* 1.593–596):

Mas ¿si es ave de estas islas?
que los del Nuevo Mundo
vuelven a España, nos cuentan
mil embelecos como estos.

[Could it be a bird native to
this isle? Those who to Spain
return from the New World
tell us such tales.]

The first passage anticipates the cultural fusion that will take place at the end of
the play — a fusion, however, that is ultimately symbolized by the amorphous
image of a body with two shadows rather than by the perfect narcissistic mirroring constructed by Viana. The second passage, on the other hand, reveals
that, although the action occurs in the Canary Islands, the New World serves as
the scenic backdrop.

From this moment on, the play sets out to cross cultural boundaries. First,
by exploring the Self as seen by the Other, Lope indulges in the humorous and
therefore less threatening pleasure that the Baroque idea of the "world upside-
down" produces in the audience; at the same time, he seriously challenges the
connotations of concepts that most chronicles of the Indies use to describe
indigenous practices. Hence, the noisy and deadly weapons of the Spaniards are
described as efficacious but cowardly, full of "deceits" and "lies" (*embustes* or
engaños) (Lope de Vega, *Los guanches,* 1.269–270, 2.1073–1074). The gifts of love
that Spaniards give to indigenous women who immediately become love-sick
are considered by the natives to be witchcraft (*hechicerías*) (2.1507), and to Dacil,
Castillo appears to be a barbarian (*bárbaro*) (3.2333).

Apart from these *mundo al revés* motifs, Lope designs an economy of cultural exchange that operates throughout the play. The first exchange occurs
between Dacil and Castillo. She gives him a necklace (*cordón*) and he recipro-
cates with feathers (*plumas*); he seems to present her with a gift that came from
the New World, while she presents him with what could very well be a European object (*Los guanches,* 1.802–810). Tinguaro, the king's brother, takes up
Trujillo's sword (2.1391–1394), while Bencomo, the Guanche king, calls his
men for battle by yelling: "We are all already Spaniards; note / that we understand their language" ("Ya somos todos españoles; mira / que ya sus lenguas
entendemos …") (3.2199–2200). Dacil adorns her primitive clothes with Casti-

llo's collar (2.1203–1215), while the Spanish captain dwells with the Guanches for one year and wears the native furs (2.1959–2010, 3.2332–2438, 3.2639–2715). Castillo indeed confesses to his double affiliation with both the European and the Guanche worlds when he is confronted and unrecognized by his friend Trujillo on the last Spanish offensive attack (*Los guanches*, 3.2665–2671):

> ¿Quién? ¿Yo?
> Mal sabes que el ser me dió
> la misma patria que a ti;
> aunque hoy *nos* habéis vencido,
> *yo*[165] no lo estoy, y la gloria
> sin mí de vuestra victoria,
> no es posible que haya sido.

> [Who, I?
> You badly know that I came
> from the same nation you do;
> though today *we* have lost,
> *I* am indeed a winner, for
> the glory of your victory,
> without me, would not be.]

The duality of the body, as a single image that projects a double shadow, as well as the numerous cultural exchanges that occur, finds a replica in what constitutes one of the most important humorous devices of the play: the treatment of Neoplatonic love.

Lope's use of Neoplatonic ideas has been discussed in the context of other works, but in *Los guanches* he takes advantage of this tradition to voice his critique of the war of conquest.[166] Lope's version of a Neoplatonic love union

---

[165] The emphasis is mine.

[166] In *The Philosophy of Love* (Edinburgh: Edinburgh University Press, 1985), 41, 109, Alexander Parker identifies Leone Ebreo's *Dialoghi d'amore* and Baldassare Castiglione's *Il Cortegiano* as the most influential Neoplatonic philosophical texts in Golden Age Spain, but he also claims that "pure Neoplatonism scarcely took root in Spanish literature; it was modified where it exercised influence." With respect to Lope's works, Parker is rather schematic and dismisses some of Lope's deeper Neoplatonic inspirations (see the review of the book by A. K. Forcione in *Hispanic Review* 58 [1990]: 269–72). As summarized by James Holloway, "Lope's Neoplatonism: *La dama boba*," *Bulletin of Hispanic Studies* 49 (1972): 236–55, here 236–40, R. Menéndez Pidal has suggested that Lope's interest in this philosophy increased when he became a priest; Margaret Wilson has identified Leone Ebreo as the source of the dramatist's Neoplatonism, while Dámaso Alonso has identified Lope's sources of Neoplatonist thought in Pico della Mirandola and Marsilio Ficino. However, Holloway has located in Castiglione the basis for the terminology of Neoplatonism that Lope used specifically in

takes as its point of departure Castiglione's famous description. The latter describes love as the desire of enjoying beauty which sets the heart of the lover on fire, unleashing certain virtues that dart out of the eyes in the form of spiritually refined vapors made of the purest and clearest part of the blood (*Libros del cortesano*, 504); true love is then the desire to ascend to divine beauty stimulated by the beauty of the body, but adulterous love is the precipitation from contemplation to touching. Although the senses of sight and hearing were the ideal vehicles of contemplation (*Libros del cortesano*, 499–500), the touching of lips was perceived as the union of souls rather than as the union of bodies. In his popular translation of the work, Juán Boscán describes the function of a kiss:

> aquel ayuntamiento es un abrir la puerta á las almas de entreambos, las cuales, traidas por el deseo la una de la otra, se traspasan y se transportan por sus conformes veces, la una tambien en el cuerpo de la otra, y de tal manera se envuelven en uno, que cada cuerpo de entreambos queda con dos almas, y una sola compuesta de las dos rige casi dos cuerpos ... por esta causa todos los enamorados castos desean el beso como un ayuntamiento espiritual. (Castellón [=Castiglione], *Libros del cortesano*, trans. Boscán, ed. A. M. Fabié, 503).

> [that bonde is the opening of an entrie to the soules, which drawne with a coveting the one of the other, poure them selves by turne the one into the others bodie, and be so mingled together, that each of them hath two soules. And one alone so framed of them both ruleth (in a manner) two bodies ... For this doe all chaste lovers covet a kisse, as a cou-

---

La dama boba, I bring up *La dama boba* because this drama closely resembles the kind of playful relationship with Neoplatonic ideas that Lope also displays in *Los guanches*.

More recently, however, Guillermo Serés (*La transformación de los amantes: Imágenes del amor de la Antigüedad al Siglo de Oro* [Barcelona: Grijalbo Mondadori, 1996], 11–398) has written one of the most comprehensive studies of "the transformation of the lovers" from Late Antiquity to the Spanish Golden Age. Serés traces certain images of love that prevailed in the poetry of great Spanish writers of the Golden Age to the influences of Plato, the Bible, Aristotle, the Church Fathers, and other popular traditions, accounting also for their metamorphosis through medieval and Renaissance appropriations. Lope de Vega, according to this critic (*Transformación*, 314, 322–32), re-elaborated the topic of the transformation of the lovers, encompassing all its variants: those derived from Neoplatonism, from songs, from Saint Bernard's *anima animat ubi amat*, and from Saint Paul's concept of *caritas*, among others.

pling of soules together.] (Castiglione, *Book of the Courtier*, trans. Hoby, 315)[167]

In *Los guanches*, the union of souls is referred to as the bequest, though perhaps less in the service of the eye and more in that of the body, of three Spanish souls onto three native women: Castillo left his in Dacil, whereas Trujillo and Valcázar left theirs in Palmira and Erbasia. The consequent search for the invaders' "secret weapon" is clearly an important comic mechanism, but it is also more freighted with meaning than critical readings of the drama have suggested.

In a scene that Menéndez y Pelayo ("Introduction," 97–98) considers puerile and insubstantial and La Nuez y Caballero ("Las Canarias," 59) dismisses altogether as a typical dramatic practice, the role of the soul-giving act transcends the superficial and provides certain insights into Lope's ideas about the act of conquering, as a displacement of the realm of war onto the realm of love.[168] Upon his return from an interview with the Spaniards, Manil, Dacil's servant, brings Castillo's message to the princess (*Los guanches,* 2.1155–1180):

MANIL.	Yo no vi
	hombre que así me agradase:
	díjome que te acordase
	que está sin alma por ti.
DACIL.	Pues ¿dónde se le cayó?
MANIL.	En ti dice que la tiene
	. . .
DACIL.	Busquemos Manil amigo,
	el alma de ese español.
MANIL.	Mira si está en el cabello.
DACIL.	¿Cómo puedo yo contar
	las hebras?
MANIL.	Púdose entrar
	a los pechos por el cuello.
DACIL.	Ya la miro, y no está aquí.
MANIL.	Pues el español no miente,

---

[167] The description of the theoretical love principles of the philosophy appears mainly in the fourth book of *Il Cortegiano*. I utilize Boscán's translation, which circulated widely in Spain: here quoting from *Los cuatro libros del cortesano*, ed. A. M. Fabié (Madrid: Bibliófilos, 1873). For the English version I rely on the 1561 translation of Sir Thomas Hoby (London: Dent, 1948).

[168] Menéndez y Pelayo ("Introducción," 97–98) agrees with the judgment already made by the Austrian writer and critic Franz Grillparzer (*Sämtliche Werke* [Munich: Hanser, 1964], 3: 576–77) who found this humorous device rather cold for the nineteenth-century sensibility.

que es gallardo y es valiente
cuanto en mi vida le vi,
    Desnúdate, y por ventura
la hallarás donde sospecho.

[MANIL.   I did not see ever
            a man so pleasing to me.
            He asked me to remind you
            that for you his soul he lost.
DACIL.   Where did he lose it?
MANIL.   He says he left it in you.
                . . .
DACIL.   Help me look, Manil, O friend,
            for the soul of the Spaniard!
MANIL.   Look for it in your hair.
DACIL.   How can I possibly count
            each strand?
MANIL.   It could have entered
            your breast through the neck.
DACIL.   I am looking and it is not here.
MANIL.   The Spaniard did not lie,
            for he is gallant and brave
            as I have never before in my life seen,
                Take your clothes off, for
            I suspect where it may be found.]

At the center of this cultural encounter, the scene establishes on one level a parodic play with the Neoplatonic ideal of love by introducing the sexual into the sphere of the spiritual. The linguistic as well as the kinesic dynamics of the scene, as imaginable today with so few surviving stage directions, also portray Dacil not only as a naive literal interpreter of the metaphoric message but also as a sexually titillating female who, as is conventional in the *comedia*, could be equivalent only to the class of her servant.[169] The Guanche figure is assimilated to the lowest ranks of the European social class system. This is further illustrated in the play by Castillo's treatment of Dacil as a "parrot," who is capable only of reproducing the same phrase, exotic enough to be taken as an unusual

---

[169] Using Lope de Vega's *La corona merecida* (1603) and *Peribáñez y el Comendador de Ocaña* (1609) as examples, Smith points out how lower-class female characters in Lope's dramas can transcend their class through beauty although they will ultimately "be unworthy of the purest emotions of love" (*Beautiful Woman*, 174). Since Smith's study deals with "honor plays," her conclusions do not apply directly to my analysis of Dacil who in the end is quite successful in attaining her aim.

gift and a provocative object to possess (Lope de Vega, *Los guanches*, 1.702–706). He also calls "barbaric" the trust which the princess places in a mountain as the loyal witness of their matrimonial engagement (*Los guanches*, 3.2420–2422); and Alonso de Lugo, the Spanish commander, addresses the Guanche king, Bencomo, as a "keeper of cows" (*guardador de vacas*) (2.1754).

On another level, the pouring of souls into the Other's body draws on a profound and keenly debated theological principle inherent in any spiritual conquest. Lope clearly indicates here that the only possible subjugation and method of evangelization should be a peaceful one where "souls" (*almas*) are substituted for "weapons" (*armas*).

This idea of a peaceful conquest finds echoes as well in *El Nuevo Mundo*, where, in three different scenes, the dramatic action played out between lovers or between Spaniards and natives emphasizes the reaching of a compromise and prefers patience and waiting for the initiative of the others rather than the use of force.[170] In *El Nuevo Mundo*, Lope's attitudes are first seen in a scene about the conquest of Granada. Images of war serve to praise the brave Gran Capitán Gonzalo Fernández de Córdoba, Garcilaso, and others (*El Nuevo Mundo*, 1.291–354), but the virtues of dialogue prevail when the Catholic monarchs claim that listening to the enemy is always wise and beneficial (1.506–508). When the Indian *cacique* Dulcanquellín kidnaps his beloved yet disdainful Tacuana, he announces that he will be willing to wait for her love as long as she demands (*El Nuevo Mundo*, 2.1308–1319). In the end, the same Dulcanquellín advises the Spaniards not to destroy the natives' idols, but rather to wait for their affection for Christ to grow so as to bring about naturally their own rejection of their pagan practices (*El Nuevo Mundo*, 3.2552–2559). Furthermore, in *Arauco domado*, as in Ercilla's text, Lope is more concerned with war itself. This phenomenon is treated as a chain of absurd violent acts that undermine the heroic model of the Spaniards while elevating the deeds of the Araucanians, especially their women, to a heroic level.[171] The phenomenon of the cruelty of

---

170 Jack Weiner ("La guerra y la paz espirituales," 65–66) deals insufficiently with the issue of the military conquest and conversion of the natives in three of Lope's *comedias* including *Los guanches, Arauco Domado*, and *El Nuevo Mundo*. However, his study suggests that Lope, perhaps influenced indirectly by Lascasian thought, chose to depict peaceful conversions rather than violent ones.

171 Francisco Ruiz Ramón ("El héroe americano en Lope y Tirso: de la guerra de los hombres a la guerra de los dioses," in *El mundo del teatro español en su Siglo de Oro: Ensayos dedicados a John E. Varey*, ed. J. M. Ruano de la Haza [Ottawa: Dovehouse, 1989], 229–48) has extensively argued the heroic dynamics constructed in Lope's *Arauco domado* to emphasize the dramatist's project of imperial critique. Another article, which I find very insightful, is Viviana Díaz Balsera, "Araucanian Alterity in Alonso de Ercilla and Lope de Vega," in *Looking at the "Comedia" in the Year of the Quincentennial*, ed. Mujica and Voros, 23–36, a study of Ercilla's *La Araucana* and Lope's *Arauco domado*. She argues that: "In *Arauco domado*, there is a considerable anxiety that there might be something unconquerable about the Other's desire

war in *Arauco domado* is highlighted by several episodes. When Gualeva, for example, is treated with deference, she changes her opinions and begins to embrace peace ("Arauco domado," 2.1711–1782). When peace negotiations are taking place between Spaniards and Araucanians, Galbarino, whose hands had been cut off, appears as a vivid reminder of the brutality of war and how cruelty engenders more cruelty (3.2417–2496). In the end, when Caupolicán surrenders, the act of peace is again undermined by violence when Fresia kills her own son (3.2904–2923). Lope's vision of war finds an echo in the words of an Araucanian leader, Rengo, who, torn by so much destruction, laments: "War, can it bring other than / plunder, death, and wreckage?" ("La guerra ¿qué puede hacer / sino robos, muertes, daños?") ("Arauco domado," 2.1413–1414).

Lope offers further reflections on the nature of war in *Los guanches de Tenerife*, but this time he explores the justification for such acts. He not only proposes a spiritual conquest — as in the Neoplatonic exchange of souls — rather than a military one, but he gives Bencomo words that protest against the Spanish invasion using the traditionally stated arguments for waging war against pagans. In a Segismundian tone, Bencomo laments to his Sun God that the Spaniards have unjustly invaded his dominion where he had ruled by divine right. Not content with the lamentation, the Guanche king goes on to refute the arguments against just war by rhetorically asking why the Spaniards had interest in his lands when he and his people had not invaded Spain, nor coveted Spanish women or territories nor any other foreign possessions (*Los guanches*, 1.232–251). In other words, Lope's Guanches are clearly constructed as distinct from the enemies of the Spanish crown; thus a military intervention on the part of Europeans was unjustifiable.

The Guanches, like King Bencomo, Tinguaro, or the loyal soldiers, are never denied access in the *comedia* to the meter of solemnity, the *octavas reales* (3.2167–2214). Thus, the native social class system is once again modeled upon the European one. In the case of Dacil the initial characterization undergoes an inversion, and by the end of the drama she has evolved from a servant-like figure to the leading female character who must be and is vindicated with the sacrament of matrimony. She firmly opposes the peace treaty that the male figures have arranged around her, and she demands personal satisfaction with respect

---

that will forever return to split the Spanish colonizer's valued fantasy of spiritual domination. The irony that a text which was to serve the colonizer's interest (Lope's) turned out to be more problematical than another (Ercilla's) which was openly critical of such interests offers an insight into the ambivalence that traversed the Spanish discourse of colonialism. It suggests that the logic of the Conquest was something never totally mastered by the conquistador" (Díaz Balsera, "Araucanian Alterity," 36). Lope's *Los guanches* reveals a similar ambivalence, although he adopted a different solution: the recovering of another locus in which to work out such anxieties. The number of critical articles that have addressed Lope's play about Arauco is considerable, but I am only referring here to the most significant ones in terms of my own arguments.

to Castillo's promise of matrimony. To the surprise of the Spanish captain, who at first had been portrayed as a brave and honest conquistador, the mountain-Virgin constitutes a very effective witness, a fact which brings out into the open the captain's dishonorable behavior and, above all, makes him recognize his equal in the person of the Guanche princess. As in the case of many old husbands of the *entremeses*, the joke is not on her but on him and ultimately on the Spaniards. The cultural allegiance between Spaniards and Guanches becomes unavoidable and legitimated by the dramatic convention of matrimony. Nonetheless, it does not occur smoothly, for the greed of the Spaniards also needs to be eliminated to achieve the ideal encounter between two cultures.

5. GOLD AND EVIL: THE WEALTH FALLACY

An important element in Lope's recreation of the Spanish war of conquest in Tenerife surfaces toward the end of the play. When the spiritual mission of the Spaniards seems about to be fulfilled, Lope introduces a biting critique of the Spaniards' greedy intentions which prove to be only the acquisition of gold and silver. Lope chooses to accuse the conquistadors of the Canaries of pursuing such riches when historically the island and islanders had no practical or ornamental use for metals. According to the first accounts of late medieval travelers to the Canary Islands, the Europeans benefited economically from the slave trade, goats, cereals, dragon-tree blood, orchil dye, and shells (Mercer, *Canary Islanders*, 155–59, 161; Fernández Armesto, *The Canary Islands*, 69–71), and later primarily from the sugar industry (Aznar Vallejo, *Integración*, 260–61, 392–99; Fernández Armesto, *The Canary Islands*, 13–32, 80–85). Although the value of gold from 1450 onward increased as the expeditions into the Atlantic Ocean and Africa proliferated (Vilar, *History of Gold and Money*, 46–52), it was clear that the islands were not part of the "geography of gold." When Lope criticizes the European thirst for gold in *Los guanches*, he is directly referring to the New World, the primary place whence gold and silver poured into Europe in the sixteenth and seventeenth centuries.

In Lope de Vega's times, Europeans held gold and silver as signs of real wealth (Vilar, *History of Gold and Money*, 161) and were very much aware of the role of the New World in the economic prosperity of Europe; in fact, Lope's dramas prominently feature the figure of the rich *indiano* who came back to Spain after making great fortunes on the other side of the Atlantic Ocean (Morínigo, *América*, 149–211). In his *El Nuevo Mundo*, the dramatist also voices a debate in which gold is at the center: holy gold (*gesta Dei per aurum*) and evil gold (*gesta Diaboli per aurum*).[172] The allegorical figure of Idolatry powerfully ar-

---

[172] Pierre Vilar's study (*A History of Gold and Money 1450–1920*, trans. Judith White [London: Verso, 1991]) is quite helpful in tracing the significance of gold and the role of the

gues that the conquests are driven by evil motives because the desire for gold rather than the will of God serves as the incentive for the Spaniards (*El Nuevo Mundo*, 1.770–774):

> Pues los lleva la codicia
> a hacer de esta diligencia
> so color de religión:
> van en busca de plata y oro
> del encubierto tesoro.

> [Then, greed pushes them
> to make of their diligence,
> under cover of religion,
> a search for the gold and silver
> of the hidden treasures.][173]

New World in the economic growth of Europe. Vilar claims (*A History of Gold and Money*, 161) that the "moral opposition to the damage done by gold came late in the eighteenth century, and was not based on an economic analysis." However, the dichotomy of "good gold" and "evil gold" prevailed throughout the narratives of new discoveries and colonization (by the way, the phrase *gesta Dei per aurum* is a deliberate allusion to the crusades in the Holy Land, referred to as *gesta Dei per Francos*). The positive mythical view of gold takes root in the search for Solomon's mines and the reconstruction of the Temple in Jerusalem, while the negative practices of Europeans showing no other motivation but greed are responsible for the association of the metal with evil. For a comprehensive study of the search for gold and the myth of El Dorado in the conquest of the New World see Juan Gil, *Mitos y utopías del descubrimiento*, 3 vols. [Madrid: Alianza, 1989], 1: 45–56; 3: 13–389. In the sixteenth century, works by humanists contributed greatly to a critical view of gold, silver, and precious stones, as in Thomas More's *Utopia* (ed. D. H. Sacks [Boston and New York: St. Martin's Press, 1999], 149–51) where, unlike in the real world, only slaves or criminals wore the metals and only the most common domestic articles were made of them. In contemporary works of our own day, like that of Gustavo Gutiérrez in the case of Peru (*Dios o el oro en las Indias: Siglo XVI* [Lima: Instituto Bartolomé de las Casas, 1989], a clear example is offered of how gold was thought to be a theological instrument for evangelization in general to the point that there could be no "God" without "Gold" — this had been first articulated in the context of the New World by José de Acosta in the sixteenth century (*Dios o el oro*, 118). Contrasting such a view, Gutiérrez (*Dios o el oro*, 9–191) explores the theology of Las Casas — perhaps in a simplified and reductive way — to show how in the Dominican's view the adoration of gold represented nothing but idolatry.

[173] In *Arauco domado*, protests against the avarice of the Spaniards are voiced by Fresia (Lope de Vega, "Arauco domado," 1.254–259). On another occasion, while Felipe de Mendoza narrates a battle between the Spaniards and the Araucanians, he also voices the natives' accusations against the invaders of Arauco (2.1101–1104):

> Venid, que como a Valdivia
> os sacaremos las almas
> donde la codicia viene

Consequently, the figure of Providence rejects this direct reference to greed by appealing to the important role of gold as a means for spiritual gain (*El Nuevo Mundo*, 1.775–779):

> Dios juzga de la intención:
> si El, por el oro que encierra,
> gana las almas que ves,
> en el cielo hay interés,
> no es mucho que le haya en la tierra.

> [God judges the intention:
> if He, for the love of gold,
> wins over the souls you see,
> there is interest in heaven;
> how could there not be on earth?]

While in *El Nuevo Mundo* the second argument seems to cast a shadow over the evil-inspired search for gold, that is not the case in the *comedia* set in the Canary Islands. In *Los guanches* the (d)evil is nowhere to be found except in three passing remarks. The most important is that of Alonso de Lugo, who, invoking religion and acknowledging the lack of gold in the islands, makes explicit his mission of banishing the devil from Tenerife as had previously been done in the other islands (Lope de Vega, *Los guanches*, 1.21–30). The modest wealth of the islands, in contrast to the references to the precious metals of the New World found in other of Lope's plays, becomes a motif in *Los guanches*. By the beginning of the second act, Bencomo's lamentation turns into a powerful statement of poverty (*Los guanches*, 2.1051–1054):

> Pues si toda mi riqueza
> es dos limpios caracoles,
> ¿a qué vienen españoles
> a conquistar mi pobreza?

> [Since all my wealth
> is two clean seashells,

---

del oro antártico y plata.

[Come! As we have done to Valdivia
we will take your souls
right where your greed meets
the gold and silver of the Antarctic.]

why are the Spaniards here
to conquer my poverty?]

Additionally, on the Spanish side, de Lugo restates his early awareness of the absence of gold and sends back a native messenger to the Guanche king to communicate the intentions of the Spaniards (*Los guanches*, 2.1753–1760):

Dile a Bencomo, tu Rey
. . .
que yo no vengo a sus islas
ni por oro ni por plata.
Vengo a obedecer, no más
lo que mis reyes me mandan,
que a reduciros desean
a la ley de Cristo santa.

[Tell Bencomo, your king,
. . .
that I have not come to his islands
in search of gold or silver.
I have only come to obey
what was ordered by my monarchs,
who desire to conquer you
for the holy law of Christ.]

There is, however, a contradiction between the explicit mission of evangelization and the implicit hope of gaining wealth rather than souls. By the end of the play, the conquistadors go so far as to create the illusion of a treasure; thus they appear as the true idolaters, who worshipped gold and who needed to be taught how to banish from themselves not the devil, but greed.

Bencomo subsequently converts to Christianity, declaring his defeat before a vision of Saint Michael who had to threaten the king vigorously and intervene in a direct evangelization of the natives. Surprised by the brightness and richness of the image, Bencomo compares the angel with the sun, which is the divinity adored by his people — at least in Lope's Inka-like patchwork of paganism. He declares immediately, however, that the vision can come only from the sun "because for a Spanish light / that brightness is excessive" ("que para rayo español / esa claridad es mucha") (*Los guanches*, 3.2763–2765). The same vision reveals itself to the eyes of Lugo to foretell the final and definitive conquest of the seven islands and to point simultaneously to the discovery of a mountain with a hidden treasure, which is the mountain where the Virgin of Candelaria will be discovered (*Los guanches*, 3.2824–2840). While Bencomo interprets the divine message correctly and converts to Christianity, Lugo misreads the message and automatically assumes that the treasure will be silver and gold. Lugo's companion, Lope Fernández de la Guerra, whom Viana had made into a great hero in his epic poem, is quick to confess that he will be the first to dig for the gold (3.2879). Thus the allegorical vision of marriage between the conquistador and the island in Viana is destroyed in Lope's play by the strength of greed.

Despite being aware of the poverty of the land, the greed of the Spaniards creates another El Dorado, an elusive source of material wealth that makes them distrust the natives and dismiss rather quickly the main purpose of their mission. After Bencomo and his subjects come to the Spaniards announcing their peaceful conversion followed by the subsequent patriotic shouting, Alonso de Lugo, without wasting any time, requests (*Los guanches*, 3.2946–2951):

> Para que yo crea,
> isleño, si esto no os cansa,
> que lo que dicen las lenguas
> es lo que sienten las almas,
> ¿a qué parte de este monte
> hay minas de oro o de plata?

> [In order to believe you,
> if it is no trouble, islander,
> that your tongue speaks
> what you feel in your soul,
> where can I in this mountain
> find gold and silver mines?]

The search for the hidden treasure results in a fiasco for the Europeans, but it also serves as a very effective vehicle for the lesson that Lope intends to give. Instead of earthly wealth, they find a heavenly treasure, the statue of the Virgin of Candelaria, whom the natives had been adoring for some time. In the image of the mountain-Virgin two very important ramifications of the plot coincide: the justice needed by Dacil and the lesson needed by the Spaniards. The Virgin proves to be an indispensable witness of Castillo's promise to the Guanche princess, but also, with her intervention, the incentive that had triggered all conquests and colonization of the Amerindians finally evaporates.

In this final scene, Spanish and Guanche roles have been inverted. The lesson of Christianity is taught to the conquistadors, who pass through a more radical conversion from wealth and sexual rapaciousness to moral responsibility; however, the Guanches, who had received the epithet of "barbarian" throughout the play, are shown to embrace more pure and civilized practices.

6. History and Utopia: Concluding Remarks

When Cohen (*Drama of a Nation*, 226–27) points out the role of the history play in the construction of an "internally harmonious nation," the pattern seems to fit the dramatic structure of *Los guanches*. Such a conclusion, however, ignores the dramatic mechanism that exposes the process in which the external becomes devoured by the internal until the boundaries disappear. In Lope's drama, as illustrated in the previous sections, this is a far more complex process than the transference of the national conflict abroad. Lope found a location which had been constructed from antiquity onward as the locus of many myths. By taking advantage of Viana's Fortunate Islands, Lope recreates the site for a textual utopia. This new "place of happiness" remains as the site where the perfect conquest finally occurred, where gold was absent, and where two cultures found a unique match. This perfect fusion occurred, however, after revealing the many undermining fissures in the European model of conquest, therefore exposing two opposing forces at war. One of these forces acknowledges the necessity for integration, for bringing the peripheral to the center, and for creating an image of totality in the inseparable marriage of the Canary Islands (symbolized by Dacil) and Spain (symbolized by Castillo). The other acknowledges the violence contained in such a colonizing project, a violence that finds some resolution in the many cultural negotiations taking place in the play and the forceful intervention of supernatural agents. Thus the image of harmony is only superficial, and what lies at the core of the drama is a destabilizing questioning of the Spanish enterprise in the New World, via the Canary Islands.

The cultural place occupied by the Canary Islands within the Spanish empire is then problematized by the literary representation of Lope's play. Such a critical vision can be further supported, not by the accountable reception of the play, but precisely by the silence or the loss that the drama experienced throughout the centuries.[174]

It is surprising indeed that the play seems to have been little known, if at all, in the Canary Islands as well as in Spain. The published documents show that in the Cathedral of Las Palmas during the Corpus Christi festivities dramatic representations took place, including serious and devout *comedias* by Lope de Vega, but *Los guanches de Tenerife* is not mentioned.[175] The absence of plays in

---

[174] The surviving documents that explore theatrical representation in Golden Age Spain and that would allow a clearer picture of the impact of the play at the time are rather scarce in the early seventeenth century. If Díez Borque's affirmation (*Sociedad y teatro*, 261) that "a printed *comedia* was a dead *comedia*" is valid, by 1618 *Los guanches*, as a dramatic spectacle, had died after a life of ten to fifteen years.

[175] The Cathedral and its public square were the designated sites of the Corpus Christi celebrations, according to Sebastián Padrón Acosta (*El teatro en Canarias: La fiesta del Corpus* [La Laguna: Instituto de Estudios Canarios, 1954], 31). Also, a document from 1604 indi-

honor of the festivities of the Virgin of Candelaria was the origin of Padrón
Acosta's complaint in recent times (*Teatro en Canarias*, 33–34). The critic is puzzled by the fact that, although the cult of the patron Virgin in the islands is very
important, no local dramatists had taken up the pen to write about the Virgin,
while in Spain only Lope and another anonymous writer had done so. As for
Spain, other than the early publications in 1618 in Madrid and Barcelona and
1621 in Madrid, no other information has been gathered except about the performance of a *comedia* concerning "Nuestra Señora de Candelaria" in a private
home in 1635.[176] In Seville, where Lope probably encountered Viana and his
poem, no records of performances seem to have survived.[177] During the eighteenth century, the historian Viera y Clavijo gave a further testimony of the loss
suffered by Lope's drama about the Guanches. From Madrid in April of 1776
he wrote to his friend, the Marquis of Villa de San Andrés and Viscount of
Buen Paso, regarding another Canarian writer who had the intention of publishing a critical edition of Lope's drama. Viera's intentions were to narrate the
difficulties of acquiring a copy of the play, without hesitating to issue a destructive judgment based on no evidence. Viera wrote the following:

> Esta comedia, que encontramos citada en el autor de la bib-
> lioteca indiana, la descubrió [José de] Vandewalle [y
> Cervellón], por encargo mío, en la Real Biblioteca, y en la de

---

cates that Cairasco de Figueroa was the habitual dramatist for the celebration, although
pieces by other dramatists (such as Lope) were also performed. After a period of plague, on
30 April 1604, the chapter of Gran Canaria requested a special favor from the bishop. The
bishop was asked to allow the performance of one of Lope de Vega's *comedias*, approved and
praised by Cairasco de Figueroa, inside the church due to the inconveniences and expenses
that a performance in the public square would require. The document was contained in the
Libro de correspondencias, years 1603–1609 (published in *El Museo Canario* 3 [1935]: 69).

[176] María José del Río has written about the incident (see "Representaciones dramáticas
en casa de un artesano del Madrid de principios del siglo XVII," in *Teatros y vida teatral en el
Siglo de Oro a través de las fuentes documentales*, ed. L. García Lorenzo and J.E. Varey [London:
Tamesis, 1991], 245–58). This private performance was known because it was used as evidence in an inquisitorial investigation of the Portuguese bed-maker Mateo Rodríguez, who
finally received one hundred lashes in the *auto de fe* of Toledo in 1637. Mateo, who wore
religious habits and spent a significant amount of time praying, also produced theatrical
events at his home, in which he also acted. That was the case of the festivities of the Virgin
of Candelaria in February of 1635 in which a play about the Virgin was performed. Mateo
was known for his disguises: he painted himself like the Indians, danced with gestures which
were said to be affronts to decency and virtue, and was also observed dressed as a woman.
Del Río ("Representaciones dramáticas," 245–58) believes that this *comedia* might not have
been Lope's, but rather the anonymous *Nuestra Señora de la Candelaria* where divine elements
(*a lo divino*) seemed to be more relevant.

[177] Sentaurens makes no allusion to the play in *Seville et le théâtre*, nor does López
Martínez in *Teatro y comediantes*. Sentaurens offers a very comprehensive study, but with regard to theater life in other cities much needs to be done.

los Carmelitas Dezcalzos ... Avisómelo; encarguéle una
copia; me la ofreció; pero despúes acá se ha ido retirando; no
me ha dado la copia ni aún para leerla; me ha ocultado el
pensamiento de reimprimirla ... y sabe Dios el batiborrillo de
especies y fárragos acapuchinados que dará a luz si logra sus
intentos. La tal comedia no tiene otro mérito que el del
asunto y el autor: por lo demás es un parto monstruoso de
aquel fértil ingenio que sin duda se valió del Poema de
nuestro valioso Viana. (Lorenzo Cáceres, "Página inédita,"
40.)

[Vandewalle searched for this *comedia* (which we found cited
by the author of the *Biblioteca indiana*) at my request in the
Royal Library and the library of the Discalced Carmelites. ...
He notified me and I asked for a copy of the play. He has
gradually distanced himself from me, and to this date he has
not given me a copy even to read it. He has hidden from me
his desire to re-edit the play ... God save us from the kind of
hodgepodge that he would edit if he ever fulfills his intentions. As for Lope's play, I see no other merit than the subject matter and the author. The play is otherwise the monstrous offspring of Lope's fertile wit which undoubtedly used
the poem of our invaluable Viana.]

This confession shows the silent fate of the play, which was not republished
until the end of the nineteenth century. The uninformed opinion of Viera y
Clavijo, who had not read the play, persisted. Perhaps such a "monstrous offspring of Lope's fertile wit" was too troublesome for public display in the islands as well as in the peninsula. Viera's comment, which apparently speaks of
the aesthetic value of the dramatic verses, might be speaking of something else:
Lope's effective critique of the Spanish enterprise overseas. After all, in the
1850s, the Austrian hispanophile Franz Grillparzer was surprised by an author
who seemed to be taking the side of the simple and innocent natives.[178]
     Lope's vision of history destabilized the model of perfect integration pro-
posed by Viana, whose vision of the heroic cultural alliance between Spain and
one of its colonies seemed to have found a warm reception in Viera y Clavijo

---

[178] The quote reads: "Die Eingebornen so einfach und unschuldig dargestellt, daß man
manchmal zu dem Glauben verführt wird, der Verfasser nehme Partei für sie" (Grillparzer,
Sämtliche Werke, 3: 576). Menéndez y Pelayo ("Introduction," 98 n. 1) mentions Grillparzer
without elaborating, but the Austrian dramatist and critic knew Calderón's and Lope's dramas well and offered his impressions on *Los guanches*.

and in dramatists of the nineteenth century in the Canaries.[179] Lope's vision, unlike Viana's, takes refuge in the past, where the fertile ground of the somewhat distant and under-recorded history of the Canary Islands allows him to offer a critical reflection on the history of Spain in the New World, as the dramatist has equally shown in other dramatic pieces like *El Nuevo Mundo* and *Arauco domado*. In *Los guanches de Tenerife*, Lope's manipulation of the Virgin of Candelaria makes the icon less of an instrument of evangelization for Spain's cultural Others and more of a policing figure of Spain's Christian values. In Lope's view, only the spiritual presence of the Virgin of Candelaria could prevent, at least on the stage, the literary image of the Canary Islands from becoming a reflection of the disturbing historical experience of Spanish colonialism. The moral lesson that Lope intends to give in this historical episode, staged in the Canaries, applied in his times not to the stable colonial structure of the islands but to the still unsettled reality of the New World.

The dramatist was indeed participating in a debate that was far from over with the death of Bartolomé de las Casas. The intellectual debates about the conquest of the New World that flourished in mid-sixteenth-century Spain continued to surface in Lope's dramatic production in the early seventeenth century because Lope was an active participant in a broader process of "national introspection" (Elliott, *Imperial Spain*, 300), in which thinking about Spain also meant addressing critically the colonial history of Spain in the New World. If the *arbitristas* were discussing solutions in the political sphere, Lope's dramatic production was exploring past conflicts which shaped the present: the first attempted to search for practical solutions, the second attempted to explore textual utopian spaces, and both acknowledged the unresolved crisis that consumed Spain and its colonies.

---

[179] Padrón Acosta (*Teatro en Canarias*, 67–90) speaks of two dramatists who found a source of inspiration in Viana's epic poem: Desiré Dugour (1816–1875), of French origin, and Ignacio Negrín Núñez (1823–1885).

AFTERWORD

The Tree of Understanding, dazzlingly straight and simple,
sprouts by the spring called Now I Get It.
>   (Wislawa Szymborska, "Utopia," 127)

In making conquests, in the early-modern period, to be
Catholic was no impediment, any more than to be Muslim or
Russian Orthodox or Chinese. What mattered was the geographical position of the potentially imperial societies. What
the seaborne empires all had in common was their starting-
place on the shores of the Atlantic ...
>   (Felipe Fernández Armesto, *Millennium*, 257)

I want to develop the suggestion that cultural historians could
take the Atlantic as one single, complex unit of analysis in
their discussions of the modern world and use it to produce
an explicitly transnational and intercultural perspective.
>   (Paul Gilroy, *The Black Atlantic*, 15)

AT THE 1997 CONVENTION of the Modern Language Association of America,
Sara Castro-Klarén, a well-known critic of Colonial Latin American history and
literature, compared the Spanish Golden Age's silencing of New World affairs
to the way that one abandons a house during vacation, covering the furniture.
The session in which the scholar spoke was planned as an attempt to bring
together — but in fact might have worked to keep apart — what traditionally
have been constructed as two separate spheres of literary study: Peninsular
Golden Age and Latin American Colonial literature. The questions raised that
day had to do less with Spain's silencing or the Amerindian's vision of Spain
than with the conceptualization of the field(s) of critical study. The session proposed to address the two sides of an ongoing polemic. On the one hand, some
scholars have been concerned with the recent legitimization of Golden Age
literature only through the possibilities offered by the study of Spain's cultural
Others; on the other hand, many others have been concerned with the legitimization of the specificity of Colonial Latin America that keeps it related to, but
ultimately separate from, Spanish Golden Age studies.

The present study has been conceived as a dual project. First, I explore the
historical and literary narratives of the two geographic sides of the Atlantic as
they meet in an important locus of transatlantic exchange at the turn of the
seventeenth century. Second, I attempt to participate in the increasingly acknowledged and significant current of contemporary literary criticism that stud-

ies the cultural production of the two shores as part of one single cultural sphere, that is, at the level of elite culture created by the Spanish empire in which is also embedded a narrative of cultural resistance to colonization. When the historical and literary production about the Canaries is taken into consideration, the investigation of the absence of the New World in Spanish literature finds new paths. Spain did not abandon the house of the New World, but rather covered the furniture and moved it to another house — the Canary Islands.

Using the important colonial outpost of the Canaries and their incipient identities, I have attempted to follow a more organic model of analysis that unveils the fluidity of cultural exchange prevailing in the Hispanic transatlantic world of the sixteenth and seventeenth centuries. In this case, the mutual and unidirectional gazing of one side at the other seems more decipherable, not through the rigidity of a dual and antagonistic model, but through a plausible triangulation encompassing other spaces. This process reveals European strategies of negotiation, which involved the exploration of alternative textual and colonial loci to elucidate the many conflicts regarding colonialism still at play in the Spanish imperial world.

Now, at the start of a new millennium, the Atlantic World has finally been valued in its function as both metaphor and practical tool of analysis with clear interdisciplinary applications. What was more evident during the early European colonial enterprises, and later systematically fragmented in the exclusionary process of the formation of fields of study and the rise of nationalisms, has regained global viability. This study, in its originality as well as its inscription in a long list of works by Atlantic and Latin American cultural historians, attests to the fact that it is possible to recover new spaces through the inclusive critical spectrum of Transatlantic Studies.

BIBLIOGRAPHY

Abreu y Galindo, Juan de. *Historia de la conquista de las siete Islas de Canarias*, ed. Alejandro Cioranescu. Santa Cruz de Tenerife: Goya, 1977.

Abulafia, David. "Neolithic Meets Medieval: First Encounters in the Canary Islands." In *The Medieval Frontier: Concepts and Practices*, ed. David Abulafia and Nora Berend, 255–78. Aldershot: Ashgate, 2002.

Acosta, José de. "De procuranda Indorum salute." In *Biblioteca de Autores Españoles: Obras del P. José de Acosta*, ed. Francisco Mateos, 387–608. Madrid: Atlas, 1954.

Adorno, Rolena. "Censorship and its Evasion: The Case of Fray Jerónimo Román y Zamora's *Repúblicas del mundo* [1575, 1595]." *Hispania* 75 (1992): 812–27.

———. "Los debates sobre la naturaleza del indio en el siglo XVI: textos y contextos." *Revista de estudios hispánicos* 19 (1992): 47–66.

———. *Guaman Poma: Writing and Resistance in Colonial Peru.* Austin: University of Texas Press, 1986.

———. "The Intellectual Life of Bartolomé de las Casas." The Andrew W. Mellon Lecture, Fall 1992. New Orleans, LA: The Graduate School of Tulane University, 1992.

———. "Literary Production and Suppression: Reading and Writing About Amerindians in Colonial Spanish America." *Dispositio* 11 (1986): 1–25.

———. "Nuevas perspectivas en los estudios literarios coloniales hispanoamericanos." *Revista de crítica literaria latinoamericana* 14 (1988): 11–27.

———. "Todorov y de Certeau: La alteridad y la contemplación del sujeto." *Revista de crítica literaria latinoamericana* 17 (1991): 51–58.

Alemany, Luis. "Antonio de Viana: una postura literaria ante la historia." *Revista de historia canaria* 37 (1980): 267–72.

Alonso, Elfidio. *Tierra canaria.* Madrid: Zacosa, 1981.

———. *El canario (Baile del siglo XVI).* Santa Cruz de Tenerife: Litoten, 1985.

Alonso, María Rosa, ed. *Comedia de Nuestra Señora de la Candelaria.* Madrid: Consejo Superior de Investigaciones Científicas, 1943.

———. *El poema de Viana.* Madrid: Consejo Superior de Investigaciones Científicas, 1952.

Aristotle. *The Complete Works*, ed. Jonathan Barnes. Vol. 2. Princeton: Princeton University Press, 1984.

———. *Poetics*, trans. James Hutton. New York: Norton, 1982.

Armas, Frederick A. de. "Fashioning a New World: Lope de Vega and Claramonte's *El nuevo rey Gallinato*." In *Critical Essays on the Literature of Spain and Spanish America*, ed. Luis T. González-del-Valle and Julio Baena, 1–10. Boulder: Society of Spanish and Spanish-American Studies, University of Colorado, 1991.

Armas Wilson, Diana de. "'Vuela por alta mar, isleño esquife': Antonio de Viana's *Conquista de Tenerife* (1604)." *Calíope* 3 (1997): 24–43.

Astrana Marín, Luis. *Vida azarosa de Lope de Vega*. Barcelona: Editorial Juventud, 1935.

Aznar Vallejo, Eduardo. *La integración de las Islas Canarias en la Corona de Castilla (1478–1526)*. Madrid: Secretariado de Publicaciones de la Universidad de La Laguna, 1982.

———. "Canary Islands." In *Medieval Iberia: An Encyclopedia*, ed. E. Michael Gerli, 193–94. New York: Routledge, 2003.

Azorín, José Martínez Ruiz. "Retratos de algunos malos españoles y de un mal español honorario." In idem, *Obras completas*. Vol. 2. Madrid: Aguilar, 1947.

Benavente, Toribio de (Motolinía). *Carta al Emperador. Refutación a Las Casas sobre la colonización española*, ed. José Bravo Ugarte. México: Editorial Jus, 1949.

Benedetti, Thomas. "The Noble Triumph of Cortés: *El valeroso español y primero de su casa.*" In *Looking at the "Comedia" in the Year of the Quincentennial*, ed. Bárbara Mujica and Sharon D. Voros, 3–12. Lanham, MD: University Press of America, 1993.

Bernáldez, Andrés. *Memorias del reinado de los Reyes Católicos*, ed. Manuel Gómez-Moreno and Juan de Mata Carriazo. Madrid: Real Academia de la Historia, 1962.

Bershas, Henry N. "Lope de Vega and the Post of Royal Chronicler." *Hispanic Review* 31 (1963): 109–17.

Bonnet, Buenaventura. "Las Canarias y el primer libro de geografía medieval, escrito por un fraile español en 1350." *Revista de historia canaria* 10 (1944): 205–27.

———. "Un manuscrito del siglo XV." *Revista de historia canaria* 7 (1940): 92–100.

———. "La obra del p[adre] Alonso de Espinosa." *Revista de historia canaria* 6 (1932): 33–42.

———. "El p[adre] Alonso de Espinosa y su historia." *El Museo Canario* 12 (1952): 31–49.

Boutier [Bontier], Pierre, and Jean Le Verrier. *Le Canarien. Crónicas francesas de la conquista de Canarias*, ed. and trans. Elías Serra Ráfols and Alejandro Cioranescu. 3 vols. La Laguna: Instituto de Estudios Canarios and Museo Canario, 1959, 1960, 1964.

Brito Díaz, Carlos. "Visiones del indígena canario en el teatro español del Siglo de Oro." *Revista de literatura* 61 (1991): 225–37.

Brotherton, John. "Lope's *El Nuevo Mundo descubierto por Cristóbal Colón*: Convention and Ideology." *Bulletin of the Comediantes* 46 (1994): 33–48.

Brooks, Lynn Matluck. *The Dances of the Processions of Seville in the Spanish Golden Age*. Kassel: Reichenberger, 1988.

Brumble, H. D. *Classical Myths and Legends in the Middle Ages and Renaissance*. Westport, CT: Greenwood Press, 1998.

Cabrera de Córdoba, Luis. *De historia, para entenderla y escribirla*, ed. Santiago Montero Díaz. Madrid: Instituto de Estudios Políticos, 1948.

Cabrera Perera, Antonio. *Las bibliotecas en las Palmas*. Las Palmas: Cabildo Insular and El Museo Canario, 1982.

———. *Las Islas Canarias en el mundo clásico*. Las Palmas de Gran Canaria: Viceconsejería de Cultura y Deportes and Gobierno Canario, 1988.

Cachey, Theodore J., Jr. *Le Isole Fortunate. Appunti di storia letteraria italiana*. Rome: "L'Erma" di Bretschneider, 1995.

———. "Petrarch, Boccaccio, and the New World Encounter." *Stanford Italian Review* 10 (1991): 45–59.

Ca' da Mosto, Alvise [Luís de]. *Viagens*. Lisboa: Academia Portuguesa da Historia, 1947.

Campos, Jorge. "Lope de Vega y el descubrimiento colombino." *Revista de Indias* 9 (1949): 751–54.

Cartagena, Alfonso de. *Diplomacia y humanismo en el siglo XV. Edición crítica, traducción y notas de las Allegaciones super conquesta Insularum Canariae contra portugalenses de Alfonso de Cartagena*, ed., intro. and trans. Tomás González Rolán, Fremiot Hernández González, and Pilar Saquero Suárez-Somonte. Madrid: Universidad Nacional de Educación a Distancia, 1994.

Cartas de Indias. Biblioteca de Autores Españoles 2. Madrid: Manuel Hernández, 1877.

Casas, Bartolomé de las. *Apologética historia sumaria*, ed. Edmundo O'Gorman. 2 vols. México: Universidad Nacional Autónoma de México e Instituto de Investigaciones Históricas, 1967.

———. *Brevísima relación de la destrucción de las Indias*, ed. André Saint-Lu. Madrid: Cátedra, 1984.

———. *Historia de las Indias*, ed. Agustín Millares Carlo. México: FCE, 1986.

———. *The Only Way*, ed. Helen Rand Parish, trans. Francis Patrick Sullivan. New York: Paulist Press, 1992.

———. *Tratados*. 2 vols. México: Fondo de Cultura Económica, 1965.

Case, Thomas E. "History and Structural Unity in *San Diego de Alcalá*." *Bulletin of the Comediantes* 32 (1980): 55–62.

Castellón, Baltasar. *Los cuatro libros del cortesano compuestos en italiano y agora nuevamente traduzidos en lengua castellana por Boscán*, ed. Antonio M. Fabié. Madrid: Librería de los Bibliófilos, 1873.

Castiglione, Baldassare. *The Book of the Courtier*, trans. Sir Thomas Hoby. London: J.M. Dent and Sons, 1948.

Castro, Américo, and Hugo A. Rennert. *Vida de Lope de Vega (1562–1635)*. Salamanca: Anaya, 1969.

Certeau, Michel de. *Heterologies. Discourse on the Other*, trans. Brian Massumi. Minneapolis: University of Minnesota Press, 1986.

———. *The Writing of History*, trans. Tom Conley. New York: Columbia University Press, 1988.

Cevallos, Francisco Javier. "Don Alonso de Ercilla and the American Indian: History and Myth." *Revista de estudios hispánicos* 23 (1989): 1–20.

Christian, William A., Jr. *Apparitions in Late Medieval and Renaissance Spain.* Princeton: Princeton University Press, 1981.

Cioranescu, Alejandro. *Colón humanista: estudios de humanismo atlántico.* Madrid: Editorial Prensa Española, 1967.

———. "'El Doctor Fiesco, historiador de Gran Canaria."*Revista de historia canaria* 25 (1959): 203–9.

———. ed. *Thomas Nichols: Mercader de azúcar, hispanista y hereje. Con la edición y traducción de su Descripción de las Islas Afortunadas.* La Laguna de Tenerife: Instituto de Estudios Canarios, 1963.

Clifford, James. "Traveling Cultures." In *Cultural Studies*, ed. Lawrence Grossberg, Cary Nelson, and Paula A. Treichler, 96–116. London: Routledge, 1992.

Cohen, Walter. *Drama of a Nation: Public Theater in Renaissance England and Spain.* Ithaca: Cornell University Press, 1985.

Coloquio de Historia Canario-Americana, III (1978). Las Palmas: Ediciones del Excelentísimo Cabildo Insular de Gran Canaria, 1980.

Dávila Padilla, Agustín. *Historia de la fundación y discurso de la provincia de Santiago de México de la Orden de Predicadores.* 3rd ed., intro. Agustín Millares Carlo. México: Editorial Academia Literaria, 1955.

Delumeau, Jean. *History of Paradise: The Garden of Eden in Myth and Tradition*, trans. Matthew O'Connell. New York: Continuum, 1995.

Díaz Alayón, Carmen. "Los estudios canarios de Dominik Josef Wölfel." *Anuario de estudios atlánticos* 35 (1989): 363–93.

Díaz Balsera, Viviana. "Araucanian Alterity in Alonso de Ercilla and Lope de Vega." In *Looking at the "Comedia" in the Year of the Quincentennial,* ed. Bárbara Mujica and Sharon D. Voros, 23–36. Lanham, MD: University Press of America, 1993.

Díaz Núñez, Agustín. *Memoria cronológica del establecimiento, propagación y permanencia de la religión católica, apostólica y romana en Islas Canarias.* Madrid: Antonio Pérez Dubrull, 1865.

Díez Borque, José María. *Sociedad y teatro en la España de Lope de Vega.* Barcelona: Antoni Bosch, 1978.

Dille, Glen F. "El descubrimiento y la conquista de América en la comedia." *Hispania* 71 (1988): 492–502.

Durand, José. "Caupolicán, clave historial y épica de *La Araucana.*" *Révue de littérature comparée* 46 (1978): 367–89.

———. "El chapetón Ercilla y la honra araucana." *Filología* 10 (1964): 113–34.

Elliott, John. *Imperial Spain (1469–1716)*. New York: St. Martin's Press, 1964.

Ercilla y Zúñiga, Alonso de. *La Araucana*, ed. Marcos A. Morínigo and Isaías Lerner. 2 vols. Madrid: Clásicos Castalia, 1979.

Espinosa, Fray Alonso de. *Del origen y milagros de la Santa Imagen de Nuestra Señora de Candelaria, que apareció en la isla de Tenerife, con la descripción de esta isla.* Sevilla: Juan de León, 1594.

――――. *Historia de Nuestra Señora de Candelaria*, ed. Alejandro Cioranescu. Santa Cruz de Tenerife: Goya, 1968.

――――. *Historia de Nuestra Señora de Candelaria*, ed. Elías Serra Ráfols, Buenaventura Bonnet, and Néstor Álamo. Santa Cruz de Tenerife: Goya, 1952.

――――. *The Guanches of Tenerife. The Holy Image of Our Lady of Candelaria and the Spanish Conquest and Settlement*, trans. Sir Clements Markham. Hakluyt Society, Series 2, 21. London: Hakluyt Society, 1907.

Fernández Armesto, Felipe. *Before Columbus: Exploration and Colonization from the Mediterranean to the Atlantic, 1229–1492.* Philadelphia: University of Pennsylvania Press, 1987.

――――. *The Canary Islands after the Conquest. The Making of a Colonial Society in the Early Sixteenth Century.* Oxford: Clarendon Press, 1982.

――――. *Millennium: A History of the Last Thousand Years.* New York: Scribner, 1995.

Fernández Shaw, Carlos. "America en Lope de Vega." *Cuadernos hispanoamericanos* 161–62 (1963): 678–83.

Fichter, W. L. "Lope de Vega's *La conquista de Cortés* and *El Marqués del Valle.*" *Hispanic Review* 3 (1935): 163–65.

Flecniakoska, Jean-Louis. "Lope de Vega propagandiste nationaliste: *La Dragontea* (1598)." In *Hommage des hispanistes français à Noël Salomon*, intro. Henry Bonneville, 321–33. Barcelona: LAIA, 1979.

Flint, Weston. "Colón en el teatro español." *Estudios americanos* 22 (1961): 165–86.

Franco, Ángel. *El tema de América en los autores del siglo de Oro.* Madrid: n.p., 1954.

Gárate Córdoba, José María. *La poesía del descubrimiento.* Madrid: Ediciones Cultura Hispánica, 1977.

García Icazbalceta, Joaquín. *Bibliografía mexicana del siglo XVI*, ed. Agustín Millares Carlo. México: Fondo de Cultura Económica, 1954.

García Ramos, Juan Manuel. "Viana entre la historia y la literatura." *Revista de historia canaria* 37 (1980): 267–72.

Gil, Juan. *Mitos y utopías del descubrimiento.* 3 vols. Madrid: Alianza, 1989.

Gilroy, Paul. *The Black Atlantic: Modernity and Double Consciousness.* Cambridge, MA: Harvard University Press, 1993.

Gisbert, Teresa. *Iconografía y mitos indígenas en el arte.* 2nd ed. La Paz: Gisbert y Cia, 1994.

Gómara, Francisco López de. *Historia general de las Indias*, ed. Jorge Gurría Lacroix. Caracas: Biblioteca Ayacucho, 1979.

Goodman, Jennifer R. *Chivalry and Exploration (1298–1630)*. Woodbridge, UK: The Boydell Press, 1998.

Grafton, Anthony. *New Worlds, Ancient Texts*. Cambridge, MA: Harvard University Press, 1992.

Greer, Margaret. "Constituting Community: A New Historical Perspective on the *Autos* of Calderón." In *New Historicism and the Comedia: Poetics, Politics and Praxis*, ed. José A. Madrigal, 33–60. Boulder: Society of Spanish and Spanish-American Studies, University of Colorado, 1997.

Grillparzer, Franz. *Sämtliche Werke: Ausgewählte Briefe, Gespräche, Berichte*, hrsg. von Peter Frank und Karl Pörnbacher, Bd. 3 (1850/1). Munich: Carl Hanser, 1964.

Gutiérrez, Gustavo. *Dios o el oro en las Indias: Siglo XVI*. Lima: Instituto Bartolomé de las Casas, 1989.

Hamilton, John W. "Las relaciones personales de Lope de Vega con el Nuevo Mundo." *Romance Notes* 8 (1967): 260–65.

Hanke, Lewis. *Aristotle and the American Indian*. Chicago: Henry Regnery, 1959.

Henríquez Ureña, Pedro. "El primer libro de escritor americano." *Romanic Review* 7 (1916): 284–87.

Herodotus. *Histories*, trans. A. D. Godley. 2 vols. Loeb Classical Library. Cambridge, MA: Harvard University Press, 1995.

Hertel, Christiane. "'Der rauch man zu Münichen': Die Porträts der Familie Gonsalus in der Kunstkammer Erzherzog Ferdinands II. von Tirol." In *Sammler-Bibliophile-Exzentriker*, ed. Aleida Assmann, Monika Gomille, and Gabriele Rippl, 163–91. Tübingen: Gunter Narr Verlag, 1998.

Holloway, James E., Jr. "Lope's Neoplatonism: *La dama boba*." *Bulletin of Hispanic Studies* 49 (1972): 236–55.

Hulme, Peter. "Tales of Distinction: European Ethnography and the Caribbean." In *Implicit Understandings: Observing, Reporting and Reflecting on the Encounters between Europeans and Other Peoples in the Early Modern Era*, ed. Stuart B. Schwartz, 157–97. Cambridge: Cambridge University Press, 1994.

Kicza, John E. "Patterns in Early Spanish Overseas Expansion." *William and Mary Quarterly* 3rd ser. 49 (1992): 229–53.

Kirschner, Teresa J. "Enmascaramiento y desenmascaramiento del discurso sobre el 'indio' en el teatro del 'Nuevo Mundo' de Lope de Vega." In *Relaciones literarias entre España y América en los siglos XVI y XVII*, ed. Ysla Campbell, 47–64. Ciudad Juárez, México: Universidad Autónoma de Ciudad Juárez, 1992.

La Nuez y Caballero, Sebastián de. "Las Canarias en la obra de Lope de Vega." *Anuario de estudios atlánticos* 10 (1964): 11–159.

La Rosa, Leopoldo de. "Bailadores canarios en unas bodas reales europeas en 1451." *Anuario de estudios atlánticos* 23 (1977): 661–63.

Lauer, Robert. "The Use and Abuse of History in the Spanish Theater of the Golden Age: The Regicide of Sancho II as Treated by Juan de la Cueva, Guillén de Castro, and Lope de Vega." *Hispanic Review* 56 (1988): 17–37.

Leavitt, Sturgis E. "Lope de Vega y el Nuevo Mundo." *Mapocho* 1 (1963): 225–30.

Lerner, Isaías. "Ercilla y Lucano." In *Hommage à Robert Jammes*, ed. Francis Cerdan, 2: 683–91. Toulouse: Presses Universitaires du Mirail, 1994.

López Martínez, Celestino. *Teatro y comediantes sevillanos del siglo XVI.* Sevilla: Imprenta Provincial, 1940.

López Pinciano, Alonso. *Philosophía antigua poética.* 3 vols. Madrid: Consejo Superior de Investigaciones Científicas, 1953.

Lorenzo Cáceres, Andrés. "Las Canarias de Lope de Vega. Una página inédita de don José de Viera y Clavijo sobre *Los Guanches de Tenerife.*" *El Museo Canario* 4 (1936): 38–40.

———. "Las Canarias en el teatro de Lope de Vega." *El Museo Canario* 3 (1935): 2–32.

MacCormack, Sabine. *Religion in the Andes. Vision and Imagination in Early Colonial Perú.* Princeton: Princeton University Press, 1991.

———. "Time, Space and Ritual Action: The Inka and Christian Calendars in Early Colonial Perú." In *Native Traditions in the Postconquest World*, ed. Elizabeth Hill Boone and Tom Cummins, 295–343. Washington, D.C.: Dumbarton Oaks Research Library and Collection, 1998.

———. "Ubi Ecclesia? Perceptions of Medieval Europe in Spanish America." *Speculum* 69 (1994): 74–100.

Madrigal, José A. "El discurso primitivista en las obras de colonización de Lope de Vega." *Círculo* 20 (1991): 147–55.

Maravall, José Antonio. *La cultura del Barroco: análisis de una estructura histórica.* Barcelona: Ariel, 1989.

Márquez Villanueva, Francisco. *Fuentes literarias cervantinas.* Madrid: Gredos, 1973.

Martínez Hernández, Marcos. *Canarias en la mitología. Historia mítica del archipiélago.* Santa Cruz de Tenerife: Centro de la Cultura Popular Canaria, 1992.

———. *Las Islas Canarias de la Antigüedad al Renacimiento. Nuevos Aspectos.* Santa Cruz de Tenerife: Cabildo de Tenerife and Centro de la Cultura Popular Canaria, 1996.

McKendrick, Melveena. *Woman and Society in the Spanish Drama of the Golden Age: A Study of the mujer varonil.* Cambridge: Cambridge University Press, 1974.

Méchoulan, Henry. *El honor de Dios*, trans. Enrique Sordo. Barcelona: Editorial Argos Vergara, 1981. (Orig. *Le sang de l'autre ou l'honneur de Dieu: indiens, juifs, morisques dans l'Espagne du Siècle d'Or.* Paris: Fayard, 1979.)

Medina, José Toribio. *Dos comedias famosas y un auto sacramental.* 2 vols. Santiago de Chile: Litografía Barcelona, 1915.

———. *La imprenta en México: 1539–1821.* 8 vols. Amsterdam: N. Israel, 1965. Repr. of Santiago de Chile: Casa del Autor, 1912.

Mejías-López, William. "La relación ideológica de Alonso de Ercilla con Francisco de Vitoria y Fray Bartolomé de las Casas." *Revista iberoamericana* 61 (1995): 197–217.

Melczer, William. "Ercilla's Divided Heroic Vision: A Re-Evaluation of the Epic Hero in *La Araucana.*" *Hispania* 56 (1973): 216–21.

Menéndez y Pelayo, Marcelino. Introduction to *Obras de Lope de Vega,* ed. idem, 82–112. Biblioteca de Autores Españoles 23. Madrid: Atlas, 1968.

Mercer, John. *The Canary Islanders: Their Prehistory, Conquest and Survival.* London: Rex Collings, 1980.

Merediz, Eyda M. "Más allá de América: Las Casas en una crónica sobre las Islas Canarias." *El Museo Canario* 51 (1996): 245–58.

———. "Traveling Icons: The Virgin of Candelaria's Transatlantic Journeys." *Arizona Journal of Hispanic Cultural Studies* 5 (2001): 1–18.

Mignolo, Walter D. "El metatexto historiográfico y la historiografía indiana." *Modern Language Notes* 96 (1981): 358–402.

Millares Carlo, Agustín. "Proceso inquisitorial contra fray Alonso de Espinosa, dominico (1590–1592)." *El Museo Canario* 1 (1933): 150–216.

———, and Manuel Hernández Suárez. *Biobibliografía de escritores canarios (Siglos XVI, XVII y XVIII).* Vol. 2. Las Palmas de Gran Canaria: El Museo Canario and Mancomunidad de Cabildos de Las Palmas, 1977.

Minian de Alfie, Raquel. "Lope, lector de cronistas de Indias." *Filología* 11 (1965): 1–21.

———. "Nombres indígenas en una comedia de Lope." *Filología* 7 (1961): 173–75.

Miramón, Alberto. "El Nuevo Mundo en el universo dramático de Lope de Vega." *Revista de Indias* 28 (1968): 169–77.

Miró Quesada Sosa, Aurelio. *América en el teatro de Lope de Vega.* Lima: n.p., 1935.

Morales Padrón, Francisco, ed. *Canarias: Crónicas de su conquista: Transcripción, estudio y notas.* Las Palmas de Gran Canaria: El Museo Canario and Ayuntamiento de Las Palmas, 1978.

———. *Sevilla, Canarias y América.* Las Palmas: Ediciones del Excmo. Cabildo Insular de Gran Canaria, 1970.

Moratín, Leandro Fernández de. *Obras póstumas.* Vol. 3. Madrid: Rivadeneyra, 1868.

More, Thomas. *Utopia,* trans. Ralph Robynson (1556), ed. and intro. David Harris Sacks. Boston and New York: St. Martin's Press, 1999.

Morínigo, Marcos A. *América en el teatro de Lope de Vega.* Buenos Aires: Instituto de Filología, 1946.

Morley, S. Griswold, and Courtney Bruerton. *The Chronology of Lope de Vega's Comedias.* New York: Modern Language Association, 1940.

Muldoon, James. *Popes, Lawyers, and Infidels.* Philadelphia: University of Pennsylvania Press, 1979.

Navarro Artiles, Francisco, comp. *Teberite, diccionario de la lengua aborigen canaria.* Las Palmas: Edirca, 1981.

Nelson, William. *Fact or Fiction: The Dilemma of the Renaissance Storyteller.* Cambridge, MA: Harvard University Press, 1973.

Oviedo y Valdés, Gonzalo Fernández de. *Historia general y natural de las Indias,* ed. Juan Pérez de Tudela Bueso. Vol. 1. Biblioteca de Autores Españoles 117. Madrid: Atlas, 1959.

Padrón Acosta, Sebastián. *El teatro en Canarias: La fiesta del Corpus.* La Laguna: Instituto de Estudios Canarios, 1954.

Pagden, Anthony. *The Fall of Natural Man. The American Indian and the Origins of Comparative Ethnology.* Cambridge: Cambridge University Press, 1982.

Palencia, Alfonso Fernández de. *Gesta hispaniensia ex annalibus suorum dierum collecta,* ed., intro. and trans. Brian Tate and Jeremy Lawrance. Vol. 1. Madrid: Real Academia de la Historia, 1998.

Palenzuela, Nilo. "El arte del retrato en el poema de Viana." In *Homenaje al profesor Sebastián de la Nuéz,* 79–91. La Laguna: Secretariado de Publicaciones, Universidad de La Laguna, 1991.

Parish, Helen Rand. *Las Casas as a Bishop. A New Interpretation Based on His Holograph Petition in the Hans P. Kraus Collection of Hispanic American Manuscripts.* Washington, D.C.: Library of Congress, 1980.

———, and Harold E. Weidman. *Las Casas en México. Historia y obras desconocidas.* México: Fondo de Cultura Económica, 1992.

Parker, Alexander A. "The New World in the *Autos Sacramentales* of Calderón." In *Saeculum Hispanum: Beiträge zu Texten des Siglo de Oro. Festschrift für Hans Flasche zum 70. Geburtstag,* ed. Karl-Hermann Körner and Dietrich Briesemeister, 261–69. Wiesbaden: Franz Steiner Verlag, 1983.

———. *The Philosophy of Love.* Edinburgh: Edinburgh University Press, 1985.

Pastor, Beatriz. "Alonso de Ercilla y la emergencia de una conciencia hispanoamericana." In *Discurso narrativo de la conquista de América,* 451–570. La Habana: Casa de las Américas, 1983.

Pennington, Kenneth J., Jr. "Bartolomé de las Casas and the Tradition of Medieval Law." *Church History* 39 (1970): 149–61.

Peraza de Ayala, José. *El régimen comercial de Canarias con las Indias en los siglos XVI, XVII y XVIII.* Sevilla: Publicaciones de la Universidad de Sevilla, 1977.

Pérez Bustamante, Ciriaco. "El lascasismo en *La Araucana.*" *Revista de estudios políticos* 64 (1952): 157–68.

Pérez Fernández, Isacio. Introduction to Bartolomé de las Casas, *Brevísima relación de la destrucción de África. Preludio de la destrucción de Indias. Primera defensa de los guanches y negros contra su esclavización.* Salamanca: Viceconsejería de cultura y deportes del gobierno de Canarias, 1989.

Pérez Morera, Jesús. "Fray Domingo de Mendoza y las primeras fundaciones de la orden dominica en Canarias y América." *El Museo Canario* 53 (1998): 327–66.

Pérez Voituriez, Antonio. *Problemas jurídicos internacionales de la conquista de Canarias.* La Laguna: Universidad de La Laguna, 1958.

Pierce, Frank. *Alonso de Ercilla y Zúñiga.* Amsterdam: Rodopi, 1984.

———. *La poesía épica del Siglo de Oro.* Madrid: Gredos, 1961.

Pratt, Mary Louise. *Imperial Eyes: Travel Writing and Transculturation.* London: Routledge, 1992.

Pulgar, Hernando del. "Crónica de los Reyes Católicos Don Fernando y Doña Isabel." En *Crónicas de los Reyes de Castilla*, ed. Cayetano Rosell. Biblioteca de Autores Españoles 70. Madrid: Rivadeneyra, 1878.

Quint, David. *Epic and Empire.* Princeton: Princeton University Press, 1993.

Rabasa, José. "Utopian Ethnology in Las Casas's *Apologética.*" In *1492–1992: Re/discovering Colonial Writing*, ed. René Jara and Nicolás Spadacchini, 263–99. Minneapolis: The Prisma Institute, 1989.

Remesal, Antonio de. *Historia general de las Indias Occidentales y particular de la gobernación de Chiapa y Guatemala*, ed. Carmelo Sáenz de Santa María. Biblioteca de Autores Españoles 175. Madrid: Atlas, 1964.

Restori, Antonio. *Una collezione di commedie de Lope de Vega Carpio.* Livorno: Tipografia Francesco Vigo, 1891.

Río, María José del. "Representaciones dramáticas en casa de un artesano del Madrid de principios del siglo XVII." In *Teatros y vida teatral en el Siglo de Oro a través de las fuentes documentales*, ed. Luciano García Lorenzo and J.E. Varey, 245–58. London: Támesis, 1991.

Riquelme Pérez, María Jesús. *La Virgen de Candelaria y las Islas Canarias.* Santa Cruz de Tenerife: Aula de Cultura and Cabildo de Tenerife, 1990.

Rodríguez-Buckingham, Antonio. "The Arm of Spain: The Content Analysis of the Material Printed in Mexico and Peru in the Sixteenth Century." In *Bibliography and Reference Series. Seminar on the Acquisition of Latin American Library Materials*, vol. 23: 249–80. Austin: Seminar on the Acquisition of Latin American Library Materials, University of Texas, 1979.

Romero Muñoz, Carlos. "Lope de Vega y 'Fernando de Zárate': *El Nuevo Mundo* (y *Arauco domado*) en *La conquista de México.*" *Studi di letteratura ispano-americana* 15–16 (1983): 243–64.

Ruiz Ramón, Francisco. "El héroe americano en Lope y Tirso: de la guerra de los hombres a la guerra de los dioses." In *El mundo del teatro español en su Siglo de Oro: Ensayos dedicados a John E. Varey*, ed. J. M. Ruano de la Haza, 229–48. Ottawa: Dovehouse, 1989.

———. "El Nuevo Mundo en el teatro clásico (Introducción a una visión dramática)." In *Celebración y catarsis (leer el teatro español)*, 69–137. Murcia: Sucesores de Nogués, 1988.

Rumeu de Armas, Antonio. *La conquista de Tenerife*. Tenerife: Aula de Cultura de Tenerife, 1975.

———. *España en el África Atlántica*. 2nd ed. 2 vols. Las Palmas: Ediciones del Cabildo Insular de Gran Canaria, 1996.

———. "Don Fernando Guanarteme y las princesas Guayarmina y Masequera en la corte de los Reyes Cátolicos." *Revista de historia canaria* 149–52 (1965–1966): 35–40.

———. *La política indigenista de Isabel la Católica*. Valladolid: Instituto "Isabel la Católica" de Historia Eclesiástica, 1969.

Russell, Frederick. *The Just War in the Middle Ages*. Cambridge: Cambridge University Press, 1975.

Russell, Peter E. "El descubrimiento de Las Canarias y el debate medieval acerca de los derechos de los príncipes y pueblos paganos." *Revista de historia canaria* 36 (1978): 9–32.

Sale, Kirkpatrick. *The Conquest of Paradise: Christopher Columbus and the Columbian Legacy*. New York: Alfred A. Knopf, 1990.

Salles-Reese, Verónica. *From Viracocha to the Virgin of Copacabana. Representation of the Sacred at Lake Titicaca*. Austin: University of Texas Press, 1997.

Sánchez Escribano, Federico, and Alberto Porqueras Mayo. *Preceptiva dramática española: del Renacimiento al Barroco*. Madrid: Gredos, 1972.

Serés, Guillermo. *La transformación de los amantes. Imágenes del amor de la Antigüedad al Siglo de Oro*. Barcelona: Grijalbo Mondadori, 1996.

Sentaurens, Jean. *Seville et le théâtre de la fin du Moyen Age à la fin du XVIIe siècle*. Talence: Presses Universitaires de Bordeaux, 1984.

Serra Ráfols, Elías, and Marcos Martínez Hernández. "Sermón de Clemente VI Papa acerca de la otorgación del Reino de Canarias a Luis de España, 1344." *Revista de historia canaria* 29 (1963–1964): 107–11.

Shannon, Robert M. *Visions of the New World in the Drama of Lope de Vega*. New York: Peter Lang, 1989.

Smith, Marlene K. *The Beautiful Woman in the Theater of Lope de Vega: Ideology and Mythology of Female Beauty in Seventeenth-Century Spain*. New York: Peter Lang, 1998.

Sommer, Doris. *Foundational Fiction: The National Romances of Latin America*. Berkeley: University of California Press, 1991.

Soufas, Teresa S. "Rhetorical Appropriation: Lope's New World Play and Canonicity." *Hispanic Review* 67 (1999): 319–31.

Stern, Charlotte. "Lope de Vega: Propagandist?" *Bulletin of the Comediantes* 34 (1982): 1–36.

Stevens-Arroyo, Anthony M. "The Inter-Atlantic Paradigm: The Failure of Spanish Medieval Colonization of the Canary and Caribbean Islands." *Comparative Studies in Society and History* 35 (1993): 515–43.

Strabo. *Geography*, trans. Horace Leonard Jones. Vol. 3. Loeb Classical Library. Cambridge, MA: Harvard University Press, 1995.

Szymborska, Wislawa. "Utopia." In *View with a Grain of Sand. Selected Poems*, trans. Stanislaw Baranczak and Clare Cavanagh, 127. New York: Harcourt Brace, 1995.

Tasso, Torquato. *Jerusalem Delivered*, trans. Ralph Nash. Detroit: Wayne State University Press, 1987.

"Testimonio de los conventos y estudios con sus estatutos, observancias y méritos de la Provincia de Santo Domingo de Canarias." Written and certified by Joseph Isidro Uque Osorio in April, 1743. Library of the University of La Laguna (call number C / IV-8).

Tejera Gaspar, Antonio. "Sociedad y cultura indígena." In *Historia de Canarias*, ed. Antonio Béthencourt Massieu, 83–129. Las Palmas: Ediciones del Cabildo Insular de Gran Canaria, 1995.

———. *Tenerife y los Guanches*. Santa Cruz de Tenerife: La Biblioteca Canaria, 1992.

Todorov, Tzvetan. *The Conquest of America*, trans. Richard Howard. New York: Harper and Row, 1984.

Torriani, Leonardo. *Descripción e historia de las Islas Canarias antes Afortunadas con el parecer de sus fortificaciones*, trans. Alejandro Cioranescu. Santa Cruz de Tenerife: Goya, 1978.

———. *Descrição e História do Reino das Ilhas Canárias antes ditas Afortunadas com o parecer das suas fortificações*, ed. and trans. José Manuel Azevedo e Silva. Lisboa: Edições Cosmos, 1999.

———. *Die Kanarischen Inseln und ihre Urbewöhner*, ed. Dominik Josef Wölfel. Leipzig: K. F. Koehler, 1940.

Valbuena Prat, Angel. *Historia de la poesía canaria*. Vol. 1. Barcelona: Universidad de Barcelona, 1937.

Valera, Mosén Diego de. *Crónica de los Reyes Católicos*, ed. Juan de Mata Carriazo. Madrid: José Molina, 1927.

Vega Carpio, Lope de. "Arauco domado." In *Obras de Lope de Vega*, ed. Marcelino Menéndez y Pelayo, 237–89. Biblioteca de Autores Españoles 27. Madrid: Atlas, 1969.

———. "Los guanches de Tenerife y conquista de Canarias." *Décima parte de las comedias de Lope de Vega Carpio, Familiar del Santo Oficio*. Madrid: Viuda de Alonso Martín de Balboa, 1618.

———. "Los guanches de Tenerife y conquista de Canarias." *Décima parte de las comedias de Lope de Vega Carpio, Familiar del Santo Oficio*. Barcelona: Sebastian de Cormellas, 1618.

——. "Los guanches de Tenerife y conquista de Canarias." *Décima parte de las comedias de Lope de Vega Carpio, Familiar del Santo Oficio.* Madrid: Diego Flamenco, 1621.

——. "Los guanches de Tenerife y conquista de Canarias." Manuscript CC-V-28032/28. Biblioteca Palatina, Parma, Italy.

——. "Los guanches de Tenerife y conquista de Canarias." In *Obras de Lope de Vega,* ed. Marcelino Menéndez y Pelayo, 302–39. Real Academia: Crónicas y leyendas dramáticas de España 11. Madrid: Sucesores de Rivadeneyra, 1900.

——. "Los guanches de Tenerife y conquista de Canarias." In Lope de Vega, *Obras escogidas,* ed. Federico Carlos Sáinz de Robles, 3: 1262–93. Madrid: Aguilar, 1955.

——. *Los guanches de Tenerife y conquista de Canarias.* Versión libre de Claudio de la Torre. Madrid: Alfil, 1963.

——. "Los guanches de Tenerife y conquista de Canarias." In *Obras de Lope de Vega,* ed. Marcelino Menéndez y Pelayo, 65–119. Biblioteca de Autores Españoles 24. Madrid: Atlas, 1968.

——. *Los guanches de Tenerife y conquista de Canaria.* Santa Cruz de Tenerife: Museo de Historia, Organismo Autónomo de Museos y Centros del Cabildo de Tenerife, Caja Canarias, 1996.

——. "Los guanches de Tenerife y conquista de Canaria." In *Obras completas de Lope de Vega,* ed. Jesús Gómez y Paloma Cuenca, 803–94. Comedias 13. Madrid: Biblioteca Castro, 1997.

——. *El Nuevo Mundo descubierto por Cristóbal Colón,* ed. Jean Lemartinel and Charles Minguet. Lille: Presses Universitaires de Lille, 1980.

——. "San Diego de Alcalá." In *Obras de Lope de Vega,* ed. Marcelino Menéndez y Pelayo, 105–57. Biblioteca de Autores Españoles 11 (Comedias de vidas de santos 2). Madrid: Ediciones Atlas, 1965.

——. *San Diego de Alcalá,* ed. Thomas E. Case. Kassel: Reichenberger, 1988.

Viana, Antonio de. *Antigüedades de las Islas Afortunadas de la Gran Canaria, conquista de Tenerife y aparición de la imagen de Candelaria en verso suelto y octava rima. Año 1604.* Edición facsimile, intro. María Rosa Alonso. San Cristóbal de La Laguna: Excmo. Ayuntamiento de San Cristóbal de La Laguna, 1996.

——. *Antigüedades de las Islas Afortunadas,* ed. María Rosa Alonso. 2 vols. Islas Canarias: Biblioteca Básica Canaria, 1991.

——. *Conquista de Tenerife,* ed. Alejandro Cioranescu. 2 vols. Tenerife: Aula de Cultura de Tenerife, 1971.

Viera y Clavijo, Joseph de. *Noticias de la historia general de las Islas Canarias,* ed. Alejandro Cioranescu and Marcos G. Martínez Hernández. 2 vols. Santa Cruz de Tenerife: Goya, 1982.

Vilar, Pierre. *A History of Gold and Money 1450–1920,* trans. Judith White. London: Verso, 1991.

Wagner, Henry Raup, and Helen Rand Parish. *The Life and Writings of Bartolomé de las Casas*. Albuquerque: University of New Mexico, 1967.

Warner, Marina. *Alone of All Her Sex: The Myth and the Cult of the Virgin Mary*. New York: Alfred A. Knopf, 1976.

Weckmann, Luis. *Las bulas alejandrinas de 1493 y la teoría política del papado medieval. Estudio de la supremacía papal sobre islas, 1091–1493*. México: Instituto de Historia, 1949.

Weinberg, Bernard. *A History of Literary Criticism in the Italian Renaissance*. 2 vols. Chicago: University of Chicago Press, 1961.

Weiner, Jack. "La guerra y la paz espirituales en tres comedias de Lope de Vega." *Revista de estudios hispánicos* 17 (1983): 65–79.

———. "Lope de Vega, un puesto de cronista y *La hermosa Ester*." In *Actas del VIII Congreso de la Asociación Internacional de Hispanistas*, ed. D. Kossoff, J. Amor y Vázquez, R. Kossoff, and G. W. Ribbans, 723–30. Madrid: Ediciones Itsmo, 1986.

Wilks, Michael. *The Problem of Sovereignty in the Late Middle Ages: The Papal Monarchy with Agustinus Triumphus and the Publicists*. Cambridge: Cambridge University Press, 1964.

Wölfel, Dominik Josef. "La Curia Romana y la Corona de España en defensa de los aborígenes canarios." *Antropos* 25 (1930): 1011–83.

———. *Monumenta Linguae Canariae. Un estudio sobre la prehistoria y la historia temprana del África Blanca*, trans. Marcos Sarmiento Pérez. 2 vols. Tenerife: Dirección General de Patrimonio Histórico, 1996. (Orig. *Monumenta Linguae Canariae. Die Kanarischen Sprachdenkmäler. Eine Studie zur Vor– und Frühgeschichte Weißafrikas*. Graz: Akademische Druck u. Verlagsanstalt, 1965.)

Wright, Elizabeth R. *Pilgrimage to Patronage: Lope de Vega and the Court of Philip III, 1598–1621*. London: Associated University Presses, 2001.

Zavala, Silvio. *Las conquistas de Canaria y América*. Las Palmas: Ediciones del Cabildo Insular de Gran Canaria, 1991. (Repr. of "Las conquistas de Canaria y América.") *Tierra Firme* 1 (1935): 81–112.

Zugasti, Miguel. *La "trilogía de los Pizarros" de Tirso de Molina*. Vols. 1–4. Kassel: Reichenberger; Trujillo, Cáceres: Fundación Obra Pía de los Pizarro, 1993.

Zurara, Gomes Eanes de. *Crónica dos feitos notáveis que se passaram na conquista de Guiné por mandado do Infante D. Henrique*, ed. Torquato de Sousa Soares. Vol. 2. Lisboa: Academia Portuguesa da História, 1981.

INDEX